Sleaze

The State of Britain

LEWIS BASTON

First published 2000 by Channel 4 Books
an imprint of Macmillan Publishers Ltd
25 Eccleston Place, London, SW1W 9NF
Basingstoke and Oxford

www.macmillan.co.uk

Associated companies throughout the world

ISBN 0 7522 1783 6

1 3 5 7 9 8 6 4 2

A CIP catalogue record for this book is available from
the British Library.

Designed and typeset by Anita Ruddell
Printed in Great Britain by Mackays of Chatham PLC

Sleaze: The State of Britain by Lewis Baston is based on the television series
Sleaze produced for Channel 4
by Blakeway Associates Ltd
Producer: Leonie Jameson
Executive Producer: Denys Blakeway

Contents

Acknowledgements

This book owes its existence to Leonie Jameson, writer and producer of the Blakeway Associates series *Sleaze* for Channel 4. Her suggestion that I should write the book to accompany the series was as unexpected as it was welcome. Nick Hornby and Guy Evans, the assistant producers, have been generous and helpful – far beyond the call of duty – with the fruits of their efforts. Their research, and the work done by Dan Hillman, have made this book possible.

I have drawn heavily on the interviews conducted for the series, and thank the people concerned for their insights and recollections. The staff of the British Library, Kingston University Library, and the library services of the Royal Borough of Kensington and Chelsea (particularly Karen Baston) and the City of Westminster have been helpful with my research. The select bibliography lists the books and papers that I found particularly valuable.

Thanks also to Charlie Carman, Sandy Holton, Katy Carrington and Mark Wallace at Channel 4 Books, Alan Williams at Denton Hall for his legal advice, and Christine King for her skilful editing.

I would like to thank Brian Brivati, with whom I am researching the postwar history of the Labour Party at Kingston University, for his patience with this – duly registered but rather extensive – outside interest which has occupied a lot of my attention since December 1998. He kindly read an early draft despite having many other things to do. Thanks also to David Butler, my former supervisor, without whom I would not have started a writing career. In something I wrote for him, I referred to disclosures about the 'sexual habits' of a politician. 'Better to say "private life"', was David's wise advice. It has not been possible to follow this guideline in what follows, for obvious reasons, but I hope what I have written shows some of that generosity of spirit to people who have suffered public humiliation.

Introduction

'Sleaze' is a word which has dominated British politics in the 1990s. The British people have become used to regarding their rulers as people of low morals who are in public life primarily to serve their own selfish interests. But the reality of the last fifty years shows that the idea of a fall from a state of honesty and integrity to an ethical swamp today is an oversimplification. In British politics, Eden means the man who lied about Suez, rather than a garden of innocence.

This book is the story of what we now call 'sleaze', although that term was unknown in politics until the early 1960s and not common currency until the early 1990s. It describes the way some politicians have used their power to feed their private desires for money or sexual satisfaction, and the way in which many of their friends – and even ostensible enemies – have engaged in a conspiracy of silence to protect their erring colleagues. It is also the story of the changing standards that the press and the public have demanded from their leaders, and how much people have really wanted to know about their behaviour.

Absent for the most part is 'abuse of power': dishonest behaviour which is not exactly selfish in motivation. Prime Minister Eden's lies and plotting over Suez in 1956 – probably the most serious misconduct in postwar British politics – were because of his distorted idea of Britain's national interest, not for personal gain. The same applies to the arms to Iraq scandal investigated in the 1996 Scott Report, and the more minor scandals over Westland Helicopters in 1986 and violations of Rhodesian sanctions by BP, part owned by the British government, during the 1960s. This book is about the standards of conduct of individuals, rather than government as a whole. I have also tended to restrict myself to writing about parliamentary politics – with the principal exception of the corrupt Newcastle boss T. Dan Smith and his partners in crime, local government hardly figures, although it has been if anything more corrupt than national politics.

In the immediate postwar period the British people knew little; political leaders were looked up to as moral leaders, and public and press did not pry into their private affairs. However, if something discreditable did come to light, there was little forgiveness; the person concerned was harshly punished and isolated by their colleagues. John Belcher, a minister in the 1945–51 Labour government, resigned not only as a minister but as an MP for unwisely accepting gifts from a shady businessman. The same fate befell Ian Harvey, a Conservative minister, when he was arrested in a gay cruising area of St James's Park in 1958; the careers of some backbench MPs never recovered from divorces or gay scandals.

In the scandal-ridden 1960s and 1970s, deference collapsed, and the veil of secrecy which protected the privacy of the political class was torn. Suddenly, starting with the Profumo affair in 1963, the public discovered that their faith in the ruling class of the 1950s had been built on illusions. A more commercial and aggressive press was steadily less willing to help sustain these illusions, and blind trust in the integrity of the political class was replaced by a general suspicion that all politicians were crooked. In the mid 1970s, with City scandals affecting members of all parties and the unravelling of the web of corruption around the architect John Poulson, this seemed an attractive idea to many voters. The Poulson affair led to the establishment of the Register of Members' Interests in 1975, but Parliament was still loosely regulated and, during the 1980s, prone to low standards.

At the time of writing, we have access to a great deal of information about the lives of public figures, and as a result we will have to forgive – or condone – a wider range of behaviour than in the past. Parliamentary standards are subject to external supervision, and the media's power to investigate is stronger than it has ever been. Very little can be concealed from a determined tabloid reporter. In addition, *The Guardian*'s parliamentary contingent now has a track record of exposing questionable dealings and conflicts of interest under Conservative and Labour governments. With links between government and business becoming ever closer, there is more and more for the regulators and vigilant journalists to keep an eye on. However, the cost of transparency in politics is that we will all have to learn to distinguish between a genuine scandal and antics which, however diverting, do not affect the way we are governed.

*

In this book I have used some general terms like 'the Establishment' or 'the political class'. I should say what I mean by them. The term 'the Establishment' is a vague one which grew in popularity in the early 1960s and has remained in use ever since. It comprised a network of people connected by family (landed aristocracy) and educational (Eton) background, with its members distributed in the Conservative Party, the City of London and the cultural élite, and united by an outlook which was unruffled and rather complacent. The web of connections which make up the old Establishment has not totally broken up, but it is a much more frayed and insubstantial thing than it was in the early 1960s. Its branches have less and less to do with each other. There is a mutual incomprehension and lack of shared life experiences between the élites of politics, big business, the Church, the arts and the media in a way which renders the idea of a unified Establishment less and less significant as time goes on. Politics has become a narrower and more professional business.

'The political class' is a more recent usage, a term more familiar in Italy than Britain. I use it here to refer to the group of people who are involved, usually professionally, in the business of legislating and governing Britain. This includes MPs, active peers, political journalists and newspaper editors, party staff, think-tank employees and lobbyists. There are a few thousand members of the political class, and they work and socialize in a relatively small corner of London. There are related smaller Scottish and Welsh branches, which will no doubt increase in size now devolution has taken place, but for the most part it is a metropolitan village.

*

I have chosen to tell the story of postwar British sleaze in a roughly chrono-logical framework, while distinguishing between the different forms of behaviour clustered under the umbrella of 'sleaze'. The first three chapters take 1945 as their starting-point: Chapter 1 focuses on ministerial standards, particularly the resignation of John Belcher, up to the early 1960s; Chapter 2 covers the growth of outside interests among Opposition and backbench MPs, plus espionage, and carries the story to the early 1970s; while Chapter 3 describes the sexual mores of the period up to 1962. Chapter 4 draws the threads of sex and spying together in the defining 1960s scandal, the Profumo affair of 1963.

The next three chapters are about the tangled pattern of public life in the 1960s and 1970s and the cynicism of the press and the public which replaced the illusions of the 1940s and 1950s. Chapter 5 is about Harold Wilson and his cronies, both the reality and the exaggerated allegations that were made against them; Chapter 6 describes the discrediting of John Poulson and Conservative Deputy Leader Reginald Maudling. Chapter 7 concerns the City scandals of the 1970s and the downfall of Liberal leader Jeremy Thorpe.

Chapter 8 is about the spread of the entrepreneurial 'get rich quick' cul-ture of the 1980s into the House of Commons, and Chapter 9 is about the curious relationship between Thatcherite economic liberalization and atti-tudes to sexual morality. If these two are about the party times of the 1980s, Chapters 10 and 11 are about the hangover of the 1990s: the cash for ques-tions affair and the rush of sleaze stories which doomed John Major's gov-ernment in the 1997 election. Chapter 12 describes the Blair government's efforts to get rid of sleaze and the mishaps that have taken place along the way. In the Conclusion, I take the risk of predicting what might happen over the next few years. But we start in the vanished age of ration books and the puritanical integrity of Winston Churchill and Clement Attlee in the 1940s.

CHAPTER 1

The age of austerity 1945-62

'It was hard to make people understand why they should have to go without what we would consider the normal things of life, when they had won the war.'

Barbara Castle, elected MP in 1945

At the end of the Second World War, Britain was financially drained but morally victorious. The country had stood alone in 1940 against a powerful and vicious dictatorship, and triumphed against all the odds. In 1945, its political leaders were admired by the electorate and the people of the world. Churchill was an icon of heroic resistance; ministers such as Bevin, Morrison and Attlee were admired for their competence and patriotism. None of these men had grown rich from the war effort, while the people as a whole had accepted self-sacrifice for the greater good.

Campaigning for the first postwar Parliament, the Labour Party stood for extending this rigour and honesty into peacetime. Its propaganda, publicized by such allies as the *Daily Mirror*, reminded voters that the peace of 1918, and the sacrifices of the soldiers of the First World War, had been squandered by the people who had ruled Britain between the wars. Mass unemployment and the policy of appeasing dictators played a great part in the betrayal; but a squalid political culture had also prevailed, and Labour now promised a fundamental change.

The interwar period had been a time not only of broken promises, but of corruption on a massive scale. While members of a later generation would compromise themselves with 'cash for questions', Lloyd George's coalition of Conservatives and Liberals had notoriously financed its activities by selling peerages and knighthoods. The system had been used before the war, but after 1918 it grew both in scale and sheer blatancy. The government even invented new honours, such as the Order of the British Empire (OBE), to extract money from those who could not afford more expensive decorations.

A scandal finally broke in 1922, with honours awarded to even more undeserving characters than usual: Sir John Drughorn (convicted for trading with the enemy in 1915), Sir William Vestey (tax evasion) and Sir Joseph Robinson (a South African fraudster). Many people were implicated in the affair, including the Conservative hierarchy (many members of the House of Lords had bought their positions), the Lloyd George Liberals and much of the business leadership of Britain. This level of involvement was hardly conducive to impartial investigation; furthermore, the only party that had not been contaminated by the sale of honours was the Labour Party, and nobody in the British Establishment wanted to risk causing a sudden surge towards socialism. The issue was buried amid hypocritical outrage, and a law was passed against the honours trade in 1925.

There was little chance of exposure from an independent press: Lloyd George had ensured that the newspaper proprietors had received free peerages and knighthoods – Max Aitken, owner of the *Express* papers, was made Lord Beaverbrook two days after Lloyd George became Prime Minister in 1916.

The fall of Lloyd George did not clean up politics. The funds generated by the sale of honours remained in circulation, while the rise of Labour provoked a new set of 'dirty tricks' from Conservative Central Office. These included the 'Zinoviev letter' of 1924, a forged document designed to show that Communists were taking advantage of Labour's alleged softness to plot revolution in Britain. There was also espionage against the Labour campaign in 1929 organized by Joseph Ball, who had gone from MI5 to Conservative Central Office in 1927. During the Conservative ascendancy of the 1930s, Central Office continued to smear its opponents, although the target of the campaign this time was Winston Churchill.

The aristocracy of the 1930s acquired, not entirely fairly, the taint of having favoured appeasement, even conniving with Hitler and his social-climbing ambassador Joachim von Ribbentrop. In the 1930s there was also a dubious subculture of political betting, which came to light in 1936 when the Cabinet Minister, Jimmy Thomas, was discovered to have leaked details of the Budget to allow a Tory MP, Alfred Butt, to place insider bets on the contents. A rigorous Tribunal of Inquiry was set up and Thomas and Butt were forced to resign in disgrace. The harsh response of the government to the Budget leak affair was one sign that the Establishment had started to realize that politics was in need of cleaning up.

The Labour victory in the 1945 election completed the triumph of 'Roundheads over Cavaliers' that the overthrow of the Conservative government in 1940 had begun. Unlike 1914–18, the Second World War did not provide a bonanza for profiteers because the government had clamped down on 'sleaze' through regulations and a confiscatory Excess Profits Tax. Parliament was also rigorous with its own during the war – Bob Boothby, one of the more colourful MPs, was a notable case. The representative of Lord Woolton, the Minister of Food, in the House of Commons, Boothby ended his ministerial career through questionable financial dealings. As a banker, he had become embroiled in helping a friend and business colleague, Richard Weininger, to recover financial assets from Nazi-occupied Czechoslovakia. Without disclosing his interest, he chaired a committee on

Czech assets and pressed the government to hurry up with assessing and paying claims. To add further murk to the waters, Boothby had borrowed money from Alfred Butt, the disreputable Tory MP who had profited from Jimmy Thomas' indiscretion, and Butt was pressing for repayment; Boothby needed the cash from his 10 per cent share in assets Weininger managed to recover.

When Boothby's involvement became public, he was suspended as a minister and investigated by a Select Committee, which in 1941 found his conduct 'contrary to the usage and derogatory to the dignity of the House and inconsistent with the standards which Parliament is entitled to expect from its Members'. It was a harsh verdict, given the vagueness of rules about declaration of interest and the greater issues raised by the situation of those relying on Czech assets. Boothby was in a paradoxically vulnerable position as someone who had strongly supported the new Prime Minister, Winston Churchill, even when it was not fashionable to do so. Churchill was so determined to be seen as clean and honest that he was willing to see an injustice done to an ally. Boothby resigned as a minister but surprisingly was able to defend his position as an MP. He had enough friends, and the case against him had sufficient holes in it, for him to survive although never to return to government. As later chapters of this book will show, his flamboyant personality was to express itself in other ways.

Churchill's action set a harsh precedent, which was followed to an even greater extent by his Labour successor, Clement Attlee.

Many Labour MPs elected in 1945 had first become politically aware in the 1930s, and were angry and disgusted by the moral corruption of the interwar period. Honesty and decency were integral to the socialist case. Labour's leader, and Prime Minister 1945–51, reflected the puritanical virtues of the party at the time. Clement Attlee set a high moral tone for his administration. When the 1947 Budget increased cigarette tax as a way of decreasing the amount of tobacco Britain had to buy from abroad, Attlee set an example by banning smoking in Cabinet. A fairly heavy smoker himself, Attlee was one of the ministers who suffered most from his own edict.

Attlee led a simple life, his main pleasures being the cricket scores and *The Times*' crossword. He saw public service, and the pursuit of the ideology he believed in, as the sole reason for entering politics. It is a testament to the high ethical standards prevailing after the war that there should have been only one serious scandal in the Attlee administration, and it was dealt with so harshly that the erring minister, John Belcher, was the object of pity rather than hatred.

The nature of the scandal was very much a reflection of the desperate economic condition of the country and the emergency measures taken to deal with it. Britain in the 1940s was a visibly shabby place, of patched clothes, queues and boarded-up buildings. It was highly regulated and austere, almost like the common perception of an Eastern Bloc country. Rationing of food and consumer goods was not lifted after the war, but was actually tightened to include items such as bread and potatoes in 1947. Industry was regulated by a complex web of government-issued permits for fuel, paper and other raw materials. Imports in particular required special licences which were difficult to obtain.

The economic restrictions on British life in the 1940s, according to Barbara Castle, then a newly elected Labour MP, 'made for a great deal of drabness in people's lives, the kind of little austerities that were hard to bear. We couldn't have fully fashioned stockings at home, because they'd all got to go abroad to enable us to pay our way again. I used to say mockingly that girls usually had to sleep with American GIs in order to get lipstick.'

The reasons for this austerity were less easily understood and supported by the public than the hardships imposed by war. During the war, imports came in at the cost of the lives of servicemen in the Battle of the Atlantic, and military demands on such necessities such as fuel, food and motor vehicles obviously had to take priority. After the war, as Barbara Castle puts it: 'It was hard to make people understand why they should have to go without what we would consider the normal things of life, when they had won the war.'

The reason for the new austerity was that Britain was nearly bankrupt. The war had liquidated much of Britain's foreign capital, cost the government a fortune and shattered traditional export markets for British goods. There was a shortage of internationally convertible currency. Britain could not afford the imports that unregulated consumer demand would generate. Imports from countries requiring payment in US dollars were discouraged by strict control of import licences for businesses and rationing of goods for consumers. The government promoted goods that could be bought in sterling, leading to the presence on British shelves of unfamiliar foodstuffs such as snoek (an unpopular South African fish).

It was no accident that the Belcher scandal took place at the Board of Trade, the ministry concerned with administering the complex regulations. The Board (now part of the Department of Trade and Industry) had grown enormously during the war and the austere postwar years and had acquired many new responsibilities. Import controls were handled in the same ministry that dealt with trade promotion. An idea of the scale of the operation can be grasped from Harold Wilson's boast that as President of the Board he abolished 900,000 licences and permits in a few days in 1948 – and that this came nowhere near to abolishing controls altogether.

In the Communist countries, such extensive government regulation of the economy produced ideal conditions for corruption and double standards, by which favoured individuals received better goods than ordinary people. Even without corruption as such, getting results required knowledge of who was important and how best to put your case to them. In postwar Britain, although there was nothing comparable, rationing created an underworld of black marketeers and 'spivs', who would evade restrictions for those prepared to pay. Most such transactions were petty, such as the black market pig in Alan Bennett's comedy *A Private Function*. But the bigger operators realized that there was more money to be made by corruptly dealing in the licences themselves, rather than merely operating around the edges.

The most successful contact man was Sidney Stanley, 'the Spider of Park Lane'. Stanley was an unsavoury character, a Polish-born confidence trickster who worked under several aliases and had managed to dodge a deportation order since 1933. Somehow, this man – shadowy, enigmatic, with a dubious past and a strange, intense manner – carved out a unique position as a contact man. He obtained substantial sums of money from businesses, claiming that he could help them find their way around Whitehall and advance their interests. Like many people before and after him, his claims to be an influential lobbyist were exaggerated to the point where his clients were being cheated, but there was enough substance to his web to provide the only significant scandal of the 1945–51 government.

*

John Belcher was elected Labour MP for Sowerby in Yorkshire in the 1945 election at the age of forty, gaining the seat from the Conservatives with a majority of 6,933. He had been a railway clerk in the ticket office at the Smithfield goods depot in London. He became involved in trade union activity and, like many intelligent working men in the interwar period, studied for academic qualifications in his spare time. According to his daughter Jill Mumford:

> *His whole heart was in Labour Party politics. He had seen the deprivation that so many people had suffered in the 1930s and was fired up with an ambition to change things. For him it was a marvellous thing to be able to be a part of the government and really have an opportunity to put his principles into action. The day he was elected was the happiest and proudest day of his life.*

He was regarded as one of the rising stars of the 1945 Parliament, and stood out as one of the most intelligent and popular members of that enormous intake of Labour MPs. He was promoted to become a junior minister at the Board of Trade in 1946 within a year of arriving in parliament, reflecting Attlee's pride in the quality of Labour MPs coming from the trade unions and the working class who were every bit as fit to govern as the traditional ruling class. John Belcher enjoyed his parliamentary and ministerial duties; by all accounts he was as convivial as he was hard-working, very likeable, with friends on the other side of the House.

The Board of Trade was regarded by many businessmen as a thicket of red

15

tape, run by a socialist government with a doctrinaire opposition to private enterprise. Belcher was a pragmatic, pro-business minister who did his best to build understanding between business and government in the common interest of prosperity. As his Civil Service Private Secretary, James Cross, recalls:

> *He was very approachable and this was his great value at the Board of Trade because businessmen were all very suspicious of the government. They thought that everywhere they turned there were rules and regulations and they wanted to get back to freedom – or some of them wanted to go back to the monopoly they had before the war. He was good at talking to them and explaining that we were moving as fast as we could. He was somebody to whom they could come, who would listen to them and put their case.*

His position of influence over business regulations, and his open approach to the representatives of British business, led to him being in contact with many people who were seeking to influence his decisions. Some businesses offered samples as a gesture of goodwill, or to impress upon the minister the quality of the product. Up to a point, this was legitimate and approved by the prevailing rules of the civil service, although most Labour ministers were uneasy about the ethics of accepting even the most minor gifts. They were conscious that they were imposing hardships on the people who had elected them to create a better society, and believed in the principle of equality – ministers and other prominent people should receive no special favours. Barbara Castle was Parliamentary Private Secretary (PPS) to Stafford Cripps and then Harold Wilson, Belcher's superiors at the Board of Trade, and remembers one of her own crises of conscience:

> *I was taken out to lunch by one of the managing directors of Kent hairbrushes, who was trying to twist my arm to persuade the Department to give him a bigger allocation of dollars for an export drive to the United States. It couldn't have come any more legitimate than that, because he said that Kent brushes were highly esteemed in the States and selling them would earn us some dollars. He gave me a brush, and I said, 'I couldn't accept that.' He told me not to be stupid and that if he was trying to bribe me it would hardly be with a hairbrush. I took it as gingerly as if it had been a time bomb, and brought it back to the Department where I asked one of the top civil servants what I should do with it. They had a solemn conclave and decided I could keep the hairbrush.*

John Belcher saw no difficulties with accepting gestures of generosity. He was a kind-hearted man who enjoyed giving presents to people, and tended to make the assumption that people who gave him things had a similar motive. He would share gifts with his colleagues around the office, such as Barbara Castle:

He regarded the temptations that came his way as harmless gifts, as a means of spreading some largesse in his Department. I remember him coming into my office one day, proudly beaming all over his face and carrying a large red box with a red bow ribbon round it, and saying it was full of little samples of Max Factor cosmetics. He said, 'I've been given half a dozen boxes of these. I've given one to my secretary, there's one for you, I'm taking one home for my wife.' It was his innocence, one couldn't snub him. But I was uneasy because Clem Attlee was extremely rigorous and austere. We had to be above suspicion of any kind.

Sidney Stanley regarded gifts in a different way, as a means of buying access and compromising people in authority. He first met Belcher under the auspices of George Gibson, a trade unionist who had been made a director of the Bank of England. Gibson was to be condemned as well as Belcher for improper use of his official position, but at the time Belcher and most other people regarded Gibson as a respectable, even admirable, figure. Stanley was introduced by Gibson as a man who was well connected in business circles, including in the United States, in addition to being sympathetic to Labour objectives, and Belcher understandably thought he might be a useful man to know. Unfortunately, he was not. He seized upon Belcher's attitude to gifts as a way of influencing the Board of Trade, which in turn would enable him to demand money from business clients to get the decisions they wanted. Stanley established a friendship with Belcher, who was under the impression that he was some sort of executive in a large company. Many other people regarded Stanley in a favourable light, and the misgivings of those who did not could be put down to anti-Semitism; the prejudice that every Jewish businessman is a shady character had survived the Nazi holocaust and was, shockingly, still present in postwar Britain.

By December 1947, when James Cross arrived in Belcher's private office at the Board of Trade, Stanley was a constant presence. He would call in or telephone most days. Cross was puzzled by the minister's strange friend:

I never knew what he did, and I asked John Belcher on one occasion what he did, and he said he didn't know either. He lived in a large flat in Park Lane and seemed to have a lot of money. He was a close friend of John Belcher, he saw him most days and the minister had developed the habit of dropping in at the Park Lane flat, for instance on the way home in the evening or between meetings. I thought it was just friendship; it seemed to me slightly odd, but I was young and I thought perhaps all businessmen were like that.

Stanley ingratiated himself with Belcher by providing him with gifts in kind. James Cross, in hindsight, feels that:

The main thing he gave Belcher was a fairly constant hospitality over a period of a year or eighteen months, either at the flat, or being taken out to meals, to the greyhound races or boxing matches. There was nothing very large that anyone could find and there was never any evidence that Stanley had given Belcher any money. I don't think Stanley would have; he was a recipient of money rather than a giver.

The largest gift was a week's holiday at Cliftonville in Margate. This arose in a chaotic way. Stanley had originally offered Belcher use of a rented house in Margate for the Labour Party conference which was held in the town in May 1947, but the minister wanted to bring along his family and mix a seaside holiday with conference business. Stanley, despite Belcher's misgivings, arranged hotel accommodation instead. The family stayed two weeks, Stanley paying for the last week in May when the conference took place, and Belcher for the holiday week. Mini-bars were not found in Margate hotel rooms in the 1940s, but, while Stanley was paying, Belcher's bar account was modest. He paid for his own sherry, a considerable £15 worth, in the second week.

Belcher was also given a gold cigarette case, and after Stanley had seen him in a patched and worn suit he was given a new one. The minister also accepted fifty-odd bottles of various spirits and sherry in two months from a distiller, Maurice Bloch, who wanted help with import licences.

The scale of the gifts from Stanley and other businessmen was not particularly massive. Belcher and his family did not get rich from his acceptance of what he was offered. They lived in the same house in a working-class part of Enfield before, during and after his time as a minister. Belcher had never known anyone as rich as Stanley seemed to be, and tended to assume that all rich people behaved generously to their friends who lived modestly. As Barbara Castle witnessed, he also tended to give a lot away.

Belcher, in return, was expected to use his ministerial powers to help Stanley and other business contacts. His reputation has been the victim of the exaggerated claims made by Stanley when he was touting for business. Some commentators feel that Stanley was reflecting, in crude form, the central dynamic of the lobbying business; as the commentator Anthony Howard says:

He was a one-man band who managed to prevail on businessmen, who are always much more gullible than people tend to imagine ... In

a sense the job he was doing was not dissimilar to that which lobby-
ists do today, but he was much more disreputable. He claimed that he
was the man who made the wheels go round. In fact I think he did
sweet Fanny Adams and they were just conned.

James Cross also believes that the 'Spider' was primarily a confidence
trickster. He would, for example, hold a party and approach a businessman
who would need an import licence or some other benefit from the Board of
Trade. Once he had got talking about the problem:

Stanley would say, 'Well, John Belcher is the man who can do this,
and he's just over there at the other side of the room. How much is it
worth to you?' And the man might say £1,000. Then Stanley would go
over and say to John Belcher, 'It's a nice day', or something and
Belcher would nod and smile. Stanley would come back and tell the
businessman that he could arrange the deal but it would cost, say,
£5,000. If the thing went through in the ordinary way, that was fine
[and Stanley would get the credit]. If not, he would tell the client that
somebody else had bribed Belcher more, or that others had inter-
vened. It's the old confidence trick, and why any businessman ever
fell for it is beyond comprehension.

The most serious real matter related to a football pools promoter, Harry
Sherman. His business was an insatiable consumer of paper, and he was dissatisfied with the ration he was receiving via the football pools trade association which negotiated with the Board of Trade. He was prepared to use
an array of bribes to acquire the necessary licences from the Board of Trade
to expand his business. Having previously infringed the regulations, he also
wanted a Board of Trade prosecution dropped. Stanley demanded cash sums
of £5,000 (now worth £100,000) each to pay for the bribery of Belcher and
Frank Soskice, the Solicitor-General, to arrange this. The prosecution was
duly dropped although Belcher had refused to discuss the matter with
Sherman and no bribery of the ministers had taken place. But Sherman continued to campaign for more paper, bombarding Belcher with enquiries,
until he made the error of saying that his firm had been exceeding its ration
anyway. Sherman dropped hints that he could blackmail the minister.
Belcher referred the matter to the civil servants involved in paper rationing
and another investigation was launched. Sherman was furious that the
money he had paid Stanley had obviously been ineffective, and started to
complain.

Stanley threw a lavish birthday party on 5 August for his ministerial contact at a dining club called the Garter Club. James Cross was invited, and
recalls: 'The guests were John Belcher and his wife, another MP, Jim

Haworth, who lived in the Belcher house, my wife and I, and various Stanley relatives. It was really a normal dinner party, although it was unusual because we weren't used to going to places like that.'

The atmosphere at the party was somewhat strained because Belcher had heard the first indications that day that Sherman had been talking about his connections with Stanley and the Board of Trade. A friend of Belcher's, David Rufus Williams, also knew Harry Sherman and had put in a word for him in official circles, but had been warned off by a threatening telephone call. Belcher believed it had come from Stanley, and before the Garter Club party began had a heated argument with him.

Allegations about a separate matter, concerning importation of amusement machines, were being investigated by the police and, after reaching Conservative Central Office, were floating around Westminster. Reports reached the President of the Board of Trade, Harold Wilson, about this matter and the Sherman affair, both of which involved Stanley. Wilson promptly told the police and colleagues, and on 9 October 1948 Attlee announced that a Tribunal of Inquiry would be set up, a procedure established in 1921 for the airing and assessment of allegations which related to public misconduct. Unusually, it was not given terms of reference relating to specific allegations. Tribunals had previously been used in cases of police corruption, and the nearest precedent was the inquiry into the 1936 Budget leak that condemned Jimmy Thomas. Belcher requested a suspension from his ministerial duties. The affair had gone public, and false rumours circulated about the involvement of ever more senior Labour figures.

The investigation was extremely rigorous. The Treasury Solicitor examined even the most minor matters. Even before the tribunal had been established, Barbara Castle was required to rummage through the dustbin to show that her Max Factor 'casket' had in fact been a small box of samples.

The Conservatives desperately wanted to believe that the Labour government was corrupt. Resentment at the electorate's ingratitude for Churchill's statesmanship in 1945 was deepened by the government's assault on middle- and upper-class life through rationing and taxation. The country houses were closing down with death duties and the ever worsening 'servant problem'. By the end of the 1940s, something near hysteria was gripping Tory England. The revelations about corruption at the Board of Trade seemed to confirm all these prejudices. Conservative Central Office had its own sources in the business community and did its best to spread the allegations. Expectations of the tribunal were stoked up higher and higher, and the more excitable Tories were looking forward to a massive scandal, of the whole government being bribed and behaving with total hypocrisy while the population endured austerity.

The tribunal hearings were held in Church House in Westminster in November and December 1948, under Mr Justice Lynskey. Not subject to the rules of evidence which protect witnesses in court, hearsay evidence was permitted before the tribunal. The Attorney-General, Sir Hartley Shawcross, who had prosecuted Nazi war criminals at Nuremberg, turned his aggressive courtroom tactics against a junior minister in his own government. In his opening address Shawcross said that gifts, even small seasonal ones, should not be permitted in public life in the way they were in commerce. Belcher was harshly interrogated by Shawcross, and tripped up over matters of dubious relevance such as his understanding of Stanley's family background and nationality. The way he was treated still arouses understandable feelings of anger and distress in his daughter, Jill Mumford:

What my parents were put through in that tribunal I believe was indefensible. My father was subjected to hours of grilling. He was not allowed to know in advance what he would be asked. He never flinched. He told the truth all the way through with courage and dignity.

Belcher's lawyer announced that the minister intended to resign his office after giving evidence to the tribunal. His wife was also given a gruelling interrogation; Jill Mumford recalls her mother's ordeal:

My mother's privacy was invaded ... she had to reveal details of her savings she hadn't even told my father and it distressed her terribly. She was so obviously honest. At one point she says, 'There hasn't been a week since I was fourteen when I haven't saved, and these are my savings.' In fact, she collapsed after giving evidence.

In the 1940s in particular, to be compelled to talk about personal finance in such a public way was a terrible injury to a woman's pride. She was traumatized by her appearance before the tribunal.

In contrast, Shawcross found his questioning of Stanley a disconcerting experience. Stanley was an accomplished name-dropper, which in the context of the hearings draped several red herrings across the path of the investigation, and he was skilled at evading questions with repartee such as, 'Do not try to trap me with the truth.' Shawcross conceded that, 'I have never had a witness with whom I could do so little.' Stanley milked the proceedings for as much notoriety as he could, holding impromptu press conferences on the steps of Church House. The public did not really know what to make of him; expecting a sinister schemer, they got a man portraying himself as a rather comic, engaging figure. Stanley's evidence was a *tour de force* of chutzpah.

After the tribunal was over, the government wanted to enforce the deportation order made against Stanley in 1933, but the conman enjoyed a last

Indian summer entertaining in London clubs because the arrangements were so complicated. The new Communist government in Poland was not interested in this disreputable capitalist, and claimed that he was not an accredited Polish citizen anyway. Israel reluctantly accepted him as a gesture of mercy on Passover 1949.

The proceedings of the tribunal aroused considerable interest among the public; there were queues outside Church House for the public gallery every day and it was front-page news. The main witnesses were treated like the starring cast members of a theatrical production. According to Shawcross, who was called to the Bar in 1925 and wrote his memoirs in 1995, 'The whole subject was reported from day to day more fully than anything I have known, either before or since.'

The report of the Lynskey Tribunal, published on 22 January 1949, found that some of the allegations against Belcher were true; that he had used his ministerial influence improperly in exchange for the gifts he had received, knowing that they were intended to influence his decisions. It did not accept Belcher's opinion that the gifts had not affected his conduct because he knew that it would have been improper to allow them to do so. Gibson was also found to have improperly and knowingly abused his powers, and continued to deny this interpretation. The report reserved its harshest words for the businessmen, Stanley and Sherman. Stanley was described as 'a man who will make any statement, whether true or untrue, if he thinks that it is to his advantage'.

Belcher insisted that he had not abused his ministerial powers. The outcome was a shock to him. He resigned his seat in Parliament immediately before the House of Commons debated the report on 3 February 1949. His resignation speech was a moving House of Commons occasion. He deplored the anti-Semitism and distrust of business that the affair had produced, and spoke about the standards expected of MPs. Belcher said that he was 'touching the very depths of unhappiness and wretchedness' and left the Commons for the last time.

Attlee spoke after Belcher. He welcomed Belcher's decision to resign but spoke with sympathy about Belcher's dignified last speech, and his family. 'What Mr Baldwin on a former occasion in this House called the "unthinking cruelty of modern publicity" has been inflicted on him in full measure.' Churchill acknowledged for the Opposition that the honesty of government had been vindicated, praising the honour of the Labour Party and the trade unions: 'I cannot feel that any party issue is involved.' But he welcomed Belcher's resignation and added, 'We must not allow our personal sympathy for men who are down to lead us to condone in any way the seriousness of the offences committed … as a democratic assembly we are bound to take action.'

A few backbenchers were perturbed about the way the accused minister was not allowed to offer a proper legal defence before the Lynskey Tribunal, and were shocked at the way Belcher had been treated for his mistakes. One of them was Michael Foot, then a rebellious backbencher and later Labour leader, who now recalls: 'The debate in the House of Commons was a wretched scene. I was one of the few people who voted against it. It didn't mean we were in favour of corruption, but it did mean that we thought people should be treated fairly when they were put in front of these tribunals.'

Another, Raymond Blackburn, reflected on the perverse outcome of the scandal: 'The result has been that the guilty go more or less scot-free and those who are innocent of any offence against the criminal law are ruined.' Stanley was made a kind of national hero and sold his story to the press while Belcher suffered. It was to be a recurring pattern in postwar history.

On reflection the Conservative politician Lord Carrington feels that the hysteria about the incident went too far:

It seems pretty trivial by the standards of today. It appeared rather shocking at the time, partly because the press took it up in a big way. There's no doubt that Belcher did the wrong thing, but he was pilloried for it in a way that was out of scale with his lapses. When you look back on it, you'd just had an enormous Labour Party victory and I suppose, as always, that the Opposition and the Conservative press made a meal of it because it was a way of attacking the Labour government.

The Director of Public Prosecutions did not believe that criminal proceedings should be started against any of the principals in the affair, and the matter ended with the report. As with all scandals in which only small fry are caught, there were rumours that the big fish had escaped. Hartley Shawcross certainly intimated in 1974 that someone more important had been involved in corrupt activity at the Board of Trade, but he made it clear that it was an official long since dead. In the 1960s and 1970s those who hated Wilson liked to hint that he had also been involved with Stanley, despite the fact that Wilson had promptly called in the police as soon as he heard the allegations.

The affair probably did not help the Labour government in the 1950 election, despite the prompt and severe action it had taken to deal with Belcher and Stanley. It served the purposes of the Conservative Opposition in enabling them to argue that Labour's belief in the moral, as well as economic, superiority of the planned economy could not be sustained. It might also have served to illustrate the greed and gullibility of the captains of British industry. In any case, the intellectual tide was turning away from physical controls and the economy was growing rapidly again by the end of 1949, meaning that rationing and controls were less necessary. Wilson's first 'bonfire of controls' was in 1948. By 1954 the Conservative government had removed the last remnants of the rationing system.

*

John Belcher was a broken man after he resigned from Parliament. He was horrified at the idea that he had done anything to harm the causes he believed in and the government he had supported. He had not been in the best of health as a minister, and was laid up in hospital for a couple of weeks in 1948 with duodenal ulcers. The shock of public humiliation made things worse, as his daughter Jill Mumford makes clear: 'It broke his spirit ... but my father was never bitter. His health continued to deteriorate and he died far too soon, he was only fifty-nine. He was just able to see the Labour government of 1964. I think he couldn't recover from the effects of the tribunal.'

He returned to his old job in the railway ticket office, and did his best to resume life as an ordinary working man. Some former colleagues behaved decently towards him. Harold Wilson, his former boss at the Board of Trade, would write to him, and on one occasion visited him and his family in Enfield. Clement Attlee, who rarely expressed his feelings, sent a letter of sympathy to Mrs Belcher. Jill Mumford recalls that he tried to comfort her mother and assure her that one day the public would forget. This was not helped by periodic press stories along the lines of 'Where are they now?' – 'fresh journalistic impeachment' as Anthony Howard puts it. The misery of John Belcher's life after 1949, and indeed the penance of a later transgressor, John Profumo, are a sorry contrast to some later survivors of scandal who have used public disgrace as a career stepping stone.

Belcher's fate was resented by many of his colleagues in the trade union group of Labour MPs. Hartley Shawcross, whom many in the Labour Party regarded as little short of an aristocrat, had humiliated a working-class ministerial colleague in 1948 and then gone on to leave Parliament and eventually the party. In his retirement Lord Shawcross was offered, and accepted, several well-paid positions with large firms, notably Ford and Shell. He also enjoyed pleasant smaller jobs such as President of the British Hotels and Restaurants Association. There was nothing in the slightest bit improper about his activities, but they did appear to confirm the rewards of an Establishment background and Establishment views. It did not go unnoticed that barristers such as Shawcross, and journalists such as Dick Crossman, could continue to practise their professions and rake in outside earnings, while working-class members could not carry on their trades and had to subsist on MPs' pay.

After the Lynskey Tribunal Attlee commissioned a report into the wider issue of lobbyists and members' interests. Sidney Stanley had been unique in the scale of his operations at the time, but he was not the only person claiming to be a contact man. During the debate, Herbert Morrison described these proto-lobbyists as 'contact parasites … these objectionable persons are a bad social excrescence, and the sooner they go the better'. This condemnation informed the deliberations of the commission. It reported in 1949 that 'common sense and vigilance' were required, a futile observation, and argued that there would be little future for middlemen because they could not provide any services that would justify extracting a fee. This complacent attitude meant that no action was taken to ensure that the circumstances that led to the rise of Sidney Stanley would not recur. It is perhaps surprising that it took twenty-five years for another major financial scandal to erupt in Westminster.

Although the licensing and regulations run by the postwar Board of Trade were dismantled in the years following Wilson's famous 'bonfire of controls', there were still substantial areas in which business and government met, particularly in the construction industry. Neither was much done to prevent future ministers from finding themselves in the sort of morass John Belcher wandered into, although the guidebook *Questions of Procedure for Ministers* (*QPM*) gradually expanded from 37 paragraphs in 1945 to 132 paragraphs in 1976. In a very British fashion, *QPM* was technically secret until 1992, so that even if the standards expected were known to ministers they were supposed to be unknown to the press and the public.

Nevertheless, the high standards of public conduct of the Attlee administration were carried over into the incoming Conservative government, and no comparable scandal was to arise – though there were a couple of noteworthy 'blips'. In 1954 Sir Thomas Dugdale, Minister for Agriculture, felt obliged to resign over the Crichel Down affair. This involved some land in Dorset which had been purchased in 1938 for use as a bombing range and was run as a model farm by the Ministry of Agriculture after 1945. In 1950 the land was sold for private use, as one large farm rather than splitting it back into its three former constituent farms. In later years Crichel Down would have been dealt with by the Ombudsman, as the relevant decisions had been taken by civil servants and it was a matter of 'maladministration' rather than punishable misconduct. Dugdale was further distanced from the mistake, if mistake it was, by the fact that he had not been minister when the original decisions were taken.

Many in the farming industry and hence the rural Conservative Party were outraged by the Ministry of Agriculture's decision, as it seemed to trample on the rights of property owners, and an inquiry was held into Crichel Down. The judicious constitutional historian Peter Hennessy called it 'a thoroughly partisan inquiry which ended up by publicly pillorying named civil servants' conducted by the Tory right and farmers. Dugdale could have allowed the civil servants to take the blame, but because he basically agreed with the decision and honourably would not sacrifice the officials, he was hounded out of office by Tory backbenchers.

On a different tack, in 1957 allegations emerged, given publicity by Harold Wilson, that insider trading in government stock had been taking place in the City of London. The Board of the Bank of England had decided to raise the standard interest rate, known as Bank Rate, and it was claimed that some firms had profited by selling holdings of bonds which would fall in value when Bank Rate rose. A Tribunal of Inquiry was set up; the City's commercial aristocracy was dragged in to face questioning by the Attorney-General in Church House. The Treasury Solicitor's office dug through the records of the relevant transactions. It was a higher-rent reprise of the Lynskey Tribunal.

The tribunal reported in 1958, and its headline conclusion dismissed the allegations as untrue. Like many another whitewash, the real cause for concern was hidden away in the detail. The evidence gathered suggested a cosy, amateurish system in which people spent more time on grouse moors than at desks and talked as if they were still at public school. It was a glimpse at the way the Establishment did business. It was also not a total clean bill of health; tucked away in paragraph 39 was the sentence, 'Although we have come to the conclusion that there was no general leakage of advance information as to a rise in Bank Rate, it does not, of course, follow that there may not have been individual cases in which dealings were prompted by the improper disclosure or use of confidential information.' However, the political side of the allegations did not add up; Conservative Party officials had not been tipped off and were not involved in insider dealing. In political terms Wilson was the main loser from Bank Rate, looking foolish for bandying around unsubstantiated allegations.

Bank Rate was quickly forgotten and the Macmillan Conservative government was triumphantly re-elected in 1959. By this time the affluence of 'You've never had it so good' had replaced the austerity of the 1940s. By the early 1960s some commentators, such as the well-paid editors of national newspapers, were starting to say that the good times had sapped the nation's moral fibre. The waves of commerce were even lapping at the gates of the Palace of Westminster through the revival of the lobbying industry.

CHAPTER 2

'Honourable Members' 1945-74

'He was considered in those days to be on the take, paid by various people … So for all his gifts, the one thing he could not be given was office.'

**Anthony Howard on Stephen McAdden,
Conservative MP for Southend East 1950–79**

Ministers of the Crown were clearly subject to harsh rules of conduct. For backbench members the position was less clear, and the lack of any external regulation meant that financial interests were policed only by peer pressure and the risk of public embarrassment. It is a testament to the ideals of the time, and the principles that drew most people into politics, that the obvious temptations were so rarely taken up.

The basic pay of an MP in the postwar period was very poor, although many Members accepted this as part of the package. Barbara Castle recalls the position of the average MP in the 1940s:

There was the view that it was a privilege to serve the public. You were underpaid and worked extraordinarily hard. The only perk you got was a free ticket to your constituency. We had no secretarial help in those days, nothing came out of public funds to help us, no research assistant, no free postage. When we got into power in 1945 an MP's salary was £600 a year. One of the first things we did was to raise it to £1,000. When I was heckled by Tories in my constituency saying that we were lining our pockets I used to say, 'I see. So you only want to be represented by rich men with a private income who can buy a seat in Parliament.'

MPs' salaries had been introduced in 1911 as a concession to Labour from the ruling Liberals, and even when Labour became a party of government its members were more affected by poor pay than Conservatives. Tory MPs were often people of considerable private means or wealthy businessmen, and if not they had ready access to connections that could procure a seat in the boardroom of an amenable company. It was much more difficult for Labour MPs. Members who had previously had working-class jobs suddenly found that their expenses had shot up, and they could not usually gain access to the kinds of employment, like law and writing, whose hours could be made to fit around parliamentary responsibilities. It was a struggle to maintain a decent standard of living and offer constituents proper services. As Albert Roberts, elected Labour MP for Normanton, a mining area in Yorkshire, in 1951, recalls:

Nobody was there for the money. In 1951 we were paid £1,000 [now worth £19,000]. You bought your own stamps. You could only have a local call in London, so it wasn't easy. It was a struggle but you got these men from all walks of life in the Labour Party. You could only just keep things going ... Some Labour members lived in poor accommodation, boarding houses with no central heating. I was one of them. And local people would put you on a pedestal and it was very difficult to live up to it.

Labour MPs from distant constituencies suffered from multiple disadvantages, not least that their constituents often had more than their fair share of problems. MPs were cut off from families and had to pay for a London flat to live in during the week. MPs who lived in London could do without a second home, and those, like Barbara Castle, who had working spouses were also more fortunate. MPs who were particularly conscientious with constituency work suffered because of the lack of assistance with office expenses. An allowance for secretarial expenses of up to the modest sum of £500 (now worth about £4,600) and free national telephone calls were introduced only in 1969. It was not until 1974 that the allowance was just about enough to pay for a full-time secretary for each MP.

A lifetime parliamentary career also offered no pension, and no financial benefits to family members. In the 1950s, as Edward Short, a Labour Chief Whip, was later to write, 'There was merely a rigorously means-tested charitable fund, and their salaries were so miserably low that few had any savings worth mentioning.' A contributory pension scheme for Members serving longer than ten years was introduced in 1965 and the qualifying period was reduced to four years in 1972. A severance allowance for MPs losing their seats was also introduced in 1972, but before these changes the position of MPs, particularly those in marginal seats, could be desperate and even pathetic. Unofficial and secret systems evolved to help some MPs to cope – there have long been rumours of a fund controlled by the Conservative whips whose purpose is to prevent MPs becoming bankrupt and hence legally obliged to give up their seats. On the Labour side a benevolent fund was set up by the colleagues of Patrick Bartley, the MP for Chester-le-Street, after his death in 1956. Bartley was an MP with a modest background, and his sudden death in his forties left his family nearly destitute.

Financial necessity led many MPs to take an interest in parliamentary consultancy, particularly if they were not able to practise law, write articles or run companies. Consultants were sought out by a wide range of individual firms, trade associations, unions and pressure group causes. A consultant's duties varied greatly between Members. Some consultancies were thinly disguised subsidies from a firm to a friendly politician; others involved a great deal of work for the MP. Consultants were expected to brief the interest which paid them about parliamentary developments, a particularly useful function for highly regulated industries such as brewers and bookmakers. They were also supposed to help with making useful contacts. When legislation was coming before Parliament they could assess its effects on the outside interest and act when necessary, usually in a Standing Committee. In particular cases, mainly those concerning pressure groups, MPs could sponsor Private Members' Bills.

The rules about declaration of interests for MPs were vague and unwritten. The rule was directed mainly at the casting of a vote, and did not explicitly affect the making of speeches or the asking of parliamentary questions. Still less did it cover what went on in party meetings or lobbying of ministers, or informal persuasion through the social networks of the Palace of Westminster. The basic text was a Speaker's ruling in 1811 that: 'This interest must be a direct pecuniary interest, and separately belonging to the persons whose votes are questioned and not in common with the rest of His Majesty's subjects, or on a matter of State policy.' This left a number of massive loopholes. The definition of a direct pecuniary interest could be, and no doubt was, subject to differing interpretations, as was the degree of harmony between the private interest and the interests of the public in general. As late as the mid 1960s the Speaker insisted that declaration of interests was entirely up to the conscience of individual members, even in cases where the convergence of the private interest and the public matter being discussed seemed obvious. Some Members were scrupulous about declaring, but others were not.

An enormous variety of interests was represented on the backbenches of both main political parties, not all of them paid. What attention was directed to the exercise of influence in Westminster and Whitehall tended to be concentrated on the more obvious pressure groups, whose supporters were clearly identifiable, but private businesses were arguably more important. A backbencher speaking up for a cause such as disability rights or joining the European Community would be talking in broad terms about what he or she believed to be desirable for society as a whole. Different issues were raised when a smaller sectional interest such as a private firm was involved. With business issues of this kind there was also a risk of conflicts of interest with the main task of an MP to represent a constituency, although in practice the interests were often easily reconciled.

Albert Roberts was a consultant for an architect, John Poulson (whose rise and fall are chronicled in Chapter 6), and describes his duties:

> *I saw him perhaps once every two months. He'd talk about his own business and how it was doing and I used to simply say, 'Is there any way I can help?', particularly abroad, which was very important. I could see people, this always happened with Members of Parliament who went abroad. You used to make contact with business people sometimes to help with all this fuss but I did it in a quite open way. I helped him where I could because he employed a good number of people in Pontefract. He was quite helpful to some people but he only employed the best, did Poulson.*

This description of Poulson and his attitude to Members of Parliament would not attract universal agreement. The fact that Poulson had employed significant numbers of Roberts' Normanton constituents counted in favour of the MP when his conduct in relation to the corrupt architect was assessed in 1977.

Getting too closely identified with a lobby, particularly if the cause being represented was below the salt, was regarded as vulgar, not the sort of thing that gentlemen should do. There was also sensitivity about the use of House of Commons facilities for outside interests and distaste for anything that smacked of advertising. Shortly after Jim Prior won his Lowestoft seat in 1959 he was approached by the Bird's Eye food company, a big employer in the fishing port Prior represented. He recalls:

> *They told me that the previous Labour Member had agreed to hold a reception in the House of Commons dining room to launch a product, and asked me to continue it. I rather naively said yes straight away and that caused a hell of a stink because that was regarded as using the House of Commons for advertising purposes. The* Daily Mirror *rang me up and said they assumed I had an interest in the firm involved, and could hardly believe it when I told them I didn't and it was only a constituency matter.*

Prior thought some of the older Conservative backbenchers 'looked down their noses a bit' at him and regarded him with public school condescension as a young upstart who did not know how to behave.

In the 1960s another Conservative MP was the contact man for Lintas, the in-house advertising agency run by the detergent firm Lever Brothers. He would ask colleagues and political journalists to address the firm's directors and in return they would receive a good lunch and 'afterwards there mysteriously arrived a case of the very best wine' according to Anthony Howard. While a flow of information from business to politics and vice versa was proper, the MP's precise reward for arranging these events was not known.

The benefits for an assiduous backbencher from gathering consultancies could be substantial. In 1971–72 a Bill extending the activities of the state-owned Tote was being considered. One clause in particular was opposed by the commercial bookmakers, who thought that Labour MP Brian Walden was making an eloquent case for an argument with which they agreed. In 1972 he was given a five-year contract at £5,000 per annum (now worth £30,000) to act as consultant to the National Association of Bookmakers. The interest was declared by Walden and was not related to his advocacy, which was a personal opinion he had argued before taking the job. Walden also refused to lobby other MPs himself. Walden had several other consultancies and interests, and his total earnings were well in excess of a ministerial salary. According to Anthony Howard: 'Wilson offered Brian a rather good job in 1974, Minister of State at the Board of Trade, and greatly to Wilson's surprise Brian said, "Prime Minister, I can't take it." Wilson asked him to explain and he said, "I can't afford it." Wilson was knocked back a bit.' A ministerial and parliamentary salary combined totalled around £10,000 and friends thought Walden was earning twice that much in (properly declared) retainers. Taken to this extent, consultancy payments had distorted the normal structure of a political career. Walden left the Commons in 1977 to become presenter of *Weekend World*.

*

Trade union sponsorship was a particular type of formal consultancy arrangement, in which the sponsoring union met the election expenses and the office costs of the Labour MP, with an understanding that the MP would advise the union on parliamentary developments and act in a way that furthered the union's interest. The Labour Party had been founded as a kind of lobby for trade union and working class interests; for a while in the 1890s it was thought that it might be possible to develop labour representation through sponsoring working-class candidates in both Liberal and Conservative parties. As the Labour Party grew – and the professional and intellectual middle class became more prominent within it – the role of sponsorship dwindled until it was abolished in 1997.

In the days of very low pay for MPs, union sponsorship did sometimes take the form of a supplement to parliamentary pay. In the 1950s the largest annual payment was £250 (now worth £4,000), compared to a parliamentary salary of £1,250. Personal payments went out of fashion in the 1970s with the general distaste for direct payment of MPs by lobbying organizations and companies, and were usually not uprated in line with inflation. In the 1980s the largest payment was £400 compared to a parliamentary salary of £17,000 and office allowance of £12,000. More usually, sponsorship took the form of a significant contribution to election expenses (themselves governed by a strict legal limit) and the costs of maintaining a constituency organization.

In return, the unions gained the presence of working-class MPs and a level of recognition as a part of the parliamentary system. Although the influence of the trade union movement as a whole was more often manifested through the TUC or the Labour Party constitution, sponsored MPs served to publicize the interests of their union and the people in the union. The relationship between union and MP has never been to give orders, even in heated moments like the 'In Place of Strife' conflict over union law in 1969 and the collapse of the Labour government's incomes policy in 1978. The public nature of the sponsorship relationship and the bureaucratic procedures of unions made attempts to abuse the link very obvious and easily dealt with. In 1975 the Yorkshire Area National Union of Mineworkers (NUM) passed a resolution threatening withdrawal of sponsorship for pro-European MPs, and was condemned by the Commons Committee on Privileges and the national leadership of the NUM. The freedom of sponsored MPs was regularly upheld; they were hardly 'kept men'.

Sponsorship and paid consultancy were not restricted to backbenchers. Cabinet ministers and, to a lesser extent, junior ministers suffered a drastic loss of income when ejected from office: they were immediately reduced to a backbencher's pay (£1,750 as opposed to £5,000 in the 1950s), with no time to unwind commitments made while being paid at the higher level. However, the expertise of former Cabinet ministers would be more attractive to commercial interests than the opinions of a run-of-the-mill backbencher. Connections with their foreign counterparts would still be in working order, and their Whitehall experience would be of great value when firms needed to deal with the British government. Former Chancellors, in particular, were of considerable interest to the City of London.

Although Conservatives found it easier to make the necessary connections, the practice of former Cabinet ministers seeking employment was bipartisan. Labour Shadow Cabinet members such as Harold Wilson and James Callaghan were consultants in the 1950s. When Wilson resigned in 1951, he turned his knowledge of East–West trade gained from his 1948 visit to USSR and his considerable experience at the Board of Trade to commercial use for a number of companies. In 1963–64 he advised Joe Kagan, who produced the Gannex raincoats that shielded him from the elements. His earnings were erratic but averaged £5,000 per annum in total in Opposition. Wilson probably worked harder for the firms which used his services than most parliamentary consultants.

One of the best-known and most respected consultancies was the position of parliamentary adviser to the Police Federation, held until the 1980s by a member of the Opposition. From 1955 to 1964 James Callaghan took on the role. In Callaghan's day the yearly salary was £500 (now worth £6,500) and £300 in expenses. His main benefit to the Federation was actually in helping it perform its functions as a quasi-trade union in arguing its corner on police pay, which had been lagging behind other workers' pay since the war.

The consultancy system was also used for explicitly political purposes by Cecil King, owner of the *Mirror* papers and many other printing and publishing concerns. As a stalwart of the right wing of the Labour Party, he was concerned at the possibility that two allies, Alfred Robens and George Brown, were about to leave Parliament in 1954. King paid them both £500 a year (now worth £8,000), later increased, as consultants to make it possible for them to stay in politics.

Robens was open about his position, but Brown was secretive – and also used his position in the Shadow Cabinet to further King's business interests. Details of the consultancy emerged in the most embarrassing fashion possible in 1962 when the Pilkington Committee on Broadcasting reported favouring a stronger role for the Independent Television Authority (ITA), giving it control over advertising and schedules, and commissioning programmes from the independent companies. This was in line with previous Labour policy and Christopher Mayhew, then the party spokesman on broadcasting, was ready to endorse it. This would have run counter to Cecil King's campaign in favour of more commercial television. George Brown, as Mayhew later wrote, 'argued passionately against me in the Shadow Cabinet and won the day ... Wilson came up to me and remarked, "I don't mind people opposing party policy, but I do think, when they do so, they should declare their interests."'

Mayhew was not aware that Brown was, as Wilson put it, 'on Cecil King's payroll' and neither, it appears, was Labour leader Hugh Gaitskell, who had taken it for granted that Brown would have declared any interest. Brown complained furiously to Gaitskell that Mayhew was accusing him of corruption. Eventually he was pressured into admitting that Wilson's allegation was true, although he only declared it publicly after he had received the impression that Mayhew would reveal it if he did not. Brown's conduct was at best questionable, at worst more corrupt than the activities of Poulson's parliamentary allies.

Brown was also parliamentary consultant for the Frederick Snow surveying and engineering firm based in his home area of Southwark in south London and he energetically promoted its interests. In 1962 Brown tried to fix up a meeting between Snow and London County Council officers via Herbert Morrison, who had led the council and was still a strong influence on it. Morrison thought the suggestion 'unwise' and improper; the high standards of honesty prevailing at the LCC during his term of office were famous. Brown took Morrison's rebuke well; he realized he had overstepped the mark.

*

Sometimes the link between the commercial interest and the Member of Parliament was made through a lobbyist or public relations firm. The principle behind a lobbying firm is that putting a case to the political establishment is a specialized business, which requires knowledge of the relevant players and how to approach them. Keeping track of the political and governmental scene involves considerable work, and the specialist firm is in a better position to get results than, say, the public relations department of a firm which has not previously dealt with government. The specialist firm then hires out its expertise to clients who want to obtain certain outcomes from the governmental process.

There had been a small number of lobbyists in Westminster since the 1920s, when Commander Christopher Powell ran a business providing secretarial services to MPs. In one case, for a Tory MP permanently resident in Monte Carlo, he did more or less everything on the MP's behalf except vote. He was reputed to have considerable behind-the-scenes power, particularly over Private Bills which are promoted by an outside interest. Powell did not directly pay MPs and thought lobbying should be restricted to industries rather than individual private companies.

In the early 1960s the larger corporations did not need to employ MPs to communicate with government, because efforts could be more successfully directed at ministers or civil servants through organized lobbying or, very often, through social contact. Ministers would be invited periodically to boardroom or club lunches and other functions and influence exercised in a more subtle way.

Many MPs had little time for the lobbying industry. According to Douglas Smith, who started work as a lobbyist in the 1960s, some Conservative backbenchers did not believe in the lobbying industry at all and had a very traditional view of the MP's role:

They, as the MP, were representing their constituency and if anyone had a complaint they didn't need an intermediary. And on the other side there were a lot of traditional trade union types who felt that if people had a complaint they went to their union and they sorted it out … People may paint them as being old blimps and trade union men with braces; they were in fact quite experienced people and you had to treat them like that. They weren't going to be fooled by you, you had to be open with them.

Certain MPs were known among their peer group and the public relations industry as having a taste for the more dubious end of the consultancy business. In 1972 an article in *The Observer* revealed that 'between twenty and thirty MPs are known to be really "bendable". Unscrupulous publicists, the pressure salesmen, pass these names around among themselves.' However, most MPs and political journalists would also have been able to guess the identity of most members of the 'dirty thirty' by observing the public actions for which the lobbyist had paid. James Callaghan observed the activities of members during the passage of the Finance Bill enacting his 1965 Budget and is quoted in Mark Hollingsworth's *MPs for Hire*:

I do not think of them as the Honourable Member for X, or Y or Z constituency. I look at them and say investment trusts, capital speculators or 'That is the fellow who is the Stock Exchange man who makes profit on gilt edge.' I have almost forgotten their constituencies, but I shall never forget their interests.

In 1974 Labour MP Joe Ashton alleged in *Labour Weekly* that 'the number of Labour MPs who can be hired can be counted on the fingers of one hand. And the rest of us know who they are. But often their constituents and constituency parties don't.' Ashton was called upon to name them, but he refused and was reported to the Privileges Committee for investigation. He was prevented from gathering evidence and was forced to apologize to the House. It was not the last time that the whistleblower was more harshly treated than the wrongdoer.

One unfastidious MP was reputed to be Stephen McAdden, Conservative MP for Southend East from 1950 until he died in the early months of the 1979–83 Parliament. Anthony Howard recalls:

Stephen McAdden was a brilliant speaker, the hero of the debating halls, always on Any Questions? *I used occasionally to ask Tory MPs why Stephen never got a job. They would pull long faces and say, 'Well, that would be a tale to tell you.' Eventually someone tipped me the wink that he was considered in those days to be on the take, paid by various people ... This was considered just beyond the pale of the Tory Party in those days. So for all his gifts, the one thing he could not be given was office because he was thought to have touched pitch and to have been defiled.*

McAdden's fate was a matter for internal sanctions by his peer group. In such a small world as Westminster it was relatively easy for the whips to detect those members who had improper relations with outside lobbies and screen them out from gaining ministerial office.

However, much as MPs thought a fellow Member was tainted, going to the press was the last thing anyone would do, and in those days the press did not engage in investigations of MPs' improper relationships of either a financial or a sexual nature. Marcus Fox, who first stood for Parliament in 1959 and was elected in 1970, recalls: 'Parliament had been immune from criticism and there were Members who did not behave perhaps as they should have done way back, and yet the system did not allow them to be criticized. Somehow they were protected, they were a protected species.'

The main academic study of outside interests and the political process in the 1950s and 1960s, Samuel Finer's *Anonymous Empire*, considered that, 'In Britain one can exclude [bribery of MPs and officials] completely.' Beyond the relatively small circle of people in the know, there was massive complacency about the honesty of British politicians. It was, and remains, part of the self-image of Britain that its politics are clean, whatever those disreputable foreigners get up to. In the same period as Finer was writing those words, John Poulson's 'consultants' were receiving their payments.

*

By the 1960s it was becoming apparent that there were large grey areas in what it was permissible for Members of Parliament to do in relation to their contracts, and the first tentative steps to disclosure and regulation were urged. Eddie Milne, Labour MP for Blyth from 1960 to 1974, opposed the developing world of lobbying and public relations. In the 1964–66 Parliament he proposed a Ten Minute Rule Bill – a gesture rather than serious legislation – to register the clients of firms engaged in the PR business. It was a not very subtle statement of opposition to the power of T. Dan Smith, the dominant figure in Newcastle politics and himself a corrupt public relations man working with John Poulson. Milne's abortive 'Bill' was a straw in the wind, reflecting growing public distaste for the industry and the secrecy in which it operated.

Foreign governments as well as commercial interests were also involved in hiring lobbyists and sometimes MPs to put their case. The Commons has long had specialist committees which are cross-party groups of MPs who share a legitimate interest of some kind, such as intellectual curiosity about the impact of holiday resort development in the Caribbean or, less facetiously, a common constituency interest such as employment on the railways. There are committees for most parts of the world, in many cases receiving official funding for their activities through the Inter-Parliamentary Union (IPU) and offering considerable opportunities for free travel. Foreign governments with a poor reputation or a recent breach with Britain have a particular need to recruit professional public relations advice. Michael Rice, one of the pioneers of political public relations in the 1950s and 1960s, recalls working for Egypt when the wounds of Suez were still very raw:

For three years after 1956 there were no formal diplomatic relations. They were restored in 1959 and the Egyptians under Gamal Abdel Nasser were conscious that the world had moved on very rapidly from 1956 to 1959 and they wanted someone to advise them and we were recommended. The Egyptians were particularly anxious to restore their tourist industry, and that was a very agreeable aspect of what we were doing. We took Members of Parliament to visit the country, and we facilitated media interest from television and press. We made films for Pathé Pictorial, that sort of thing.

Spain, with its Fascist regime under General Franco, also had an image problem in Britain – which the continuing dispute over Gibraltar did nothing to help. Albert Roberts was more or less alone in the Labour Party in supporting the regime, publicly and privately, to the point of taking the Spanish side in the Gibraltar quarrel. He also had good contacts in Portugal, where a rather less sinister but still repressive dictatorship under Dr Salazar was in power. These contacts were not the result of payment, although he was an honoured guest in Spain and his good standing with the dictatorships was useful for British firms seeking contracts in the area. John Poulson felt that Roberts gave him value for money because the connections he was able to make in Iberia, and particularly in the Portuguese colony of Angola, generated such good business.

Another Labour MP who became entangled with a Fascist regime was Gordon Bagier, this time in Greece, where the 'Colonels' took power in a military coup in 1967. The regime thought itself misunderstood, and re-cruited a public relations firm, Maurice Fraser and Associates, to press its case. In its autumn 1968 report to the client to renew the contract, Fraser made the error of referring to a British MP lobbying behind the scenes and the report reached *The Sunday Times*. Bagier had in fact been a paid con-sultant to Maurice Fraser for £500 (now worth about £5,000) a year plus commission on any business he could find for Fraser. He denied 'lobbying' for the Colonels. In March 1969 he admitted the Fraser payments, having denied this when the allegations were first made in October 1968.

It was almost as embarrassing for the public relations industry as it was for Labour or for Parliament. PR was virtually unregulated, as Michael Rice points out: 'In those days there was absolutely no reason to prevent anyone putting up a brass plate on their door calling themselves public relations consultants, taking money from unsuspecting clients and doing whatever, and this indeed was a problem that faced us all.'

The Maurice Fraser agency was small, with an extremely restricted client list and a nationalistic sympathy for Greece, and the ill-advised report to the Colonels' regime showed that the firm was operating in an area that it did not understand very well. The Fraser–Bagier affair was the opportu-nity to introduce a certain amount of self-regulation in the industry by set-ting up what was then called the Public Relations Consultants' Association, initially from twelve of the largest London firms.

The first time the affair came to light, in October 1968, Richard Cross-man, then Leader of the House, recommended setting up a special select committee of the House to advise on lobbying firms, foreign governments and declaration of interests, but the Crossman minute was apparently lost in other business about proposed select committees. After Bagier's admission, more ministers in the Labour government became concerned about the lobbying activities of foreign governments, and the question of members' interests in general. Harold Wilson was 'tremendously excited' about the need to clear up the definition of appropriate members' interests through a piece of government legislation, but other Cabinet colleagues were not as keen. The Parliamentary Labour Party was already in a state of indiscipline; the reform of the House of Lords was stalled and ministers were already worried about the prospects for proposed trade union legislation. To try to ram through a measure on MPs' outside interests would have been disastrous for the government's relations with its backbenchers and might have failed in Parliament. There was also the political calculation Crossman attributed to Callaghan and Richard Marsh and recorded in his *Diaries* to the effect of: 'What do we get out of this? All we shall do is expose the two or three other Labour MPs who may well have been working for PR firms. If we set up a committee of inquiry into this, don't we merely damage the government at this stage?'

The issue was referred to the House of Commons for an inquiry, and there was no promise of government legislation. There was never a serious threat to self-regulation, but the Select Committee which investigated Members' Interests in 1969 produced a mild report which recommended some changes to improve the clarity of the situation. The report said that questions in Parliament and correspondence with ministers should be brought clearly within the disclosure requirement. It also effectively banned paid advocacy, although it stopped short of recommending a public register of all outside interests held by MPs.

The hurried calling of the June 1970 election meant that the Select Committee report was not implemented before the Labour majority which had favoured it was overturned. The incoming Conservative government was even less keen than its predecessor on imposing regulations on Members' interests and the Select Committee report was buried. It took the exposure of the payment of MPs by the corrupt architect John Poulson, and another Labour-led Parliament, for reform to take place in 1974.

*

Some governments used intelligence agencies instead of public relations firms. Compared to spying, PR is a highly regulated and reputable industry. Since the end of the Cold War concern about sleaze generated or exploited by intelligence services has diminished, to the extent where paranoia has probably been replaced by complacency. During the Cold War the most active foreign intelligence agencies on the British scene were those of the USSR, the USA, Czechoslovakia and South Africa. American influence was generally wielded subtly, for instance through a CIA subsidy for the magazine *Encounter* which was closely aligned with the pro-American

Gaitskellite wing of the Labour Party.

The operations of the Eastern Bloc and South African agencies were more crude and sleazy. Czechoslovakia targeted MPs and had a relationship with the only MP since 1940 to be charged with acting for a foreign power. (In that year a Tory MP publicized Nazi radio stations and was interned as an enemy.) Will Owen, Labour MP for Morpeth, had been passing documents to the Czech intelligence service. Owen was not a minister and the only work he did that was of conceivable interest to the Czechs was as a member of the Commons Defence Estimates Committee. Most of the information that went to the committee was publicly available. In exchange for £500 (now worth about £5,000) a month – plus free holidays – Owen was giving the Czechs information which could be found in broadsheet newspapers and the academic press; he was apparently known as 'Greedy Bastard' to Czech intelligence. The scam came to an end when a Czech defector named him to MI5 and he was brought to trial in 1970. When it was pointed out that the documents Owen was charged with supplying did not count as secrets, he was acquitted.

South African operations under the apartheid regime came to the attention of British politicians in 1976 when Harold Wilson convinced himself that they had seriously destabilized British democracy, a fear which proved greatly exaggerated. The most serious operations in Britain were the assassinations of South African exiles. However, the machinations of the South African BOSS (Bureau of State Security) certainly deserve a mention in the context of sleaze. Some right-wing Conservative MPs had sympathy for South Africa and the rebel Ian Smith regime in Rhodesia, and pleaded their cause out of ideological conviction. It is still not clear to what extent some MPs colluded with South African intelligence. Gordon Winter, a BOSS agent in Britain, alleged that he was on friendly terms with several Conservative MPs, and was told on several occasions by BOSS to use them to further the interests of South Africa. These included Harold Soref, the right-wing Member for Ormskirk 1970–74, who was described as 'a good friend of South Africa' and colluded with Winter in several propaganda operations in favour of South Africa and against British anti-apartheid campaigners.

Some Russian intelligence operations aimed at the British political class were blatantly hostile. Yevgeny Ivanov, naval attaché and Soviet spy in London from 1960 to 1963, was aware of the importance of digging dirt:

It is an open secret that the GRU and the KGB actively used all available means (even blackmail and bribes) to obtain the materials they needed. In certain conditions, information about the scandalous habits of MPs and high-ranking officials (such as homosexuality ... drug abuse or greed) could be used to discredit the highest echelons of power in Britain.

Anthony Courtney, Conservative MP for Harrow East, was the victim of an unpleasant set-up by the KGB, following his campaign to improve security at British embassies in the Eastern Bloc. He was photographed having sex with a female friend in Moscow in 1963, at a time when he was not married, and in 1965 photographs were circulated to newspapers, politicians and his constituency officials under the heading 'I'm not a Profumo, but ...' It was such an obvious set-up that Fleet Street journalists nearly unanimously thought the story was not worth printing. Only *Private Eye* published a reference to it, a decision subsequently regretted by the Editor, Richard Ingrams, who took a generally wary attitude to stories that smelled of espionage. But the KGB's operation against Courtney managed to ruin his second marriage and sowed division in his constituency party which did not help Courtney's (unsuccessful) efforts to hold the seat in 1966.

Usually, though, the approach was friendly. In the 1950s and 1960s Soviet diplomats were a recognized part of the social and political environment, although despite a common belief to the contrary at the height of spy mania there were few if any MPs on the payroll or bearing secret ideological affinity. Instead, diplomats and KGB officers (there was little difference) would act more or less as journalists, gathering political 'intelligence' (which is really a grander name for gossip).

Most politicians were well aware of this game, and would report social contacts and any information they had managed to glean back to the British security service. A few, such as Tom Driberg, got a thrill out of the rustle of cloaks and daggers. It is well known that in rigid hierarchies – such as the KGB – subordinates tend to distort their activities to serve their own interests when reporting to superior officers, so officers on the ground in Britain would boast of 'running' agents who were nothing more than people they had chatted to at a party. Some spies used fictitious agents as a way of making false expense claims to pay for a drink problem or a mistress. The ludicrous allegation that Michael Foot was a KGB agent emerged from this hall of mirrors, and the September 1999 disclosures from KGB archivist Vasili Mitrokhin's papers should be treated with some caution.

Many Labour intellectuals were conversant in Marxism, if as a kind of foreign ideological language, so Russians found it easier to communicate with the British left. However, some Conservatives also enjoyed the company of the Russians – Yevgeny Ivanov was able to gain access to the circle around Lord Astor and John Profumo. Ivanov's social success led to the classic 'scandal' of postwar Britain, but to acquire that legendary status the Profumo scandal had to have more than just espionage. It needed to tear the curtain protecting the political class from discussion of their sex lives.

CHAPTER 3

Private lives
1945-62

'If anything, I became more promiscuous after my election to parliament.'

**Tom Driberg, in his posthumously
published autobiography, 1977**

P owerful people have always been free to exploit their position for financial gain, but money is not the only driving passion – or, as some may have it, perk. There have always been those in the political and social élite inclined to indulge their particular private lusts – for the opposite sex, or the same sex, or for mind-altering substances – that would be deemed off-limits to 'ordinary' people.

Absolute power confers absolute licence: the ruling class carries on without regard for the sensibilities of its population or any fear of exposure. The advent of democracy, as one might expect, has not eliminated the fundamental connection between self-indulgence and power, but has weakened its effect on the lives of the rulers. The dispersal of political power among a larger ruling class means that the sexual and other personal rewards of power are shared out to a greater extent, and democracy has reduced the distance between the ruling class and ordinary people. The governors are accountable to the governed, through elections; and the ability of the popular press to publicize their behaviour exposes them to the envy – and censure – of their fellow citizens.

Certain elements of the privileged classes in Britain have not been reluctant to take advantage of their position. Sexually, aristocratic morals of the 1920s accepted as routine extra-marital affairs between social equals, while casual sex between young members of the metropolitan avant-garde was common then, probably more so than at any other time until the 1970s. Women in the 1920s had more legal and political rights than ever before, and were also starting to assert their right to sexual fulfilment.

There was also more knowledge about, and tolerance of, homosexuality among the élite than before or since, at least until the 1990s. Oxford in the 1910s and 1920s was suffused with a gentle homo-erotic current. In the late 1920s the circle around W. H. Auden was the most prestigious in the university, and drew in Tom Driberg and Richard Crossman. As Anthony

Howard's biography of Crossman says, 'Dick never sought to conceal the fact that in his early years at Oxford he had operated predominantly as a homosexual.' He had several gay relationships at college, a relatively normal thing to do in his circle, including a brief affair with Stephen Spender (which was not revealed until after the poet's death).

The unwritten private scandal of the political class in the 1930s involved Bob Boothby. He was one of the more flamboyant Conservatives in a rather dull age, and therefore someone of recurrent interest in this book (his public downfall was described in Chapter 1). Boothby had seemed a rising Tory star when elected in 1924 at the age of twenty-four: articulate, popular, liberal-minded and dynamic. He was also self-confessedly a 'bit of a shit'. He was always running out of money because of his gambling habit. He had a string of affairs with married women, resulting in several children. His authorized, and generous, biographer admits that 'Boothby's affections were consistently rather too easily aroused, and he was often outrageously indiscreet and weak'. The longest-lasting and most significant of these affairs was with Dorothy, Harold Macmillan's wife, which began in the early months of the 1929–31 Parliament and lasted for decades. Dorothy found Macmillan cold and was drawn to Boothby's emotional and sexual warmth. Boothby may have been a bounder, but Dorothy also used him selfishly, damaging him politically and psychologically. From 1930 she campaigned for a divorce, but Harold Macmillan would not agree to it. Boothby married, unsuccessfully, to try to escape his relationship with her.

As the journalist Geoffrey Goodman says of Boothby and Macmillan, the relationship wrecked the Boothby marriage and accentuated Macmillan's pessimism and depression:

The situation was fairly well known to a lot of people in politics and journalism, but nobody would think of breaking that story, not simply because of the personal tragedies involved but because you would be offending a certain unwritten ethical code. There was a consensus among journalists as well as politicians that there were certain things you didn't do. There was an element of real tragedy in Harold Macmillan's life – his relationship with Dorothy had been shadowed and marred for so long by her relationship with Boothby.

The last act of the tragedy was in 1966, when Dorothy Macmillan died. Harold Macmillan said that he burned the letters Boothby had written her, telling Boothby, with whom he remained on decent terms: 'I didn't want some Arizonan professor writing a thesis about you and me.'

Ironically to a later generation, Boothby's 1937 divorce brought him more censure than his flagrant affair with Dorothy. Divorce was still something of a problem for politicians, because it was a public matter and, before the law was reformed, required sordid evidence to be trailed through a court-room. The stigma against divorce was, for upper-class men, accompanied by a permissive attitude to prostitution and mistresses. The career of one dash-ing young Conservative MP, Somerset de Chair, was cut short in 1950 because of his divorce, not because of the censure of his colleagues but the disapproval of his Paddington South constituency association. He had been followed since before the election by private detectives hired by his wife, who proved his adultery and fatherhood of a child by another woman.

Anthony Eden, who became Prime Minister in 1955, had been divorced in 1950. He remarried, with some trepidation, in 1952 but other than some criticism from the churches it was generally welcomed. The problems posed by the issue were complicated by the abdication crisis in 1936, which had imposed a stringent moral code on the royal family. The previous marriages of Wallis Simpson were a public reason for forcing the abdication of Edward VIII, but the political class led by Baldwin was also concerned at his sym-pathies with Fascism and the possibility of his making active use of the con-stitutional powers of the monarchy. In the case of the forced break between Princess Margaret and Peter Townsend in the early 1950s there were no constitutional implications; it was a pure case of moral judgement against Townsend as a divorced man. It reminded the ruling class of the 1936 abdi-cation, although public opinion was broadly sympathetic to Townsend.

The Labour government had, under pressure from some backbenchers and the rise in divorce cases after legal aid was introduced in 1949, set up a Royal Commission into the laws on marriage and divorce in September 1951. It reported in highly inconclusive fashion in December 1955, two gen-eral elections later, and significant divorce law reform waited until 1969.

*

Back in the 1920s, on the Labour side, left-wing thinkers were increasing-ly interested in alternatives to traditional marriage; in *Marriage and Morals* Bertrand Russell argued that married couples should loose the shackles of sexual possessiveness (but failed to acheive this himself). The new genera-tion of Labour politicians, at least the most intellectually and socially con-fident among them, started to relax the restrictive morality that had domi-nated the Party. The early Labour Party had been influenced by a puritani-cal nonconformist religious conscience, and by the working-class self-advancement embodied by the trade unions, whose members often saw dis-cipline and clean living as part of the socialist life. Gradually, the middle- and upper-class intellectual left, with new political ideas about personal life, became more influential in the party, as did the early feminism of the peri-od. Jennie Lee, a fiercely independent Scottish woman of twenty-one when she was first elected an MP in 1929, rejected the expectation that women should 'submit' to their husbands only once married, and enjoyed several partners before her unconventional marriage to Nye Bevan in 1934.

Michael Foot and Jill Craigie were an unmarried couple for a while, at the risk of scandalizing the press, although Michael Foot as a journalist had a way of fighting back. Jill Craigie recalls the time they returned from a holiday together in the mid 1940s:

When I came back to the little house in Hampstead where I was living it was surrounded, the little alleyways by it full of the press. They said, 'You've been off to the south of France with Michael Foot.' This was the sort of thing that wasn't done in those days at all. I telephoned Michael and when I came back I told the press, 'Michael says if you publish anything at all he will print in Tribune *everything he knows about Lord Beaverbrook and his various mistresses, Lord Thomson and what goes on there, Lord Rothermere who has a disgraceful record,' and right through the list of all the proprietors. All the press vanished.*

Attlee was himself an uxorious man who had high personal moral standards. He found affairs, such as Herbert Morrison's relationship with his Cabinet colleague Ellen Wilkinson, distasteful but would not hire and fire ministers on the basis of their personal lives alone, still less want to see them exposed. Another of his ministers, Philip Noel-Baker, conducted a cross-party extra-marital affair with Megan Lloyd George, who was then a Liberal MP and therefore a member of the Opposition. Attlee warned ministers that Labour Members were more harshly punished for any lapses than Tories, using a sexual metaphor for the entire range of misconduct: 'A Tory minister can sleep in ten different women's beds in a week. A Labour Minister gets it in the neck if he looks at his neighbour's wife over the garden fence.'

Hugh Gaitskell, Attlee's successor as leader of the Labour Party (1955–63), has an unfair historical reputation as a 'desiccated calculating machine' – a jibe Nye Bevan was in fact aiming at the ageing Attlee. He had the same stiff-backed posture and stilted tones of many of his age and class (Winchester and Oxford), but when roused, as at the time of Suez, he was capable of fierce oratory. He was also, in private, a passionate man who enjoyed the good things in life like fine wine and dancing late into the night. Much as he loved his wife, Dora, she did not share this side of his life and Gaitskell instead formed a romantic attachment with Ann Fleming, formerly Rothermere, who was married to Ian Fleming, author of the James Bond books. She was a high-society hostess of pronounced Conservative views ('I suppose I shall have to go dancing next Friday with Hugh Gaitskell to explode his pathetic belief in equality, but it will be a great sacrifice to my country'). It was entirely separate from Gaitskell's political or family life; he was able to compartmentalize his life and his feelings. Their affair apparently lasted until Gaitskell died, and was no secret in London society, not least because Ann Fleming was inclined to gossip. Gaitskell's political colleague Tony Crosland let them use his flat to meet; Ann Fleming joked that she would fantasize about Crosland when she was in bed with Gaitskell.

The relationship was never publicized, not least because of the incestuous way the political and media establishment worked. She remained on good terms with Rothermere after their marriage ended, and she was also close to Beaverbrook, to whom she wrote frequently and candidly about 'twinkle-toes' Gaitskell. These connections saw to it that even relatively clear evidence could be suppressed and inquiries called off. When she discovered a *Daily Express* reporter had been curious about Gaitskell's presence at Goldeneye, the Fleming retreat in Jamaica, she cabled Beaverbrook:

> *EXPRESS PURSING [sic] HUGH PLEASE DARLING MAX PREVENT GOLDENEYE PUBLICITY URGENT PASSIONATE LOVE AND GRATITUDE ANNIE.*

Over-enthusiastic journalists in London also found their progress barred, as Jill Craigie points out:

> *It was well known at the time that a young journalist photographer had taken a picture of Hugh Gaitskell when he was drunk, as happened now and again. He was slouched on the pavement with his arm around a lamp post and Ann Fleming was standing right by. The journalist thought he had the scoop of a lifetime, he was going to sell it for £50,000. Anyway, he tried every single newspaper and there wasn't a single one which would publish it, although lots and lots of people in Fleet Street had seen it.*

This not surprisingly led to many journalists chatting about the affair in Fleet Street pubs, or teasing Gaitskell who was thin-skinned about it. Ian Aitken, then *Daily Express* correspondent in New York, was waiting with Lord Beaverbrook for a flight to Jamaica.

> *The people who had got off the plane came flocking in and among them were Hugh Gaitskell and his mistress, Annie Fleming. Gaitskell spotted us almost immediately and they scuttled straight across the room to the very far end. Beaverbrook saw them and, that impish grin on his face, said to me, 'Ian, go over there and invite Mr Gaitskell to join us.' He loved this sort of situation and would screw every ounce of embarrassment he could out of it. I went across and Gaitskell flatly refused, as we knew he would.*

But most of all, private lives were governed by a code of silence of the sort which governs most closed societies. The working population of the Palace of Westminster is the size of a fairly large village, though this is perhaps a less exact metaphor than an enormous Oxbridge college. Six hundred or more MPs and several hundred attending peers work alongside a multitude of research and secretarial workers, catering and security staff and many others. Like a college or a village, it is a breeding ground for gossip and rumour, and it is very hard to keep a secret for long from one's neighbours. The whips of all parties considered it part of their duty to monitor the personal lives of MPs, as Labour's Chief Whip from 1964 to 1966 Ted Short recalled in his book *Whip to Wilson*:

> *Whips are also welfare officers who must make themselves aware of the personal problems of their Members and give whatever assistance they can, particularly where attendance at Westminster may be affected … When I arrived at No. 12 [the Chief Whip's office in Downing Street] I was told that it had been the practice to keep a 'dirt book' in which unsavoury personal items about Members were recorded. I gave strict instructions that no such book was to be kept in future.*

The compilation of a 'dirt book' in the 1960s by the Tory whips was confirmed by Lord Whitelaw in 1995 for a BBC documentary on the Whips' Office, *Westminster's Secret Service*. The recording of discreditable stories means that the whips can threaten some pretty rough tactics to pressure dissenting MPs into following the party line. Tim Fortescue, a Conservative whip in the 1970s, gave an interview for the documentary: 'When you were trying to persuade a member that he should vote the way he didn't want to vote, it was possible to suggest that perhaps it would not be in his interest if people knew something about him.'

The threat rarely had to be acted upon. To publicize the contents of the dirt book would cause embarrassment to the party as well as the MP, and reduce the confidence MPs have in the whips' discretion which is necessary for their effectiveness. The dirt book, and the use chief whips can make of their knowledge, is a popular theme for fictional writers such as Michael Dobbs (*House of Cards*) and Sara Keays (*The Black Book*). All papers of the whips' office are the personal property of the Chief Whip, who can choose to destroy them (as Ted Short did) or to keep them. There are presumably some dirt books sitting in the archives of some former chief whips.

But in general, Westminster's inhabitants see no reason to share the secrets of their institution with outsiders, in the way that colleges rarely wash their dirty linen in public, and strangers get short shrift when they arrive in a village asking questions.

The code of silence is more than a social fact. It is combined with the same sort of professional discretion that policemen, doctors and lawyers have often exercised when dealing with erring members of their professional community. To be a politician is to be a member of an unusually self-regarding profession, whose legitimacy comes from nothing less than the will of the people, and whose tradition of self-regulation was the guardian of political rights in ancient struggles with the Crown. Most Members feel a justifiable pride in their popular mandate, and their participation in such a time-honoured institution.

The British public was complicitous in the illusions which were perpetuated about the morality of the political class. By the early 1950s public opinion seemed inflexibly conservative on 'moral' issues. For the Conservative Party in particular, the grip of moral conservatism on the party's membership and voters had to be reflected in the party's policy and rhetoric. The influence of the Church was still strong, and the internal politics of the Church of England ('the Tory Party at prayer') were still dominated by traditional views. The Tory Party was compelled, by the nature of its electoral and ideological base, to pretend to be the Church of England in Parliament – despite the sophisticated sexual tastes of many of its leading members. As Christine Keeler, a leading player in a later national scandal, was to put it, 'The hypocrisy of the middle-class British was to drive the prostitutes off the streets in a feeble attempt to pretend they didn't exist. Meanwhile, sex orgies flourished behind the doors of the grandest homes.'

One such grand home was Cherkley, the country house of Lord Beaverbrook, although 'orgies' is perhaps pushing it as a description of the parties he held there and at his Fulham house, The Vineyard. As his biographers Anne Chisholm and Michael Davie record:

> When [the writer William] Gerhardie was encouraged to hurry straight round to The Vineyard with a problem, he found a dinner party in progress that included Lloyd George, and guests waiting to hear the latecomer's troubles. The next night he attended a rather different kind of party, consisting of 'young lords and chorus girls'; he opened a bedroom door to find Beaverbrook busy with two young women.

Beaverbrook found decadence amusing, and would use his money and social connections to put temptation, be it alcohol, gifts, hospitality or chorus girls, in the way of people who could be interesting or useful to him. Some people such as Aneurin Bevan knew how far they could go without selling their soul to Beaverbrook. Bevan and Jennie Lee tactfully refused the offer of a lodge on Beaverbrook's estate and treatment from his doctors.

Beaverbrook was not just another peer. He was the most powerful newspaper baron that Britain has ever seen, controlling the *Express* papers, the London *Evening Standard* and at one stage the Mirror Group as well. He cheerfully used his newspapers as propaganda for his own political agenda, which was an eccentric mix of right-wing Conservatism and Stalinism, and to promote the interests of his friends and political allies. He was included in Cabinets in 1918 and from 1940 to 1945, on Lyndon Johnson's famous principle that it is better to have people like that inside the tent pissing out than outside pissing in.

The other press barons, despite commercial rivalry, were also firmly part of the political establishment. The power of the barons, particularly Beaverbrook, meant that keeping the peccadilloes of politicians out of the public eye was relatively easy given the consent of a small group of powerful men. This was forthcoming, especially from Beaverbrook who was as much a beneficiary of the system as the most dissolute politician.

Editors and journalists, as well as proprietors, mixed socially with politicians, and heard a lot of stories that they knew would never see print, whether because the proprietor would not allow it, it seemed in bad taste, or simply that it would be a libel risk. Partial insider status was terrific fun for journalists. Patrick Marnham in his history of *Private Eye* described journalists in the postwar period as 'accustomed to finding out what was going on and keeping it to themselves … That was, after all, one of the great insidious attractions of being a journalist. By suppressing the information one automatically increased the value of it to those chosen few who were let in on the secret.'

The most privileged journalists were given a kind of formal associate membership of the political class through the lobby system. Accredited lobby journalists were, and are, allowed to mingle freely with politicians in the Palace of Westminster and given regular off-the-record briefings by press secretaries and politicians of all parties and privileged early access to official documents. Newspapers were initially restricted to one lobby pass each, which was usually held by the senior political correspondent. It was governed by a committee of the most senior among the lobby correspondents. Journalists such as *The Sunday Times*' James Margach had longer parliamentary careers than most politicians. Terence Lancaster, an experienced political journalist, recalls the way the lobby bound political journalists into the parliamentary system: 'The main difference between political journalism now and then is the introduction of the investigative reporter. I wouldn't say the lobby were servile, but they were certainly deferential … A lobby journalist in those days would be horrified at the idea that he had to investigate a minister's sex life.'

The rules of the political class do not apply just to unorthodox sexual behaviour, but also to other embarrassing matters such as drinking and drug use. Through the ages, many politicians have been heavy drinkers. It is only to be expected in a job that involves wasting considerable time hanging around waiting to cast routine votes, separates many people from the stabilizing influences of home and family, and requires the sort of confident self-presentation that can be found in the bottle. Some of the greatest figures in British political history – Winston Churchill and Asquith, for example – have had serious alcohol problems.

Because the allegation is so often justified, imputations of being drunk on duty are severely frowned upon by the traditions of the House. Garry Allighan MP fell foul of this rule in 1947 and was kicked out of Parliament. Allighan's offence was to write an article in the *World's Press News* on how exactly it was that details of private meetings such as the Parliamentary Labour Party were published with such accuracy in the newspapers, particularly the London *Evening Standard*. He explained that lobby journalists would pay for this information with cash, personal publicity or alcohol, and he alleged that MPs were frequently drunk.

Allighan's claims were investigated by the Privileges Committee, and it was discovered that he owned a press agency which supplied the *Evening Standard* with political information from none other than Allighan himself. Allighan's leaking was not punishable because it involved party meetings rather than parliamentary proceedings, but his comments about drunkenness and his hypocrisy were dealt with harshly, and he aroused little sympathy among his colleagues. Another MP, Ernest Walkden, who had been paid for gathering political intelligence, was only reprimanded.

The next case related to drinking was the 'Venetian Blind' libel action of 1957. Aneurin Bevan, Richard Crossman and the Labour Party General Secretary Morgan Phillips had attended the Congress of the Italian Socialist Party in Venice. An article in *The Spectator* alleged that the trio had 'filled themselves like tanks with whisky and coffee' and that the Italians 'were never sure whether the British delegation was sober'. The burden of the paragraph was that all three had been drinking heavily in Venice.

Despite the fact that, although one or two of the details were astray, the substance of the article was true, the *The Spectator* lost the libel action. Jenny Nicholson, who wrote the piece, had been unwise to break the taboo against publicizing the drinking habits of politicians, even in a light-hearted and possibly approving way. The punishment of the *The Spectator* through costs and £2,500 (now worth about £35,000) each for the plaintiffs deterred anyone from doing so in future. The story had a number of sequels, mainly thanks to the indiscretion of Richard Crossman. In 1972 he went to a *Private Eye* lunch and Auberon Waugh, who was present, has a clear recollection that he had boasted that he and Bevan had been 'pissed as newts' (the term is Waugh's rather than Crossman's) in Venice. In 1981 Crossman's backbench diaries were published, which revealed that Morgan Phillips had been 'tiddly by midday and soaked by dinnertime' and that Bevan had been, at the very least, in ebullient and expansive form at the conference. After the end of the case Crossman told his diary, 'I still think the risk we took was appalling.' One can only agree.

In Bevan's defence, his action against the *The Spectator* was partly because he had grown sick of the amount of criticism and innuendo that had been aimed against him in the press. His ally Jill Foot thinks he was not covered by the general code of silence about personal lives because his political views were considered beyond the pale:

> *They wanted to get Nye. Once they tried to set him up as he was walking at night; he used to go walking at night to think. A prostitute approached him and a flashlight went on. Nye was really quick and pushed the camera out of the way. He was absolutely furious. Now, if they'd got a picture of Nye with a prostitute you could be quite sure that that would have been published.*

Public trouble has generally only started when MPs misbehave outside the protective environment of the Westminster social circle. According to Terence Lancaster: 'In the 1950s if an MP was disgraced in any way it was either because of a court case in a sexual matter or some financial irregularity. But there was no probing into private lives unless it was served up to the newspapers on a plate.'

This was particularly the case during the 1950s for homosexuals. From 1885 until 1967 all male homosexual contact was illegal, thanks to an amendment dubbed the 'blackmailer's charter' by a Victorian judge. Oscar Wilde, and many less famous than him, suffered the punishment of imprisonment for expressing their feelings. Enforcement of this law ebbed and flowed over the years, and was always harsher on the powerless and unlucky than the upper class. There have always been gay politicians of all parties, and for the most part they have been able to rely on the discretion of their colleagues regardless of political differences. The political class as a whole connived at the hypocrisy of maintaining the criminalization of homosexuality while extending a more tolerant approach to their friends.

After the Conservatives returned to power in 1951, the Home Secretary Sir David Maxwell-Fyfe intensified police efforts against homosexuals. Maxwell-Fyfe bore a sanctimonious hatred for homosexuals; in addition the flight to Moscow of Guy Burgess, a flamboyant gay man, and Donald Maclean in 1951 confirmed the prejudice that gay men were unreliable and security risks. A 1956 conference of Privy Councillors decided that 'personality defects' such as homosexuality, heavy drinking and promiscuity were reasons to deny security clearance for people working in sensitive positions in the civil and security services. Logically, the same sort of standards could be demanded from politicians themselves.

The anti-homosexual witch hunt led to the downfall of two bright but unfortunate MPs in the 1950s, before its cruelty caused a shift in public sympathy symbolized by the Wolfenden Report (1957) which led ten years later to the decriminalization of gay sex in private places between men aged over twenty-one. William Field, Labour MP for North Paddington, was entrapped by police in a public lavatory at Piccadilly Circus in 1953. He was found guilty of a trivial offence, and resigned his seat. In 1958 the Conservative Foreign Office Minister Ian Harvey was caught with a guardsman in St James's Park, and resigned his office and his seat. Both men realized the hostility they would encounter in their constituency associations.

Harvey and Field might have looked enviously at the career of Parliament's most celebrated homosexual, Tom Driberg. His career is perhaps the most extreme example of how favoured members of the political class got away with behaviour for which ordinary citizens would have been persecuted.

Tom Driberg was MP for Maldon in Essex from 1942 to 1955, the first three years as an independent, then Labour; and Labour MP for Barking from 1959 to 1974. From 1949 until 1972 he served on the National Executive Committee of the Labour Party. He was ennobled as Lord Bradwell in 1975 and died in 1976.

Such a bald summary does little justice to one of the most exotic figures ever to have sat in Parliament. At Lancing School, and immediately afterwards, he acquired the three loves of his life: 'all, it seemed, mutually irreconcilable, yet each, in its different way, expressing rebellion against the values of my home: "deviant" sex, "exotic" religion – and left-wing politics'. Driberg was a promiscuous homosexual, and a keen churchman who was a devotee of the highest Anglo-Catholic ritual. In his autobiography he recalled his first orgasm (in an underground lavatory in Tunbridge Wells) and his first High Mass (in St Andrew's Church, Worthing) 'with absolute and equal clarity'. He joined the Communist Party while a student at Christ Church, Oxford.

In the 1920s he knew the occultist Aleister Crowley, who claimed to have found a reference to the young Driberg in the Egyptian Book of the Dead, and nominated him his successor as World Teacher (Driberg was apparently not alone in this honour). As a journalist at the *Express*, he invented the modern gossip column in the form of 'William Hickey' and became a favourite of the paper's autocratic proprietor, Lord Beaverbrook. He played games with the security services of Britain and the USSR. In 1942, shortly after leaving the Communist Party, he won a celebrated by-election, and found another closed society replete with high camp ritual to belong to, in the cosy form of the House of Commons. Sir Henry 'Chips' Channon, a wealthy right-wing Tory MP, himself very well known in society as homosexual, welcomed Driberg to the Commons and to parliamentary gay life, as Driberg recalled in his autobiography: 'Only a few hours after I had been introduced to the House, when I was still wandering around in a daze, and lost, Chips kindly showed me round the most important rooms – the Members' lavatories. This was an act of pure, disinterested, sisterly friendship, for we had no physical attraction for each other.'

Driberg had never known much restraint, but his exploits during his parliamentary career were truly extraordinary: 'if anything I became more promiscuous after my election to Parliament, relying on my new status to get me out of tight corners'. He most enjoyed oral sex with young, working-class men he would never have to see again, and was a devotee of 'cottaging' – anonymous sexual encounters in public lavatories. His tastes were well known to his colleagues, and he enjoyed regaling them with lurid tales. Some did not wish to listen: Tony Crosland was keen to avoid hearing about 'Tom's sordid sex life', and made up a pretext rather than share a car all the way back from Gloucestershire to London. In September 1957 Richard Crossman shared a railway carriage with him on the way to the Labour Party conference in Brighton, and recorded in his *Diaries*:

> *Interspersed with these bouts of anxiety [about whether his enemies would stop him from becoming Chairman of the Labour Party 1957–58] was a fountain of items about homosexuality, including a long and extremely obscene story about the Anglo-Catholic Rector of a local Brighton church, who had come into the room of a friend, to find him in bed with a boy and, after saying it was a deadly sin, had jumped into bed to join them.*

Plenty of journalists had witnessed Tom Driberg's taste for casual gay pick-ups. Geoffrey Goodman, a reporter with excellent knowledge of the Labour Party, recalls:

> *There were times at Labour Party conferences, open to the full glare of the media, when Driberg's behaviour was quite extraordinary. He would be seen soliciting, particularly young boys or waiters, and there were photographers there, and reporters. It was never reported. I remember a time when I and a* Daily Express *journalist were having a meal with Driberg. He ignored us when a waiter he found attractive came along and spent the rest of the evening trying to solicit him. This was commonplace, it was almost a joke. If you bought Driberg a drink or a meal then you knew this sort of thing might very well happen.*

Driberg's colleagues knew that he was an accident waiting to happen. Barbara Castle recalls that 'we used to feel terribly vulnerable about Tom Driberg, we lived in fear lest he be discovered in the middle of some of his antics in public lavatories'. The worst headaches for the Labour Party were when he was indeed Chairman of the Party in 1957–58. Although the Chairman's job is less significant than it sounds, a headline reading 'Labour Chairman Arrested in Public Toilet' would go down badly. According to his biographer Francis Wheen he 'sort of behaved himself that year. Well, by his standards anyway.'

Driberg felt a sense of grievance that he had never experienced the ministerial office he thought his talents deserved. He blamed the 'puritanism' of Attlee and Wilson. The more broad-minded Gaitskell had considered the idea. Driberg's biography records his friend Gore Vidal pressing the MP's claims to office:

'How can we?' Gaitskell replied with an incredulous laugh. Vidal suggested Archbishop of Canterbury as a suitable appointment: this would both please Tom and extinguish Christianity in England, he pointed out. Gaitskell, an enlightened atheist, was delighted by the idea. Then he said, seriously: 'I suppose we could make him Minister of Works. The old thing would love that, mucking about with curtains for embassies.'

Few seriously considered Driberg of ministerial calibre. He was no political philosopher – his socialism was based on emotion rather than reason. As the journalist Terence Lancaster puts it: 'He was a left-wing snob. He had a romantic idea of the workers, particularly when he met them in public lavatories.'

Aside from the risks of being caught trawling for sex in public toilets, his chances of ministerial office were blighted by his far left political beliefs and his inability to resist the bizarre, in whatever form it presented itself. No government would risk having a member in ministerial office when he was on intimate terms with both Guy Burgess and Ronnie Kray. Attlee would never have given a job to anyone so recently in the Communist Party, and Gaitskell and Wilson would also have been impressed by MI5 reports suggesting that he would at the very least have been a serious security risk because of his Russian connections. He was appreciated more for his 'splendid love and mastery of the English language' as that most literary of politicians, Michael Foot, put it in his postscript to Driberg's autobiography. He helped to turn the stilted bureaucratic prose of Labour manifestos into something approaching good English. In later life he compiled the famously smutty *Private Eye* crossword, which no doubt helped keep his exploits away from Lord Gnome's celebrated organ.

Even if it had been within the rules of the club for his political enemies to expose Driberg's sexual habits, to do so would risk Driberg publicizing homosexual Conservatives more senior than his friend Chips Channon. As Driberg's biographer Francis Wheen says:

His ultimate sanction was what used to be known as mutual assured destruction in the days of the Cold War. If the Tories tried to expose him he would drag them down too. He used to mutter, 'Well, if they ever try to do the dirty on me I'll tell everything I know about Derick Heathcoat-Amory, for example.' Heathcoat-Amory was a mild, harmless bachelor who was Chancellor of the Exchequer from 1958 to 1960.

(Wheen did ask the Heathcoat-Amory family what Driberg may have meant, but they knew of no evidence.)

Driberg was safe enough with politicians, journalists and London society, but the main threat to prominent homosexuals in those days was from police officers. He had an astonishing run of luck, despite his compulsion for sex in public lavatories and the practice of the police of using young officers to entrap homosexuals. He only faced court once, in 1935 before he was an MP. Two young miners alleged that he tried to grope them after he had offered to put them up in his flat for the night, and reported the incident to the police. He was acquitted after doggedly arguing that he had been misunderstood, and producing impeccable Establishment character witnesses such as Lord Sysonby, whose address was given as St James's Palace. In any case, the trial had taken place in a news blackout, despite being well known to most of Fleet Street. 'Dog,' as Lord Justice Goddard said in the famous 'Venetian Blind' libel case of 1957, 'does not bite dog.' Goddard meant that journalists did not, or even should not, write derogatory stories about other journalists.

As well as goodwill from fellow journalists, an agreement not to publicize the case was organized by his benevolent employer, Lord Beaverbrook. There was only one reference, in the trade paper the *World's Press News*, that teased Driberg, whose *Express* gossip column was headed 'These Names Make News': 'That was a curious case that Fleet Street was talking about last week. Not all names make news.'

Driberg never faced charges again, despite the fact that his sexual appetite only increased as his life went on. His apparent immunity from prosecution has led to some elaborate theories being formulated. According to Chapman Pincher his links with MI5 helped him to escape:

When he was caught he was able to say, 'Not only am I an MP but if you consult with Special Branch you will find I have a relationship with MI5. They will vouch for me.' They always did, and this is what I think got him off in the most serious instances because the last thing MI5 wanted was for Tom to be in the dock answering questions about what he did and for him to say that he worked for MI5.

Driberg's own explanation found more favour with his biographer, Francis Wheen. Unlike Field and Harvey, who were in agonies of guilt about their sexual preferences, Driberg was proud. He would not collapse with remorse under questioning, but put on an impressive display of pompous bluster, threatening the police with character witnesses, eminent genito-urinary consultants appearing as specialist defence witnesses and a massive legal battle. In most 'cottaging' cases, the prosecution depended on extracting guilty pleas based on the shame of the defendant and his fear of the police. Driberg had no fear, and no shame.

In a way which is now incomprehensible, Driberg's fame actually protected him from exposure. In his account of his near arrest shortly after becoming an MP, 'almost wet-handed' with a Norwegian sailor in an Edinburgh air raid shelter, he says that the policeman who interrupted them was a regular reader of the William Hickey column. Driberg engaged him in conversation about this, and also argued that it would only assist German propaganda if a famous MP and journalist was charged in such circumstances. Driberg and the Scottish policeman parted on good terms:

I lied to him as convincingly as I could, swearing that if he would let me off I would never do such a thing again; it worked. In twenty minutes or so, we were good friends, on a writer and reader basis ... he had a ruddy face, and a markedly cleft, strong chin. I liked him and thought him attractive (but judged that it would be going too far, under the circumstances, to make a pass).

Driberg told friends of this close shave, and the incident became the basis for Compton Mackenzie's *Thin Ice*, a novel about the precarious life of a homosexual politician. For less appealing officers, Driberg boasted that he carried around a wad of banknotes, although this was running the risk of adding attempted bribery to the charge sheet. As well as escaping arrest, Driberg never suffered from 'kiss and tell' stories, despite having an astonishing number of sexual partners. His taste for rough trade involved him with semi-criminal youths and rent boys who would do anything for money, several of whom stole from him but none of whose sexual confessions ever ended up entertaining the readers of Sunday tabloids. One, a 'seductive psychopath' called Steve Raymond, stole a draft obituary of Harold Wilson from his desk and caused Driberg some other unpleasant moments in 1970–74 because of his criminal activities.

Gossip, another of Driberg's favourite pastimes, also involved keeping his mouth open all the time. He was extremely indiscreet. The idea that he was a particularly valued asset of either MI5 or the KGB is fanciful, because he had none of the self-restraint required of a spy, and his tales often grew in the telling. Nor did he have access to subjects of real interest to spies. He was a friend of Maxwell Knight, an MI5 officer with a shared interest in homosexuality, and was almost certainly 'debriefed' by MI5 after he returned from Moscow with exclusive interviews with Guy Burgess. Without doubt he talked freely over lunch to people who turned out to be KGB officers, particularly if they were rugged-looking young men, but in the words of his biographer: 'he wasn't a KGB agent in the sense that he was getting regular sums of Moscow gold. You only have to look at his bank statements to see that the poor bloke was perpetually overdrawn.'

In fact, he talked freely to a lot of people. He was valued by journalists as a source because of his openness, as Geoffrey Goodman confirms: 'He was a great leaker. If you wanted a story about what was going on inside the Labour Party Executive, or any other area of politics, Driberg was an extremely good informant. He was a very shrewd journalist himself, and knew what we would consider a good story or a useful tip.'

Ironically, despite the need to conceal his sexual desires from the world, Driberg hated secrecy. In the same way that Richard Crossman intended the publication of his Cabinet diaries to smash the cult of secrecy in British government, Driberg's posthumously published autobiography, *Ruling Passions*, was intended to reveal all about himself, and the private hypocrisies of the political class, and by doing so change the rules for ever after. His biographer, Francis Wheen, explains:

> It was an act of revelation, of honesty, and a sort of squaring of accounts with himself and with the public. I think he also hoped that by being so open about it he would cause a great scandal and shock people, which he always enjoyed doing ... but also perhaps to make it a bit easier for future public figures to be more open about their peccadilloes.

No doubt to the relief of many prominent people, he had not described his Commons career much beyond his introduction by the time he died suddenly in 1976. He had described some of his own escapades, however, in such graphic detail that there would have been no chance of publishing *Ruling Passions* had the courts not relaxed the obscenity laws in the 1960s. Tom Driberg had been a passionate supporter of the campaigns of the 1960s, not just decriminalizing homosexuality and free expression but also advocating racial equality, a lower voting age and cannabis legalization.

Driberg enjoyed the 1960s and approved of the social changes that took place. The same could not be said for most politicians. The defining event of politics in the 1960s was the Profumo scandal, in which the sexual morality of the political class became discussed – and condemned – outside the charmed circle. It was launched by a chance collision of politics, high life in country houses and low life in drinking dens – and brought to public attention by the ever intriguing subject of spying.

CHAPTER 4

The climate of scandal 1962-63

'Miss Keeler and I were on friendly terms. There was no impropriety whatsoever in my acquaintanceship with Miss Keeler.'
John Profumo, 1963

In the late 1950s and early 1960s spy stories were at their most popular. The James Bond-style drama was made more serious by the belief, widespread at the time, that the Communist Bloc was overtaking the West economically and militarily, and the international crises of the Berlin Wall (1961) and the Cuban missiles (1962). Spy scandals sold newspapers. Derek Jameson, then with the Mirror Group, recalls: 'It was an offshoot of the Cold War. Fleet Street was looking for a Red under every bed. There was a spate of espionage stories, and we were very conscious of the need to find out whether security was on the right lines, and whether the country was safe.'

In 1961, MI5 uncovered a KGB operation in Britain, aimed at infiltrating the Portland naval base in Dorset. The Russians had paid a clerk who worked there to pass on secrets he learned about nuclear submarines to a KGB officer who was posing as a Canadian businessman called Gordon Lonsdale; these would be transmitted to Russia via another two KGB agents who lived in Ruislip and posed as booksellers. The professionalism of the Lonsdale operation was astonishing to the public, as was the incongruous revelation that there really were Russian spies operating undercover in the suburbs.

'Security' was a dangerous issue for politicians. The flight of Guy Burgess and Donald Maclean, two diplomats who had been spying for the Soviet Union, to Moscow in 1951 caused great anxiety throughout the 1950s. There were well-founded worries that other spies – Kim Philby and the 'fourth man' (Anthony Blunt, as it happened) – had got away. Burgess was a heavy-drinking, promiscuous homosexual, which the authorities believed to be a sign of bad character as well as a blackmail risk. If civil service clerks were to be held to a strict code of conduct, it would only be reasonable to expect ministers and MPs to be similarly bound, a connection that started to be made in the 1960s.

The overture to the eruption of scandal on to the British political scene was the 'Vassall affair' of 1962. John Vassall was a young civil servant working for the Admiralty who served a tour of duty at the British Embassy in Moscow from 1954 to 1956 at the height of the anti-homosexual witch hunt in Britain. It was an unwise appointment, because Vassall was homosexual, lonely and unhappy in his drab Moscow posting. His sexual interest in men was quickly detected by the Russian intelligence services, who arranged for Vassall to be photographed in graphic detail at a wild homosexual party in Moscow. They threatened him with imprisonment in Russia for homosexual offences unless he agreed to spy. Vassall failed to report the blackmail to his employers and was eventually sent back to Britain.

Nearly a year after returning from Moscow and his unpleasant experiences there, Vassall served as assistant Private Secretary to the Civil Lord of the Admiralty, Thomas Galbraith, from 1957 to 1959. (As with John Profumo, 'War Minister', Galbraith's title was a hangover from Britain's days as a great power. The Wilson government was later to reorganize the Defence ministries to create a single Minister of State for the Armed Forces.) Vassall found this office much more pleasant, and liked Galbraith – although he was still meeting his KGB controllers in London. Galbraith, a Scottish aristocrat of courtly disposition, treated Vassall with kindness and saw him on several occasions after he was reshuffled out of the Admiralty. Vassall remained keen to work with Galbraith again. It was not to be, because two KGB defectors alerted Western intelligence agencies to the existence of several of their spies, including Vassall. Vassall was arrested in September 1962 and confessed.

Then the trouble began. Lord Carrington was First Sea Lord, in overall charge of the Admiralty, and as he says: 'The difficulty in handling the publicity was that having tried very hard to locate the spy in your department, you felt triumphant that you had caught the spy – and then all hell broke loose and you got blamed for having the spy in the first place.'

When the press discovered that Vassall had worked in Galbraith's private office, demands began for the resignation of the minister, who was now at the Scottish Office. It was argued, foolishly, that Galbraith should have identified Vassall as a homosexual and therefore assumed him to be a security risk – despite the fact that the security service itself had given the clerk a clean bill of health on his return from Moscow. Lord Carrington chivalrously offered to resign because of the security lapse, but the offer was rejected by the Prime Minister; he found himself unjustly traduced in the press: 'The Beaverbrook press actually accused me of withholding from the Prime Minister the fact that we knew there was a spy in the Admiralty, which of course was absolute nonsense. They called me a traitor.'

A further dimension was added by the discovery of Galbraith's 1959–62 correspondence with his former civil servant, which was distant but polite and warm. Ludicrously, the letters were held to be evidence of a homosexual relationship, particularly one which began 'My dear Vassall'. Vassall himself sold the letters to the *Sunday Pictorial*, and never did much to discourage rumours about his relationship with the minister. When these were published in November 1962 Galbraith resigned on the grounds that his informal style of running his private office had embarrassed the government, but in reality his position had been untenable because of the hounding he was receiving in the press and from some Labour MPs – particularly George Brown.

After the resignation of Galbraith a judicial inquiry was set up into the 'Vassall affair', Lord Radcliffe presiding. The Vassall tribunal was a humbling experience for the press. Looked at in calmer circumstances, the innuendo against Galbraith was indefensible. Any historian working in an archive has seen the 'My dear [surname]' mode of address used between men who are not particularly close, both on official and private correspondence. The minister was cleared and restored to office. The Labour Party had to engage in some deft legal footwork courtesy of the solicitor Arnold Goodman to avoid Brown having to justify his slurs against Galbraith, and was left with a sense of unease about being seen to exploit scandal.

Galbraith was reinstated as a transport minister in 1963, although at a more junior level, and after 1964 continued as the backbench Conservative MP for Glasgow Hillhead until his death, which caused a famous by-election in 1982. Vassall left prison in 1972, after which he became a clerk at the British Records Association, a professional association for archivists. He died in 1996.

The 'Vassall affair' had left the press and the government confused and antagonistic. For the press, the embarrassment of going too far over Galbraith was replaced by anger at the imprisonment of two journalists for failing to reveal their sources for Galbraith stories to the Radcliffe Tribunal. The Beaverbrook journalist Ian Aitken recalls:

We in the press gallery and Fleet Street realized that the Macmillan government was out to get us. Not revealing your sources is absolutely required of any member of the House of Commons Lobby and it's the MPs themselves who insist on it. When we saw them putting the screws on fellow journalists to reveal their sources our whole attitude changed radically.

Working journalists were not inclined to give the Macmillan government an easy ride, but at the same time were worried about being shown up again for printing sensational stories without the evidence to back them up. The Conservatives were furious over the shabby treatment of Galbraith and Carrington and resolved to resist any further press attacks on ministers as toughly as they could. Meanwhile, the bigger storm was brewing.

*

The central events of the Profumo scandal were not startling. John Profumo was one of the more talented middle-ranking members of the Macmillan government, serving as 'War Minister', outside the Cabinet, a job the modern equivalent of which would be roughly Minister of State at the Ministry of Defence. In July 1961 he went to a party at Cliveden, home of Lord Astor, and met Christine Keeler, a beautiful young woman who enjoyed mixing in high society and who happened to be larking around nude at the swimming pool in the grounds. Profumo saw her again a few days later, and they had a brief affair that summer. It ended abruptly when the Cabinet Secretary, Sir Norman Brook, warned Profumo that there was a potential security risk and he broke off the relationship gently, with an affectionate note on 9 August 1961 – although he met Keeler again the following December. These events were totally unremarkable. Lord Beaverbrook's country house at Cherkley had seen much more decadent goings-on than the Cliveden party, over many years, with people just as prominent as Profumo.

It was Profumo's bad luck that the affair broke during the spy mania of the early 1960s. Christine Keeler was a close friend of Dr Stephen Ward, a man who cultivated many acquaintances in the worlds of politics, high society and intelligence. He was an osteopath with many prominent clients, including Winston Churchill, and enjoyed portrait painting. He also took pleasure in introducing glamorous young women to important men and seeing what happened: 'Stephen didn't believe that class distinction should prevent attractive and intelligent girls from humble backgrounds appearing in society', wrote Christine Keeler, and he became a kind of Pygmalion, dressing and educating girls – such as Keeler herself and her colleague Mandy Rice-Davies – to fit in with high society.

One encounter involving a Ward girl and the strange worlds in which Ward dabbled was between Christine Keeler and Yevgeny Ivanov, naval attaché at the USSR Embassy. This also took place in summer 1961, although it was more of a friendship than an affair, with only one alcohol-fuelled sexual episode. Ivanov had been monitored by MI5, who had hopes of pressuring him into defecting, and during this observation Profumo was spotted and tipped off via the Cabinet Secretary. Ward, too, dabbled in security matters – mainly for the excitement of being mixed up with spies – and may well have been involved in a scheme to compromise Ivanov. Despite these cross-currents, there was in fact no real security angle to John Profumo's involvement, despite the best efforts of Ivanov.

Ivanov, as was widely suspected at the time, was a spy. He was working not for the KGB but for the GRU, a more secretive Soviet spying organization, and had managed to make contact with several Establishment figures in Britain. He was introduced to Stephen Ward by Sir Colin Coote, editor of *The Daily Telegraph*, who Ivanov claimed passed on financial gossip gleaned from Bank of England and City contacts in clubland as if nothing had changed since the 'Bank Rate' affair. Ivanov was also able to use his Ward and Cliveden connections to photograph selections of their mail and other documents left lying around while they were distracted. He claimed in his book *The Naked Spy* to have gained advance knowledge of the cancellation of the 'Skybolt' missile programme and that without the 1963 scandal he would have been an even more successful spy. He was planning to use his knowledge of the affair with Keeler to blackmail Profumo, but the plan was yet to be put into action when the scandal broke.

Ward was if anything a British agent of influence rather than a security threat. Ward did ask Keeler (as a joke, according to her) to ask Profumo a question relating to US–West German traffic in nuclear material, but it is unclear whether this information was genuinely secret anyway. He could have been testing Profumo's discretion, for his own purposes or to see if there was a genuine security problem with Profumo. The question was never asked.

By the end of 1962, Whitehall insiders had known about the summer 1961 affair since MI5 told the Cabinet Secretary. There had also been some gossip in political and aristocratic circles – Profumo had not been particularly discreet and had taken Keeler for a drive in a car borrowed from another minister.

Profumo was unfortunate in having made an enemy of George Wigg, Labour MP for Dudley and a man of generally paranoid and excitable disposition who had good contacts in the security services. Wigg's politics were strongly influenced by his time in the British Army, an organization he loved and felt could do little wrong. This brought him into contact with Profumo, who had ministerial responsibility for the Army, and Wigg felt that Profumo had failed to honour an agreement they had made during a debate on the preparedness of the force sent to Kuwait in 1961. Wigg blamed Profumo personally, did not consider him a fit person to be in charge of his beloved Army, and had a ready ear for any damaging information about him, which he also did his best to spread. Julian Critchley, the Conservative backbencher, recalls Wigg boasting to him in 1962 that Profumo was about to be exposed as 'a massive homosexual' – which as Critchley comments could hardly have been further from the mark.

Wigg's 'first authentic information about the business was sent to me, unasked', as he later wrote, by a man called John Lewis, who had been Labour MP for Bolton in 1945–51, and had run into Keeler at a party and discovered her relationship with Ward by chance. Lewis hated Ward because he believed, erroneously, that Ward had slept with his then wife, and wanted to see him ruined. Lewis taped conversations with Keeler about her relationships with Ward, Ivanov and Profumo, and according to Keeler used money and threats in a failed attempt to persuade her to sleep with him. He passed them on to Wigg, whom he knew from political and horse-racing circles.

Most of his Labour colleagues found Wigg an odd and unsavoury figure, and journalists were sharply divided. Ian Aitken had little time for him; he says: 'He was a menace, he poisoned anything he touched ... He was always creeping up on you in the lobby and talking in complete riddles with every appearance of telling you something of enormous importance. I could never understand what the hell he was talking about so I didn't use the stuff.' However, the new party leader Harold Wilson trusted him on security matters and when the story was breaking provided an official platform for Wigg's vendetta against Profumo.

Keeler herself had fallen upon harder times. She and Stephen Ward, as well as mixing with high society, were intrigued by the Notting Hill demi-monde of the early 1960s. Their Establishment friends knew little of this world. Immigrants from the West Indies had settled in the then-squalid streets around Westbourne Park Road, often exploited by slum landlords like Peter Rachman, and the victims of racist attacks that culminated in the riots of 1958. Keeler remembered that 'Notting Hill Gate was pretty rough then. You never knew when a fight might break out or a full-blown riot would erupt on the streets. A lot of the whites living there were convicts, pimps and prostitutes. Throw in a lot of generally misplaced people of assorted age, colour and nationality and you got trouble.' But there was a vibrant black nightlife of music, drinking clubs and marijuana (then virtually unknown in Britain), into which Christine Keeler was welcomed. Attractive women like Keeler have traditionally found class barriers more permeable than people in general, but the fact that she could run a social life, more or less on her own terms, in black Notting Hill and white high society around Astor and Profumo, was a sign that the barriers themselves were starting to dissolve. As the commentator Anthony Howard points out:

In the early 1960s there was a great breaking of social barriers. A whole lot of talented people were getting into what until then had been toffee-nosed society, and you saw that at Cliveden. Of the people who went to those swimming pool parties at Cliveden, some were very respectable, including the President of Pakistan, but there were also people who a few years earlier had been described as riff-raff: photographers, models, people on the fringes of society ... Of course, the middle classes were always much more snobbish than the upper classes and thought this was very inappropriate.

As Wayland Young put it eloquently in his 1963 book *The Profumo Affair*: '[Keeler] was someone who filled highly divergent bills; someone who could be rough to the smooth, smooth to the rough: a sort of social equalizer in the world of sexual endeavour.'

Christine Keeler had little luck in the men she met: 'Lucky' Gordon was a possessive and violent man who stalked her. Fleeing Gordon, she turned to Johnny Edgecombe, who wanted a more permanent relationship and became jealous of Stephen Ward. Edgecombe fired a gun at the window of Ward's flat, where she was hiding. Edgecombe was arrested and a date was set for his trial. The exciting life of Christine Keeler was confidently anticipated to be spilled out in open court, where it could be reported free of the risk of libel.

She was also out of money and still hiding from Lucky Gordon. She realized her main financial asset by selling the August 1961 note from Profumo to the *Sunday Pictorial*, then the Mirror Group's main Sunday paper. She was brought in one Saturday night to the paper's offices to speak to the Editor, Reg Payne. Derek Jameson, who worked for the Mirror Group at the time, remembers:

> *Christine Keeler told this story of strange goings-on. Reg Payne was very cautious and said to her, 'Yes, a likely story. Can you prove it?' and Christine Keeler emptied out her handbag on his desk, all bits and pieces, lipstick, this and that, and there among all the bits and bobs of her handbag was the evidence everybody had been looking for, including a letter on House of Commons notepaper from Jack Profumo in which he was quite clearly infatuated with her. This was the missing evidence, this was what we needed.*

An old-style Establishment cover-up was wheeled into action when senior management at the *Mirror* discovered that Payne and Jameson intended to publish. The Chairman of the Mirror Group was Cecil King, nephew of the newspaper baron Lord Northcliffe – who founded the *Daily Mail* – and in the words of the *Mirror* editor Mike Molloy to John Pilger, 'one of the grandest human beings you could ever imagine ... he made the royal family seem quite common'. King, despite his reforming views which were expressed in the *Mirror*, was a pillar of the Establishment if anyone was. Derek Jameson takes up the story:

> *Cecil King was summoned to Downing Street to meet Macmillan, who told him, 'Nothing in it, old boy. I've looked into it, heard all about it, it's rubbish. I've spoken to Jack Profumo, he assures me there's nothing improper going on. I believe him. I would rather you did not publish this story. It would not be in the national interest.' Cecil King came back to the office. We were ready to go with it, we had the evidence, and the whole thing was squashed, banned, we weren't allowed to use it. We were appalled, this was the biggest story we'd had for years. So we did what we always do in such circumstances, we gave a nod and a wink to our rival paper, the* News of the World, *and they broke the story.*

When the scandal fully broke in June, the text of the letter was published in the *Sunday Mirror* (as the *Sunday Pictorial* had now been renamed), plus an explanation that they had received it much earlier and returned it to Profumo in April.

Fleet Street and Westminster were already awash with rumours about Profumo and Keeler. The Russians knew in January that things were going wrong, and withdrew Ivanov. Newspapers teased those in the know by juxtaposing stories about the Edgecombe incident and those about Profumo's ministerial activities. The first explicit story about the minister and the call girl, complete with the aggravating factor of Ivanov's involvement, was published on 8 March 1963 in *Westminster Confidential*, a newsletter published by the parliamentary journalist Andrew Roth, which had a select circulation among politicians and journalists. He had been told the story by the Conservative MP for Arundel, Captain Henry 'Bob' Kerby, and recalls:

> *Bob Kerby was very right wing. He was a friend of mine, partly because I had been an intelligence officer during the war and he worked for MI6 behind German lines. We were both outsiders; I am an American of Hungarian origin, and he was a Scot who was born in pre-revolutionary Russia. He hated the domination of the Conservative Party by what he called the 'Kissing Ring' of the Establishment, who had been to the same private schools and so on. He felt John Profumo was particularly unfit to be War Minister; Profumo had been to the right school, the right regiment, and was therefore accepted, but Kerby considered him a playboy.*

Kerby hated the Conservative Establishment so much that he was a regular informant on Tory matters not only to Roth, but to George Wigg and Harold Wilson. He passed on damaging gossip and inside information to Wilson's Number 10 throughout the 1960s and in 1969 offered Labour all the secrets of the forthcoming Tory election campaign in exchange for a life peerage, a demand later reduced to a knighthood (but still refused).

Roth did not intend to publish the Profumo tip right away, but to try to check it out further. The newsletter for 8 March was intended to have been about a plan the Chancellor, Reggie Maudling, was considering to abandon the Bretton Woods system of fixed rates of exchange and 'float' the pound, but, as Roth recalls: 'on the very day that I was planning to do that newsletter, I found out that Maudling had abandoned the idea. I was left with nothing to write about and so I hurriedly moved up the Profumo story and wrote it for publication that day, having only had the chance to recheck with a source who knew about the Russian side.'

Roth's rushed decision to break the code of silence brought the affair a step closer to being a public scandal. The Chief Whip, Martin Redmayne, was furious about the article and demanded action. Profumo resisted his advice to take out a libel action, arguing that *Westminster Confidential*'s circulation was too small to justify it, so Redmayne tried a pettier form of revenge on Roth. Richard Lamb, a Conservative candidate in 1950 as well as a contemporary historian, recalls:

> Westminster Confidential *went to all the lobby correspondents and journalists and to a great number of MPs. Although it may have had a tiny circulation, its circulation was so terribly important. The worst thing Redmayne did was to suggest to Macmillan's Private Office that they remove the lobby pass from Andrew Roth, which was not government business at all and entirely up to the Serjeant-at-Arms in the House of Commons. He was slapped down, and rightly so.*

In the following week Keeler failed to appear as a witness in the Edgecombe case, and it was alleged that the government had arranged that she should leave the country to avoid her connections being exposed in court (in fact, her disappearing act seems to have been the result of some extremely poor legal advice). The eruption of the Profumo affair into the public gaze could not long be delayed, and took place late at night on the floor of the House of Commons.

In the light of the Vassall case, and the rumours alleging that Keeler had been hidden, and the possible security implications about the role of Ivanov, Barbara Castle came to the view that it was ridiculous not to have a full discussion, and she was determined to go ahead, as she now remembers:

> *My husband and I had a small dinner party. The main guests were Dick Crossman and George Wigg, and I remember saying to them, 'We can't just let this just go.' 'Don't be silly, Barbara,' was the reaction, and I said, 'But imagine what the press would make of a Labour Minister of War found sharing a call girl with a Russian military attaché. Why should we be too squeamish to point out the obvious dangers? Well anyway,' I announced, 'I'm going to raise it in the House as a security issue.' They were shocked, but having tried to make me abandon the idea they obviously had to get in first ... And so the taboo about talking about people's private lives was broken at my dinner table.*

Crossman's recollection is different in detail, but confirms the broad picture. The main purpose of the dinner at Barbara Castle's house on 10 March had been for Harold Wilson, newly elected Labour leader, to talk freely to his old colleagues on the left, but like other dinner parties the subject of 'Profumo and the disappearing model' came up. Crossman recorded the final decision he and Wigg took in the Commons chamber during the Vassall debate on 21 March:

> *George Wigg came up to me ... and said, 'I hear that Barbara has been briefed by the* Daily Herald *to spill the Profumo scandal during this debate. She's bound to do it wrong, Dick, you and I must get in first. If the story is to be broken we must break it in a reasonable way.'*

Wigg was first to speak openly about the fact that 'rumour upon rumour involving a member of the government front bench' was circulating, named Christine Keeler and demanded that the government either deny the rumours or set up a Select Committee to investigate them. In claiming the use of parliamentary privilege he criticized the failure of the press to handle the story.

Crossman endorsed the demand for a Select Committee, and Castle weighed in to refer to the allegations that people in high places knew where Christine Keeler had gone.

The Conservative leadership panicked. Profumo was roused from bed at 2.45 am, mentally fuzzy from sleeping drugs he had taken, and before he had been allowed the chance to talk in private to his wife. He was taken to the Commons and interrogated by the Chief Whip and the Attorney General. They insisted that he make a personal statement denying the rumours. Profumo's problem was that he had been accused of several things: a relationship with Keeler, lax security and perverting the course of justice, only the first of which was true. But in the panic meeting all three were woven together and he took the fateful step of denying everything.

Profumo made a personal statement in the House of Commons next morning, in which he disputed the rumours about any involvement in Keeler's disappearance and described the occasion at Cliveden at which they met, pointing out that his wife was at the party but not mentioning the swimming pool frolics. Fatally, he concluded his statement: 'Between July and December 1961 I met Miss Keeler on about half a dozen occasions when I called to see [Stephen Ward] and his friends. Miss Keeler and I were on friendly terms. There was no impropriety whatsoever in my acquaintanceship with Miss Keeler.'

This claim strained credulity among people in the know. Richard Lamb recalls, 'I knew Profumo quite well at Oxford and he was a very charming man, but I would never have thought he would have had anything to do with an uneducated girl like Christine Keeler unless he was going to make her his mistress.' But Profumo's statement seemed to have drawn a line under the whole business. Wigg, Crossman and Castle were exposed to the disapproval of their peer group for breaking the taboo on personal matters, though their use of parliamentary privilege was, surprisingly, endorsed by a leader in *The Times*.

Profumo went on to sue French and Italian publications for alleging that he had a sexual relationship with Keeler. But in the weeks that followed the line could not be held. Stephen Ward had been accused of being a security risk and in an attempt to clear his name contacted George Wigg and Harold Wilson, who passed the information on to Macmillan; in the course of this Ward revealed the truth about Profumo and Keeler.

The scandal moved into its most serious phase. Several members of the government had been aware that Profumo's statement had been false, but nothing was done. Instead, Stephen Ward was the victim of an extraordinarily severe police investigation. The basis of the case came from the vindictive John Lewis, who supplied information he had gathered to make Ward seem like a controller of prostitutes. The police took 140 witness statements, including some obviously perjured testimony which interrogations had wrung from two prostitutes. The police had gone on a fishing expedition to find whatever evidence they could against a man who had made powerful enemies.

The Ward investigation and trial is the shabbiest aspect of the scandal, although quite how shabby was kept even from Lord Denning's official inquiry at the time and only became known when papers were released in 1994. The government at least considered tampering with the course of justice, the very allegation that had panicked Profumo into his lying statement. At the end of May 1963 Macmillan ordered the Lord Chancellor, Dilhorne, to investigate the security aspects to the relationship between Ward and Ivanov. Dilhorne was empowered to ask questions among civil servants and politicians. The government was anxious to see that criminal proceedings against Ward did not start before the Dilhorne inquiry had ended, so that they could take action to control the impact of the disclosures. On two occasions Macmillan's Private Secretary Tim Bligh met Sir Joseph Simpson, Commissioner of the Metropolitan Police, to discuss the two inquiries. The surreptitious nature of these meetings was made clear to the historian Richard Lamb by an exchange at the end of the second one, as he describes:

> *Sir Joseph Simpson said, 'There's rather a crowd of reporters outside and when I go out I'm going to be asked what I've come about.' And Bligh said, 'Well, you'd better say you've come about the traffic arrangements for Trooping the Colour.' That is rather descending into the depths, isn't it, if the Head of the Metropolitan Police had to tell a lie to say why he'd been in to see the Prime Minister's Private Secretary.*

But Profumo's career could not be saved. He would have to give evidence to Dilhorne. Profumo, confronted with a personal and political crisis, came back from a holiday in Venice with his wife and decided to admit the truth and resign. He did so on 4 June, also resigning his parliamentary seat at Stratford upon Avon.

Profumo's resignation was for lying to the House of Commons in a personal statement, a particularly serious breach of the rules, but the wider ramifications were troubling. *The Economist* presciently wrote: 'Mr Profumo's properly forced resignation is game, set and match to the popular press. The floodgates to a self-righteous scurrility have thereby been opened in precisely the wrong place. Nobody can be sure of the ultimate effects on press, politicians and the whole tenor of public life.' In the short term, it unleashed the 'satire boom' in which the old-fashioned Tories were savaged by a new generation of satirists, most notably in TV's *That Was the Week That Was*, the 'Establishment Club' and *Private Eye* (founded in 1961, the magazine now discovered the opportunity it had always wanted).

The official Labour line was to criticize the government on the security aspects of the case rather than delve into personal morality, but a new front was opened up by the editor of *The Times* with an editorial stating baldly 'It *is* a moral issue'. The import of the piece was that material affluence had made Britain morally weaker and Profumo's conduct was a symptom of that moral decline. The criticism struck a chord with Conservatives across Britain and was echoed by *The Daily Telegraph* which declared that 'at present the Conservative Party is a shambles'. Lord Hailsham, from the Cabinet, weighed in with a brutal denunciation of Profumo's moral character, including the hope that 'a great party is not to be brought down because of a squalid affair between a woman of easy virtue and a proven liar'.

Following the resignation of Profumo, the government had no alternative but to concede an adjournment debate in the House of Commons, which took place on 17 June (Parliament had been in recess when Profumo resigned). At the debate the tensions that had been developing within the Conservative Party burst into the open. Senior Tory MP Nigel Birch, who had represented West Flint since 1945 and had long been critical of Macmillan, called on him to resign, pouring scorn on the acceptance of Profumo's story by the Prime Minister and his allies. Twenty-seven Conservatives abstained at the vote which closed the Profumo debate, a Tory rebellion on a scale not seen for many years. The impact of the debate was to dramatize Tory divisions and paint a picture of Macmillan as irresolute, out of date and lacking grip on his government.

After the debate the government set up an inquiry into the events under Lord Denning. It was a departmental inquiry rather than a tribunal such as Lynskey or Bank Rate, and Denning took evidence in private into the Profumo affair and other rumours that were circulating. Profumo's admission of guilt had launched an astonishing period in which bizarre rumours were told and retold among the political class and, for once, achieved a rather wider circulation. According to the journalist Anthony Howard: 'The climate for a time was absolutely febrile, people would believe anything. Macmillan himself is supposed to have said [on hearing tales about who was at an orgy], "Eight High Court judges! Two or three I could believe, but eight! It passes comprehension."'

The two most celebrated rumours were 'the headless man' and 'the man in the mask'.

The 'headless man' appeared in evidence in the salacious Argyll divorce case which was under way in 1963 and had no relation to the Profumo affair. An item of evidence was a photograph of the Duchess of Argyll and a man whose face was not in the frame engaged in oral sex. The headless man was widely assumed to be a leading politician, and the name of Duncan Sandys, the Commonwealth and Colonial Secretary, was mentioned so often in this connection that he told the Cabinet he would resign because the rumours were undermining the government. Bill Deedes, then in charge of government publicity, thought that such an announcement would be the end of the government and Sandys was persuaded to adopt another course.

During the Denning inquiry Sandys underwent an examination of his penis and feet. The man in the photograph was not him, as Richard Lamb knows: 'The papers were full of rumours about sexual scandals and Duncan Sandys was always at the top of the list. Well, I think he was a pretty erotic fellow and because he'd had a lot of lovers people focused on him. But as the headless man, that was right off beam.'

Another candidate more durably associated with the role of the headless man was the actor Douglas Fairbanks Junior, and the Denning papers are reputed to confirm this. Fairbanks still denies that he was the headless man.

The 'man in the mask' was a masochist who appeared at parties to serve drinks and get whipped by other guests, and was reputed to be someone so famous that he had to hide his face. Rumour associated the name of Tory Cabinet minister Ernest Marples with this man, but it appears that he was actually a London solicitor rather than a politician.

Moral indignation rained down on Profumo and his former associates, without much care being taken to distinguish decadent aristocrats from Notting Hill nightlife. Harold Wilson inveighed against 'the diseased excrescence, a corrupted and poisoned appendix, of a small and unrepresentative section of society that makes no contribution to what Britain is, still less what it can be'. Richard Crossman expressed disgust in the privacy of his diary at 'the sleaziness of those Tories who get mixed up with this kind of society' – incidentally, the first mention I have found of 'sleaze' in this context. Crossman also maintained that the account of the 'trial of Keeler and her Negro friends must have been the biggest shock to public morality which has been known in this century. I can't think of a more humiliating and discrediting story than that of the Secretary of State for

War's being involved with people of this kind.' This was a trifle ungenerous of Crossman, whose first wife, as his biographer Anthony Howard points out, was a Communist morphine addict he met in Berlin in 1931 (Oxford legend has it that Crossman boasted to his friends that she was a prostitute), and whose second wife was married to someone else when their relationship began. Unappealing as Labour moral outrage was, it killed nobody, which cannot be said of its Conservative counterpart.

Stephen Ward was charged on 8 June with living off the immoral earnings of several 'prostitutes' he was friendly with, including Christine Keeler. In reality he had done nothing more than accept the odd contribution to housekeeping expenses at his flat, and almost certainly had made a net financial loss on the girls, most of whom were not really prostitutes at all. His osteopathic practice and his portraits made Ward enough money for a comfortable living.

The trial of Stephen Ward symbolized the vindictiveness of the Establishment in general, which had set up Profumo and Ward as scapegoats for its own sins. In desperation Ward tried to warn the government that he would name names if the prosecution was not dropped, but was dubbed a blackmailer. Even when he had nothing to lose, he did not make good his threat. His case was fast-tracked through the judicial system within weeks.

Ward's famous friends, who had flocked around him when he could introduce them to pretty girls, vanished when he was in trouble. The royal family was also anxious to erase evidence of its connections with Ward. Ward had drawn several portraits of family members, including his friend the Duke of Edinburgh, and they featured in an exhibition of his work at the Museum Gallery in Holborn. On the second day of the exhibition the royal work was bought up and did not surface until the 1980s.

At the trial in July 1963, Ward was pilloried by the prosecuting counsel, Mervyn Griffith-Jones, who had already distinguished himself as a sanctimonious relic by asking members of the *Lady Chatterley's Lover* obscenity jury whether it was a book one would wish one's wife or servants to read. Ironically, the judge had made the jury pay for its own refreshments – 'to avoid any suspicion of favours' – despite the fact that the whole trial was itself a corruption of the judicial system.

Ward killed himself while the jury was considering its verdict.

*

The Denning Report published in September 1963 was an anticlimax and a disappointment to the thousands of members of the public who rushed to government bookshops to buy copies. It examined the events of the Profumo affair, and concluded that there had been no breach in security and that the allegations about Keeler's disappearance having been arranged were false. Denning also found the rumours about the sexual behaviour of prominent people he had investigated over the summer to be mostly hot air, although the impression that was given by the government was that the allegations had been roundly dismissed. It was a familiar pattern of inquiries from Bank Rate to Franks to Scott. In an unpublished letter to Macmillan, found in Denning's archive by Richard Lamb, he advised the Prime Minister that in two cases the allegations seemed to have substance, as Lamb describes:

The letter said that Ernest Marples, the Minister of Transport, and a junior minister were security risks. Marples was because he had engaged in disgusting practices with prostitutes, and the junior minister he said had been involved in homosexuality, and that these were security risks. In his remit Lord Denning was given the task of pointing out any ministers who might be security risks, and his letter says that Marples was a risk. In my view Denning failed completely in discharging his duty.

The junior minister, Denzil Freeth, insisted in 1995 that the person who informed Denning had 'got the wrong end of the stick' and that the account of his presence at a homosexual party was not true. Freeth resigned as a minister and left the Commons in 1964, although Marples, against whom the allegations were both more serious and better substantiated, continued in office.

By omitting the allegations from his report which he believed (the sole hint was a paragraph indicating that homosexuality and perverted sex with prostitutes would be considered security risks) Denning saved Macmillan: 'he was prepared to whitewash the Establishment' according to Richard Lamb. Denning's reticence also embarrassed the Opposition, which had insinuated that there was more to tell. One MP who was particularly embarrassed was a well-informed Liberal, Jeremy Thorpe – of whom more later – who had alleged that two ministers would be forced out.

The Denning Report closed the season of scandal, and the 'satire boom' fell away rapidly, although only superficially could one claim that normal service was resumed. It is often said in retrospect that the Profumo affair 'brought down' Harold Macmillan, but this is at best a simplification. His resignation in October 1963 was a considerable surprise, as the Denning Report had shored up his position and an election was anticipated relatively soon. It was ostensibly for health reasons, although general weariness and depression played their part. Conservative popularity was severely dented for most of 1963, running up to twenty points behind Labour.

Barbara Castle was delighted at the way the Profumo affair had punctured Macmillan's confidence, but even more so at the destruction of a false image of the Conservative Party, as she now says:

This really did make people feel that some of their betters, as they considered they were, had feet of clay ... by his acquiescence and silence [Macmillan] had become tarred with the same brush, and so there was nobody they felt they could really trust on the Tory benches any more ... It undoubtedly helped the Labour Party to get judged on its merits and not just as a second best to a marvellous Tory Party which was full of gentlemen and well-behaved people.

However, by the summer of 1964 enough time had passed to bring the Tories back into contention. Labour's victory in the 1964 election was so narrow that the voters who remembered the Profumo affair and held it against the Conservative Party may have tipped the balance.

So much for party politics. The cultural shift prompted by the events of 1963 affected the media and politicians more profoundly. To Richard Ingrams:

The Profumo affair was the central event of the 1960s in a way. It represented a groundswell of criticism of politicians that was already going on, perhaps going back to Suez and Eden ... although I still had a kind of image of the Cabinet rather as if they were the same sort of people as bishops, and the Profumo affair changed all that. The Christine Keeler affair was not really the issue, it was much more the Stephen Ward trial which looked as if he'd been made a scapegoat for the whole thing to draw attention away from Profumo.

John Profumo had been held up by the Opposition as a symbol of the dishonesty of conservatism, and denounced by his former colleagues as a disgrace and a liar. After leaving public life he started work for East End charities, particularly Toynbee Hall, for which he was awarded the OBE in 1975. It was one of Harold Wilson's better-judged honours. His wife, Valerie Hobson, stayed with him until her death in 1998. Profumo's long penance won him much sympathy in later years. Christine Keeler's full story sat in the vaults of the *News of the World* from 1963 until 1969 when the new owner of the paper, Rupert Murdoch, arrived. According to Derek Jameson:

Rupert came in like a storm from the Antipodes, took over the News of the World *and the first thing he wanted to know was 'What have you got?' He meant what properties, what stories, what features, what buy-ups have you got in the safe. The then editor Stafford Somerfield said, 'Well, we've never told the Keeler story.' They had bought Christine Keeler's story for £23,000 [now worth about £275,000] and they used bits of it but they'd never used the first-person account, so Rupert said, 'Run it! Run it!'*

Keeler's story was duly published in 1969. Murdoch's commercially motivated decision was denounced as raking over old news and hurting Jack Profumo. Murdoch was ostracized by some sections of British society and criticized by the Press Council and the Catholic Church. When Murdoch appeared on David Frost's television programme the one-time scourge of the Establishment made a verbal assault on the publisher, as Derek Jameson recalls: 'Murdoch got the most fearful barrage of criticism. He was lambasted left right and centre. "Why has he done this, the dirty digger, this awful man from Australia?" and it was really nothing to do with the ethics of the Keeler story. It was having a bash at this upstart from Oz.'

Unlike previous newspaper proprietors, Murdoch did not care very much about what people, even London's grandest, thought of him. His newspapers were the future of the British media; Cecil King and his ilk looked remarkably dated within a few years. Something had broken for the public as well as the press. Deference to the ruling class never recovered from the events of 1963. Geoffrey Goodman believes that:

> *The Profumo scandal really did shock people. They still expected a better example from their political leaders, and oddly enough from the Conservatives. People would have been surprised if Labour leaders had behaved in that way, but particularly because the Conservative Party always postured as being superior, the aristocracy of the human condition, people regarded Conservatives as special upper-class people who behaved properly ... But you had here a combination of personal morality, political naïvety, stupidity, and a form of behaviour that was not only politically unacceptable but also socially unacceptable.*

Great hopes were placed on the positive side of the Profumo disillusionment. One of the most sadly misplaced conclusions from the Profumo affair was that of Wayland Young, who wrote: 'The name conservatism will survive, but it will not again mean the blatant purchase of that which should be built, enjoyed, loved and celebrated – and the words fit whether we speak of sexual relationships or city centres – as it did in 1963.'

Conservatism came, for much of the electorate, to mean just this at the end of another long spell in government in the 1990s, and the blatant and corrupt purchase of city centres was tainting both conservatism and socialism at the time Young was writing. John Poulson's corruption of city councils was underway in 1963 although the truth only became generally known ten years later. Rather than the optimistic values that Young celebrated, the lasting legacy of the Profumo affair was cynicism. It was ironic that Harold Wilson, who had handled the affair so well in the short term, was the biggest victim of the new mood in the long term. Nobody suffered more, and more unjustly, from the attitude that 'they are all at it'.

CHAPTER 5

The Wilson circle 1963-76

'I would go in to see the Prime Minister and find Marcia, her brother, her sister, her boyfriend. The place was like a bloody railway station.'

George Wigg to Chapman Pincher, 1965

Harold Wilson was loathed by most of the old Establishment. His successful manipulation of the Profumo scandal had helped the Labour Party, but infuriated many Conservatives who condemned his actions as hypocritical, given that the private lives of Labour leaders were not above reproach. He was often dismissed as a cynical conjuror of illusions, a temporizing failure as a national leader. These points are at least arguable, but Wilson's historical reputation has been tarnished by the perception of him as the recent Prime Minister with the lowest standards of personal integrity. Although Wilson was not without his faults, the allegation that he was a sleazy Prime Minister is a travesty.

Wilson did not have the same access to the old boy network as Macmillan or even Gaitskell. His political beliefs in the early 1960s were regarded as being too far to the left and too challenging to the traditional way of doing things for him to have strong allies in the Establishment. He was lower middle class, with lower-middle-class tastes in food, music and entertainment, He was also political to an extent that people like Gaitskell found him a terrific bore; he found in-depth conversation about trade statistics more interesting than the company of society hostesses. He had also made powerful enemies. His championing of trade with the Eastern Bloc, both as President of the Board of Trade in 1947–51 and as a consultant to companies in the 1950s, had aroused suspicions among the cold warriors of the defence and security organizations. His accusations against the City during the Bank Rate affair caused lasting resentment.

Political leaders, however, need networks of political and personal support and Wilson assembled a clique of personal supporters who did not owe particular allegiance to either side of the 1950s civil war within the Labour Party, nor to the old Conservative Establishment. Members of the Wilson circle were a variegated lot, ranging from respected scientists and economists such as Solly Zuckerman and Nicholas Kaldor to dubious businessmen like Joe Kagan. Many of them, like Wilson himself, were political buffs – such as Marcia Williams, Joe Haines and Gerald Kaufman, then a journalist. Some of Wilson's entourage, like the Labour MP Albert Murray, were valued for their jovial company. Bearing in mind the damage done to Macmillan by the Profumo affair, Wilson had two scandal-control specialists, George Wigg and Arnold – from 1965 Lord – Goodman. Wigg was brought into government as Paymaster-General with a watching brief over government security. Goodman was a successful solicitor with experience in entertainment, media and commercial property law, and a vague sympathy with the progressive side of British politics; as a Jew, he was excluded from the innermost counsels and clubrooms of the old Establishment. He had acted for Bevan, Crossman and Phillips in the 'Venetian Blind' case, and for the Labour Party in attempting to stop leaks from National Executive Committee meetings. When Wilson became leader he acquired Goodman as a camp follower.

One of the first things Wilson and Goodman had to do after Profumo was to put the lid on one of the most outrageous of Tom Driberg's escapades. Because Driberg was not the first politician named in the affair, the scandal, on the surface, involved a Tory figure, but without Driberg almost certainly nothing would have happened.

PEER AND A GANGSTER: YARD INQUIRY
Probe of Public Men at Seaside Parties

The headline was a promising start for another summer of scandal. The *Sunday Mirror* story in July 1964 suggested something that would make the Profumo affair look tame by comparison, alleging that a famous politician was homosexually involved with London's most notorious criminal.

The politician was Bob, by now Lord, Boothby. His career had been sidetracked since the early days of the Second World War, partly because of the bitterness of the more powerful Macmillan and partly because of his own mistakes such as the Czech assets affair. After the war he became a public figure because of his abilities on radio and in the new medium of television, although he was never an approved voice of the Conservative Party, being too far to the left even in those days when the party supported the Welfare State. Harold Macmillan took a little revenge for years of pain by kicking Boothby upstairs as one of the first of the new, *déclassé*, life peers in 1958 and ended his mainstream political career.

After the peerage, Boothby played a considerable, and honourable, part in the campaign to decriminalize homosexuality after the Wolfenden Report. Michael Foot, who supported the campaign, recalls him as saying that he was 'a sort of non-playing captain, I suppose' of the lobby to persuade the Home Office to legislate. But Boothby could be persuaded on to the field. As well as being a notorious heterosexual philanderer, he sometimes enjoyed having sex with men – these gay relationships being based more simply on sexual satisfaction, as opposed to the emotional tangles of his heterosexual life. He was well known in the gay underground of the 1940s and 1950s. The journalist Terence Lancaster remembers 'Guy Burgess telling me in Moscow that the first man who had kissed him, fully, on the lips, was Bob Boothby. Everyone knew that Bob was ambidextrous.'

Boothby was never at risk from exposure from his Westminster friends. His rackety life added to his considerable charms, and he was regarded fondly by members of all parties as good company and generous of spirit. His colleagues rallied round when he was accused of being mixed up with decidedly the wrong sort of person.

The Kray twins, Ronald and Reginald, were in the process of building up a fearsome criminal organization. They had been engaged in violence and extortion in the East End of London for several years, and at the start of the 1960s they became interested in moving operations 'up West' to take advantage of the lucrative markets for gambling and prostitution in the West End. Ronnie Kray was a psychopath, whose fits of rage terrified fellow gangsters almost as much as his periods of cold implacability. Among the many illegal services Ronnie provided was commercial gay sex, both live shows on stage and sexual partners for friends who shared Ronnie's taste for young men. Among these friends in 1963 were Tom Driberg, who could never resist rough trade or the tang of decadence. He introduced the irrepressibly sexually curious Bob Boothby to gangland. In return, the two politicians gave the Krays the thrill of mixing with high society, and the possibility of much more.

The Krays dreamed of establishing a political network under the control of organized crime. Their adversaries, the Metropolitan Police and the prison service, were after all run by the Home Secretary, who was answerable to Parliament. Driberg proved able to use the normal channels of constituency work to get a Kray ally moved from Dartmoor back to a London prison. Ronnie's musings on the 'politics of crime' had started to pay off. The Krays aspired to the organization and political influence of the Mafia in Chicago or New Jersey, if not in Italy, but Ronnie's mental instability made it impossible for them to develop a thriving criminal empire. The Krays were not the equal of Lucky Luciano, and Tom Driberg was hardly the equivalent of Giulio Andreotti. Their ideas of a criminal lobby remained a dream, as Driberg was an unreliable figure and Boothby was marginal to say the least. However, even such a poor network, when combined with more complicated political calculations and the ability of the political class to protect its own, served to protect them for a few crucial years.

In 1964 the Kray organization was coming under threat from a concerted police investigation, and the police picked up rumours of politicians' involvement with East End criminals. Such a juicy story was naturally the stuff of gossip with crime reporters. The link between police and crime reporters is closer if anything than the parliamentary lobby, and this channel has provided much more revelation of scandal over the years than political journalism. The *Sunday Mirror* reporters pieced together a story that 'a prominent peer' (Boothby was not named in a vain attempt to libel-proof the article) was involved in a homosexual underground with 'a leading thug', Mayfair high society and clergymen in Brighton.

Boothby returned from holiday in France to find Westminster buzzing with rumours about a peer being involved with gangsters. Naturally, he consulted Driberg. According to his official biography, he did not recognize himself as the subject of the story and Driberg had to tell him: 'Bob, it's you.' But it seems a coincidence too far that he should innocently have sought out the one politician who *was* indisputably involved both with the Krays and gay priests in Brighton. Boothby was actually in a desperate panic and turned to wherever he could find assistance.

Driberg persuaded Wilson that Boothby had to be saved, and Wilson's own legal entourage of Arnold Goodman and Gerald Gardiner took over the handling of the case. Gardiner was an ascetic, other-worldly lawyer who became Lord Chancellor in Wilson's Labour government. Boothby was interrogated by the pair, who were convinced of his innocence and outraged on his behalf. They decided on punitive legal action. Ronnie Kray also considered suing the paper for describing him as 'London's leading thug' but his legal advisers told him not to push his luck.

One of the more striking aspects of the Boothby affair was the fact that it was the Labour Party, rather than the Conservatives, who came to his aid. Boothby was a politically independent free spirit rather than a Tory Party loyalist and sat on the cross benches in the House of Lords. He had not held office since 1940 and his disgrace would not have implicated the Conservative Party in much, beyond reminding the electorate of the previous scandal-soaked year. It was much more risky for the Labour Party because of Tom Driberg's involvement.

Driberg was a much more senior figure than Boothby, as an NEC member and a former Chairman. Driberg's promiscuity, and his taste for the exotic and louche in all aspects of life from High Church ceremonial to the lowest profane enjoyment London had to offer, were well known in Labour circles. Even without knowing the details of this particular incident, Harold Wilson feared the worst, and shuddered at the thought of Driberg's life being raked over in public, only months before an election.

The danger worsened. A photographer appeared at the *Mirror*'s offices with a photograph of Boothby sitting on a sofa with Ronnie Kray, but suddenly changed his mind and took out an injunction against the *Mirror* to prevent publication of the photograph. *Stern* magazine published an article, 'Lord Bobby in Trouble', on 22 July in Germany, naming Boothby for the first time as the subject of the allegations. Boothby and his lawyers went on to the attack with a witty rebuttal which was published as a letter to *The Times* on 2 August. In it, Boothby declared:

> *I am not a homosexual. I have not been to a Mayfair party of any kind for more than twenty years. I have met the man alleged to be 'King of the Underworld' only three times on business matters, and then by appointment in my flat, at his request and in the company of other people. I have never been to a party in Brighton with any gangsters, still less with clergymen ... In short the whole affair is a tissue of atrocious lies ... let them print it and face the consequences.*

The *Mirror*'s journalists had trouble corroborating the story in public. Their police sources, unsurprisingly, would not go on the record. Scotland Yard officially denied that an investigation was under way. The senior executives of the Mirror Group, Cecil King and Hugh Cudlipp, decided to fold after the threats they received from Gardiner and Goodman, and indications from Wilson that they should drop the story. Derek Jameson was then working on the *Sunday Mirror*, and recalls:

> *We could have proved that Boothby's relationship with the Krays was improper and dangerous, but we weren't allowed to because Cecil King told us that we mustn't fight the case and we had to pay him out of court. The official reason was that he didn't want it to look as if the Mirror newspapers had a vendetta against homosexuals, but it was the old boy network.*

'Lord Boothby: An Unqualified Apology' grovelled the *Sunday Mirror* five days after *The Times* letter. The case was settled with damages of £40,000 to Boothby (a tidy sum, now equivalent to about £440,000). Reg Payne, the editor responsible for the story, was sacked.

Even after 1964 Driberg and Boothby continued to ask parliamentary questions in the interests of the Kray twins and members of their 'firm'. Boothby's libel win did not make him happy. Despite his precarious finances, he gave the money away. He always regarded it as 'dirty' and unearned and in 1970 confessed to the journalist Susan Barnes (Crosland) that he regretted the whole business. Boothby's attack of conscience does him some credit, but he never wanted the truth told about the Krays, and made vigorous efforts to suppress John Pearson, the writer on the Krays, from writing about him until he died in 1986.

The severe punishment meted out to the Mirror Group for dabbling with the Boothby story was a warning to the entire press. A solid-looking story could collapse into thin air when sources failed to back it up. Worse, the political Establishment could do deals behind the backs of editors and journalists to kill stories and damage the careers of those involved. The intimidating legal power of Arnold, shortly to be Lord, Goodman – and, more particularly, his developing network of friends in all corners of public life – cast a bulky shadow over the efforts of press muckraking for ten years.

*

The satire boom of 1963 faded; *That Was the Week That Was* was not screened again. But *Private Eye* survived and prospered. The magazine was a way for journalists to short-circuit the censorship that people like Cecil King had been able to impose. If a story was spiked as a favour for a member of the old boy network, it was almost guaranteed to be passed on to *Private Eye*. But even when serious investigations were printed in *Private Eye*, they occupied a curious middle position between Fleet Street gossip and facts put on the record. Goodman, a lifelong target of the magazine, hated the threat it posed to the privacy of the Establishment.

Ironically, Goodman may have had a bigger skeleton in his closet than many of the people he protected. One of his clients was the wealthy Portman family, whose client account was depleted under Goodman's management by something of the order of £1 million between 1955 and 1993. A settlement was reached in 1993 in which Goodman repaid around £500,000 to the family. In 1999 *The Independent* alleged that Goodman had stolen the money and used it to buy influence through generosity to senior Labour figures in the Wilson era. The allegation has been disputed by Goodman's many friends.

The 1964–70 Wilson government suffered from no serious public scandals affecting ministers, despite the almost fanatical hatred Wilson inspired in parts of the Conservative Establishment. It was not a ministry of saints, but none of Wilson's ministers were forced out by sleaze of any kind. The press was still somewhat reluctant to print personal stories of public figures, while the Wilsonian Establishment, particularly the brilliance of Goodman in using the law and his connections to stop allegations from being publicized, turned out to be highly effective at controlling public knowledge of what was happening within the political class – more so than the bumbling Tory Establishment that the Profumo affair had shattered.

The political ally on whom Harold Wilson relied more than anyone was Marcia Williams (Lady Falkender after 1974), who, rather than suppressing adverse stories, attracted much criticism, fair and unfair. She became his secretary in 1956, having previously worked for Morgan Phillips 'until she changed sides and came over to Harold with all her files and secrets' according to the conspiratorial Crossman in his *Diaries*. It was a far-sighted political move by Williams to metaphorically buy shares in Wilson near to the bottom of the market, and build up a strong alliance that took her into Downing Street as his most trusted adviser.

Most politicians and journalists were unfamiliar with the concept of such a political alliance, and jumped to the erroneous conclusion that a sexual relationship was the bond between Wilson and Williams. This interpretation gained popularity when she and her husband Ed divorced in 1961, and rumours multiplied that Harold Wilson had paid off Ed Williams to avoid being named as co-respondent. In reality, Ed Williams had been living and working in Seattle, where his job had taken him, and he had met a woman there whom he wished to marry.

The allegation that Wilson and Williams were having an affair circulated among Conservatives and even Gaitskellites, now dispossessed of the Labour Party leadership. In the highly charged political atmosphere of 1964, the matter became a submerged part of the election campaign. Although Labour had been well ahead in May 1964, the Conservatives rallied during the summer as the leadership of Alec Douglas-Home gained respect and the economy boomed. By the time of the election campaign in the autumn the parties were nearly level and looking for any advantage they could find.

Labour believed that there was an organized attempt on the part of elements within the Conservative Party to spread smears about Wilson in 1964, alleging that he and Williams (and/or, absurdly, Barbara Castle) were having an affair, that he had been the cause of the Williams' divorce, and so on. The effectiveness of Profumo as a weapon for Labour in 1963 led these Conservatives to believe that Labour could be similarly damaged by a sex scandal. The nearest the allegations came to the mainstream media was when Quintin Hogg, heckled over Profumo during an election speech, snapped back: 'If you can tell me that there are no adulterers on the front bench of the Labour Party you can talk to me about Profumo.' Wilson and Williams angrily took this, a sharp retort to a heckler and nothing more, as a reference to the rumour. There was talk of taking out a writ, but wiser counsel prevailed.

Labour went on to win the election, although with a majority of only five, and Harold Wilson became Prime Minister. Speculation about the precise nature of the relationship between Wilson and Williams has continued ever since, although while Wilson was in power it was more of a political parlour game, with occasional snide printed allusions by journalists such as John Junor and Auberon Waugh, than a subject of public discussion. Wilson's biographers characterized it as a sort of marriage, with a strong element of 'sex-in-the-head'. The emotional current of co-dependence always flowed strongly, and the issue of whether there was ever, however briefly, a sexual side as well is of secondary importance. Lady Falkender, when asked by Simon Freeman in 1995, said: 'Did I fancy Harold? No. He had a wonderful brain and I thought he was God. I absolutely adored him but he used to tell smutty jokes and put milk bottles on the table. How could I have an affair with a man like that?'

Wilson was not much of a womanizer. His parliamentary colleague Leo

Abse told the following anecdote about the visit to Britain of a female academic from the United States to research Bevanism in the early 1950s. Part of her research involved shadowing Wilson in his constituency for a week. Thirty years later Abse met her again and, as he wrote:

Wilson, I discovered, had remained in touch with [her], meeting her when he was in the States and when, very occasionally, she came to Britain. Perhaps it was not surprising; she had been a dazzling young woman and Wilson, as ever more talk than passion, evidently retained some romantic attachment, as ill defined as when she had first met him.

Abse's unkind interpretation is not the only one. Perhaps Wilson liked her but thought it was not worth breaching his rather conventional moral code.

The changes in society under way at the time of the Profumo affair and after also played their part in redefining the rules of privacy for politicians. Under the first Wilson government of 1964–70 the government withdrew from regulating areas of sexual morality that the previous Conservative government had tried to enforce. Gaitskell and Crosland had rejected moralizing before the 1959 election. Within the Labour Party Wilson was outflanked from both left and right on social and moral issues. Roy Jenkins carried the torch of Gaitskellite liberalism into government and gave fair wind to liberalizing measures on abortion and homosexuality. The climate in the Parliament elected in 1966 was unprecedentedly favourable to social reform. The Labour landslide had brought in a lot of professional middle class and academic members who had more interest in liberal issues than the solid trade union core of the party. Wilson was inclined to dismiss 'permissive' legislation as 'Hampstead intellectual issues' but in 1966 for the first time Hampstead went Labour and elected left-wing MP Ben Whitaker.

The Labour government of 1964–70 had its share of ministers with colourful private lives. George Brown would often behave in a lecherous way with young women, and before his remarriage in 1964 Tony Crosland had led a remarkably dissolute life. One member of the Cabinet, the Agriculture Minister Fred Peart, had an extra-marital affair and was warned sternly by George Wigg that he was behaving too indiscreetly for the government's comfort.

There was a certain amount of excitement in the late 1960s when Marcia Williams, a divorced woman, had two children, and the more simple-minded assumed that Wilson was the father. In reality the father was Walter Terry, a senior political journalist then working for the *Daily Mail*. It is therefore hardly surprising that Williams and Terry managed to preserve their privacy as far as the readers of national newspapers were concerned. Even the editor of *Private Eye* at the time, Richard Ingrams, shied away from the story, as he now recalls:

That was never, ever referred to, perhaps because the father was a journalist, I don't know. It wasn't until she was made a peeress that anyone referred to it. We never even mentioned it in Private Eye. *It's very hard to explain, but it isn't always the case that stories don't get into the press because of the laws of libel.*

Private Eye did eventually break the story, as Ingrams says, in 1974. George Wigg, who bore no love for Marcia Williams, had written about her children in his 1972 autobiography. These passages were excised by the publisher on the advice of Lord Goodman, although they did mysteriously end up in *Private Eye*'s files where they sat for two years.

Some of the background to this affair emerged in 1998. George Wigg had been edged out of the inner group around Wilson by Goodman and Williams and was bitter about it. Wilson and his allies heard that Wigg was going to attack Williams, and engaged in a bit of counter-blackmail. Wilson asked John Silkin to investigate Wigg, and Silkin engaged a private detective to follow him around. The detective discovered that Wigg stayed overnight with a woman friend, who was herself a single mother. In the light of this discovery, Wigg decided that discretion about the Williams family would be wise. According to Chapman Pincher, Wilson's team had not finished with Wigg after this episode. Wigg was arrested and charged with kerb-crawling but acquitted in rather inconclusive circumstances. It was a messy end to an effective if dubious political partnership.

*

One particular taboo that remained, long after the 'Venetian Blind', was discussion of the drinking habits of politicians. This was fortunate, because Wilson's was a heavy drinking administration. Several of its Cabinet ministers – most famously George Brown – were frequently incapacitated by alcohol, which in a more intrusive age might have provided a 'public interest' angle on an investigation into the drinking habits of public figures.

George Brown drinking stories were told with almost as much glee as Tom Driberg sex stories throughout Westminster. The unofficial slogan of his leadership campaign in 1963 was 'Better George drunk than Harold sober'. A favourite story was about the occasion when he had overindulged at a diplomatic banquet and felt that he should start the dancing when the band struck up a tune. He turned to his neighbour with the words, 'Will you dance with me, beautiful lady in red?' The neighbour replied, 'Certainly not, and for three reasons. First, you are disgustingly drunk. Secondly, that is not a waltz, it is the national anthem of Argentina. Thirdly, I am not a beautiful lady, I am the Papal Nuncio.' It probably didn't happen, but it should have.

Brown's heavy drinking, and his tendency to behave stupidly when drunk, were alluded to only indirectly in public, even on occasions such as the 1963 Kennedy assassination broadcast when Brown made a maudlin and aggressive spectacle of himself on television. *Private Eye*'s transparent euphemism for drunk, 'tired and emotional', was coined for Brown and was the title of his biography. Even to make such a patently true allegation as to accuse George Brown in print of being a drunk was a libel risk, and for many political journalists a rather hypocritical thing to do in any case. The various codes of confidentiality applying in their different ways to civil servants, fellow politicians, lobby journalists – and bartenders – would make it very unlikely that enough witnesses could be found to defend a libel action.

*

Sexual smears against Wilson and Williams were only part of the campaign against him. More serious was the persistent allegation that he was a security risk at best, a Soviet agent at worst. His visits to Moscow for one of the firms he worked for were bad enough for some spies, but the sudden death of Hugh Gaitskell in 1963 made matters worse. A Soviet defector, Anatoly Golitsyn, turned up with a tale of a KGB operation to assassinate a leading Western politician. Gaitskell was supposedly poisoned at the Russian Embassy in London with a drug that caused the immune disorder lupus erythematosus, to make way for Wilson, their man in place.

The theory was total rubbish. Golitsyn was an extremely unreliable source (who may even have been sent over by the KGB to generate paranoia in Western intelligence services) and his claims about an assassination were made only after prompting. Gaitskell had been ill long before his visit to the Embassy, his successor might well have been George Brown, and he may not even have died of lupus anyway. Wilson, of course, had no allegiance to the USSR whatsoever. But right-wing elements in the security service did not see it this way. Their strange world was best described by Edward Heath in a Commons debate on the 'Spycatcher' affair in January 1988:

> *I ... met people in the security services who talked the most ridiculous nonsense, and whose whole philosophy was ridiculous nonsense. If some of them were on a tube and saw someone reading the* Daily Mirror, *they would say 'Get after him, that is dangerous. We must find out where he bought it.'*

Once the paranoid fantasy about Wilson had taken hold, all evidence was distorted to fit. The chaotic condition of the country in 1974–76 led some on the far right to believe that Wilson was deliberately wrecking the British economy. The fact that Wilson's friend and benefactor Joe Kagan played chess with a Soviet diplomat who was also a KGB agent was adduced as 'proof' that Wilson was under Russian control. The KGB's central archive finally disproved the slur when details were published in 1999.

Britain in 1974, as in 1963, was a seething mass of rumour about misconduct in high places. The corruption revealed in the Poulson affair (detailed in the following chapter) had already given the electorate a glimpse that public life was more rotten than they had believed possible, and the Labour government started life beset not only by economic crisis and no parliamentary majority, but a populace more cynical than ever before about politicians and their motives. It started badly, with the 'slag heaps' affair.

The story, which bears certain similarities to the troubles of Peter Mandelson at the end of 1998, involved a much less glamorous location than that MP's des. res. – some slag heaps just outside Wigan. Marcia Williams' brother, Tony Field, was one of her many friends and relations she introduced to Wilson. (George Wigg resented this 'colonization', complaining to the journalist Chapman Pincher, 'I would go in to see the Prime Minister and find Marcia, her brother, her sister, her boyfriend. The place was like a bloody railway station.') Field set up a firm and bought the famous slag heaps in 1967 with the intention of selling the slag to road builders; another of his companies which ran a quarry had Marcia Williams as a director. The venture was not very successful and in 1973 Field started to sell the land off, with planning permission for industrial development. There was nothing legally wrong with Field's actions, but it was embarrassing for the Labour Party at a time when the party had been harshly criticizing 'land speculation', particularly when untrue accounts started to circulate that Wilson had been secretly involved in making money through the Wigan deal.

One of the purchasers of the slag heap land was Ronald Milhench, who forged a letter from Harold Wilson in order to press his claims and later went to prison for this action. Wilson and Goodman were able to hold off press interest, which had been developing during 1973, until after the February 1974 election but a public row broke out the following month when Wilson was back in power. Wilson was exposed to even more ridicule after defending the slag heaps deal as 'reclamation' and therefore different from 'speculation' but the press firestorm that broke around Wilson and Williams was out of all proportion to the affair. Wilson's embattled Press Secretary Joe Haines reflected in his book *The Politics of Power* that:

> *Harold Wilson's relationships with the press were never worse than at that time, and neither were mine… the behaviour of some of the journalists outside Marcia's house was disreputable – the worst in my experience, and I had been a journalist myself for more than twenty years … We saw behind the land deals affair the larger ambition of discrediting the Labour government.*

The exposure of the Milhench forgery reduced the pressure over the land deals affair. Wilson showed what he thought of his critics by elevating Marcia Williams to a life peerage as Lady Falkender, telling the Queen that he was going to 'do a Harvey Smith' (i.e. raise two fingers) at the press. But it was the start of a torrid year. As in 1963, most of the allegations that were circulating proved not to be true. Among the more outlandish and baseless rumours were that a senior parliamentarian attended orgies where he took perverse pleasure in stabbing white rabbits while having sex, and that Tony Benn smoked cannabis in a mansion flat near Baker Street. Marcia Falkender was convinced that attempts were being made to set her up, and Ted Short was the victim of a forged document purporting to be a Swiss bank account. Wilson became convinced that the October 1974 campaign would be ruined by a Zinoviev letter-style smear, although his attack on a 'cohort' of journalists combing the country for any information, real or fabricated, to damage the Labour Party was counterproductive.

In 1974, unlike 1963, there was real malice and fabrication of evidence behind the torrent of sleaze allegations. It now seems reasonably clear that a disaffected element of MI5 and other security agencies, including Peter Wright, plotted to overthrow the Labour government. Members of the Establishment who were not actually part of the plot were sufficiently alienated and frightened by the crisis of 1974 to pass on the allegations that were made. Exploiting real and faked sleaze was central to the project of forcing Wilson from office, which involved officers in Britain and Northern Ireland and was known as operation 'Clockwork Orange'. Colin Wallace, an information officer based in Northern Ireland, assembled notes of the allegations he and his colleagues were to use to discredit not only Wilson but other Labour figures and even Tory moderates. In late 1974 he drew up a chart like this:

VULNERABILITIES

	Financial	Moral	Political
Wilson	X	X	X
Heath		X	X
Thorpe	X	X	
Callaghan	X		
Paisley	X	X	
Maudling	X	X	
Steel		X	
Slater	X		
Walker	X		
Foot			X
Benn			X
Short	X		

It should be emphasized that this checklist was a smear campaign rather than a factual analysis of the behaviour of the people named. Only in the case of Thorpe, and the financial aspects of the case against Maudling, was there substance to the claims. The effect of the 'Wilson plot' is hard to assess. Wilson's surprise resignation in March 1976 was the result of a decision he had taken two years earlier, about which he had told some of his colleagues, rather than the result of the campaign. If it achieved nothing else, the Wilson plot accentuated the general public's disgust and impatience with the leading politicians of the period.

The most lasting taint on Wilson's record was from the businessmen he associated with and to whom he awarded honours. Wilson gravitated towards other people who were outsiders as far as the traditional British Establishment was concerned. Many businessmen with an interest in East–West trade were themselves of East European origin, having come to Britain as refugees from political persecution or anti-Jewish pogroms under the pre-Communist regimes. A certain proportion of the hostility towards them in Britain was also motivated by anti-semitism. Business practices which would, if carried out by people from the right sort of background, be considered sharp but not worth making a fuss about, were scandalous if outsiders did them.

Terence Lancaster, a sympathetic journalist, feels that:

It's quite true with hindsight Harold Wilson should not have associated with a number of people with whom he did associate. At the beginning I think it was because they were mostly Jewish incidentally. They had been socialists when young and had retained a certain amount of socialist faith – not much, but they believed in a Labour government. They offered money to his office, but not to him as a person. When he lost the 1970 election his budget from Labour Party headquarters was £10,000 a year, the same figure that Gaitskell had years ago. From that he was supposed to maintain an office, research assistants, secretaries, even Mary Wilson. I think the party paid for his train tickets. It was peanuts for what he had to do.

Leaving aside the salaries of his secretary (Marcia Williams) and a Press Secretary (Joe Haines), the costs of the office were nearly £30,000. Wilson was fortunate in concluding a spectacular publishing deal for his book about the 1964–70 government which cleared £260,000 (now worth over £2 million) in serialization, which helped fund the office and his personal spending which included houses in London and Great Missenden in Buckinghamshire and a cottage in the Scilly Isles. In addition he relied on the generosity of his business friends. Joe Kagan had helped on a small scale with the expenses of the political office at Number 10 during the 1964–70 government. In 1970 Lord Goodman and Lord (Wilfred) Brown contacted sympathetic businessmen including Rudy Sternberg, Jarvis Astaire and Samuel Fisher, and established a trust to pay for office expenses.

Goodman also had secrets to conceal. In spring 1999 it was alleged that he had stolen a large sum of money from the client account of the wealthy Portman family over several decades, and diverted some of the money to help his (unwitting) friends in the Labour Party. £500,000 was paid in settlement of the Portman claim in 1993 without admission of liability. Goodman's many friends refused to believe that he had acted wrongly, and suggested that the family's own instructions were at fault. The affair cast a shadow over Goodman's undoubted record of public service.

The incoming Labour government in 1974 had introduced the 'Short money' which provided public assistance to the Opposition in parliament, although the funding was not enough to avoid future problems. The problem of how to fund their office was to affect other leaders of the opposition, including Tony Blair in 1994–97, and no wholly satisfactory way was found of funding the necessary degree of research and secretarial support. The 1970–74 office fund's existence was revealed in 1977 when the correlation between donors and subsequent honours proved embarrassing.

The Wilson circle, and its more dubious members, came into most prominence at the end of his term as Prime Minister in 1976. His resignation honours list was the most controversial since the 1920s, and not just for its contents. It became a symbol of Marcia Falkender's domination of him because it was allegedly drafted by her on a sheet of lavender notepaper. In hindsight it appears that all she had done was to compile various scraps of paper on which Wilson had written suggested honours; she also prefers to describe the notepaper as 'pale pink' rather than lavender.

Harold Wilson never set much store by honours, and used them as a way of distributing pleasant baubles and, as in the OBEs for the Beatles, promoting the image of his government. The stuffier part of the Establishment took the honours list extremely seriously, condemning the rewarding of cronies and the frivolity of awards to the entertainers and impresarios Wilson admired. The entire Political Honours Scrutiny Committee, a toothless tiger set up in 1924 after the Lloyd George scandal, resigned.

Although anti-semitism, and snobbery about the entertainment awards, played a part, some of the awards were provocative or ill-judged, and the list was open to charges of cronyism. One citation on the 'lavender' list was apparently a private joke, explained by the writer Francis Wheen: James Goldsmith was given a knighthood for 'services to ecology'. Goldsmith's brother was an environmentalist, but what Wilson and Falkender meant was that James Goldsmith had done his best to remove what they saw as toxic pollution of the political environment through his legal attack on *Private Eye*.

The businessmen who had helped with his private office were given honours. Kagan, who received a peerage, had been closer to Wilson for longer and was firmly associated with him in the public mind because Wilson famously wore 'Gannex' raincoats produced by his textiles firm. In the 1970s Kagan's business interests grew but he also became greedy and dishonest; in 1980 he received a fine and ten months in prison for theft and false accounting.

The worst-judged honour in the list was Sir Eric Miller's knighthood. Miller and his firm, Peachey Properties, had grown rapidly in the 1960s and 1970s and Miller distributed favours to friends within the political class in return for the social acceptability he craved. He was most assiduous with the Labour Party, lending Harold Wilson a company helicopter for the October 1974 election and providing champagne to the value of £3,304 (now worth over £12,000) for Wilson's resignation party. He became Treasurer of the Socialist International. Miller was a friend of Marcia Falkender, taking her to Annabel's nightclub, a fascinating place to be in the mid 1970s where Goldsmith and his extreme right friends rubbed shoulders with Harold Wilson's cronies.

One Tory recipient of Miller's generosity was the leading Conservative Reginald Maudling (see next chapter), who was given a highly advantageous leaseback deal on his Hertfordshire house. Peachey bought the freehold for £5,000, took over the cost of building work (including a swimming pool), and rented the property back for a nominal sum. Miller also pandered to Maudling's expensive tastes, feeding him baked potatoes stuffed with caviar. Miller was sacked by the Board of Peachey for his extravagance in May 1977, and in September 1977 he killed himself while under investigation by Department of Trade and Industry inspectors. In December 1978 its report estimated that £1 million (now worth £4.5 million or so) of Peachey money had been misused by Miller, using the company 'as his private bank', although the recipients of his generosity, including Maudling, were cleared of acting improperly.

The 'lavender' list was followed by Wilson's attempts to strike back at his enemies in MI5 and South Africa by setting himself up as a sort of Deep Throat for a pair of investigative journalists he sent chasing red herrings. 'I see myself as the big fat spider sitting in the corner of the room,' he told Barrie Penrose and Roger Courtiour. 'Sometimes I speak when I'm asleep. You should both listen. Occasionally when we meet I might tell you to go to the Charing Cross Road and kick a blind man standing on the corner. That blind man might tell you something, lead you somewhere.'

Wilson was ridiculed, understandably enough, for launching this investigation, although he and Marcia Falkender gave the journalists an amazing amount of accurate information about the plotting against his government and various glimpses of the underside of British politics such as a clue to the identity of the 'Fourth Man' still at the heart of the Establishment. Ironically, the main consequence of his attempt to vindicate his suspicions was the political demolition of his friend, Jeremy Thorpe.

This venture into investigative journalism was Wilson's last substantial contribution to political life. He remained an MP until 1983, and went to the Lords as Baron Wilson of Rievaulx in his ancestral Yorkshire. Wilson did not live in luxury in his retirement – confounding those who had suspected him of financial dishonesty. During his long final illness he was comforted by his family and his surviving true friends, most particularly the loyal Marcia Falkender.

CHAPTER 6

Poulson: corruption by design 1957-77

'I was hoping to build up a little pot of money for my old age.'
Reginald Maudling, 1969

Harold Wilson was not corrupt, but the allegations and the corruption of some of his Labour colleagues and Conservative opponents lent credence to the weary view that all politicians were crooked. The worst corruption in British politics since the sale of honours was revealed in the mid 1970s. It centred on a corrupt architect, John Poulson, who built a business empire on bribing councillors and MPs.

The postwar building boom fuelled the growth of the construction industry, including Poulson's business. There was an unprecedented demand for new building all over the country. The Attlee government started a massive programme of housing construction, which was accelerated when the Conservatives came to power in 1951 promising to build 300,000 houses a year.

Housing was not the only growth area. Town centres were being re-planned to replace the damage of the wartime bombing raids and to cope with the consumer boom that developed in the 1950s. A town centre redevelopment would involve a shopping area, either an open 'precinct' or a centre under a single roof, and the infrastructure of highways, car parks and service bays to support the shopping facilities. Often, rebuilt bus and train stations would be included. Such schemes involved a great deal of relatively expensive land, and were under the control of local authorities which had the powers of compulsory purchase to assemble large enough packages of real estate. It would be a badge of pride for a local authority to have a 'comprehensive' and 'imaginative' town centre redevelopment, whether one was needed or not, and there was considerable civic competition and posturing.

Poulson's architectural practice was an innovative business in legitimate ways. It offered a full service to the client including design and quantity surveying, which was an attractive feature. Dr Ken Williams, who was his business partner on some international contracts, admires this vision:

John Poulson, though he wasn't very creative and he was certainly flawed, was highly talented. He had seen a very important problem, that the ordinary architectural approach was beginning to fail ... It now required more engineering and communication awareness, and the whole thing was broken into different professions. Poulson said that we should put it into one group, with architects, engineers and surveyors working together in one practice.

However, it was frowned upon by the architectural profession. Poulson was thrown out of the professional body, the Royal Institution of British Architects, albeit only after he had gone bankrupt in 1972.

John Poulson was a complex character. Despite corrupting British public life, he had his own strange sense of right and wrong. His firm would deliver on its contracts, and if he personally promised to do something, he would do it. He even considered his corrupt gifts morally superior to those offered by his competitors: 'I saw the provision of holidays or cruises as far healthier than the usual so-called refreshment – so seldom criticized and yet so lavishly applied – of unlimited alcohol and rich food.' He regarded himself as religious, even devout, and was on the Board of Methodist Guild Homes. He would also always travel with his Bible, and read a chapter every night before he went to bed. All this went with a censorious approach to what he saw as sexual immorality. It is easy to be cynical about this, but very few people are ever consciously 'corrupt'; like others who have objectively been guilty of the most flagrant misconduct, Poulson was not without his own scruples and morality. He almost certainly convinced himself that his better nature was being taken advantage of by greedy politicians.

A certain amount of generosity, particularly at Christmas, has long been a recognized and accepted feature of business life, although in the 1990s rules have become progressively tighter in many businesses about accepting gifts. Drawing the precise dividing line between goodwill and corruption is a matter of fine judgement, but Poulson was flagrantly on the wrong side of it by the late 1950s. He had realized early on that manipulating influence with officers and politicians provided an easy route to business success. He was known in the early part of his career as 'Pullman Poulson' because of one of his techniques of meeting clients. Barnard Humphries, a police officer who later investigated him, remembers the story that:

Just after the war he had a contact in the Pullman booking office in Leeds railway station and that contact would tell him when somebody important to Poulson's business was likely to travel, and conveniently Poulson would make a trip to London, finding himself sitting opposite the person in question. As happens on a long journey, conversation would ensue. I can't vouch whether it's true or not, but it sounds pretty plausible.

Poulson insinuated his way into the local business and political establishment, joining the Masonic lodge in his home town of Pontefract. It is one of the ironies of the scandal that a staunch Tory such as Poulson worked so closely and corruptly with predominantly Labour figures; one can speculate that their greed confirmed Poulson in his low opinion of socialism. His political allegiance was technically to the National Liberals who had adhered to the Conservatives in 1931 and lingered on, dependent on them. The party maintained only a vestigial existence after 1948, until it was wound up in 1968 in a meeting in John Poulson's office, a fittingly ignominious end to a party whose sole rationale was careerism. The remnant of the National Liberals provided Poulson's first introduction to national politics, because in a small, stagnant pond a medium-sized fish like Poulson could quickly become a prominent figure.

Sir Herbert Butcher, the National Liberal MP for the flatlands of Holland with Boston in Lincolnshire, was one of many politicians in the 1950s who stood little chance of gaining high office and was dissatisfied with the amount a backbench MP was paid. He was interested in making money through directorships, and in 1957 co-operated in a plan with Poulson and a corrupt British Rail property surveyor to obtain the contract for an office development on top of Cannon Street station in the City of London. Subsequently Butcher, a tax law specialist, helped Poulson to put together his network of companies. By the time Butcher died in 1966 Poulson had hit the big time as an architect and corrupter of public figures. He had been involved since 1963 in the successful Aviemore project to build a ski resort in Scotland, and had recruited the help of George Pottinger, a civil servant in the Scottish office. Pottinger was highly regarded by his bosses, but his vanity was his weak point. He took holidays and money from Poulson, and began to live lavishly on the proceeds.

In the mid 1960s Poulson started to go international. The market in the Third World for new housing, infrastructure and grand prestige projects was booming, and Poulson's formula seemed as if it would travel well. To move into foreign markets he needed national-level connections, and started to take an interest in MPs as the means of boosting his profile in target areas. He and Butcher recruited the Labour MP Albert Roberts for his connections in Fascist Spain and Portugal, and the Tory John Cordle for his West African links. His proudest coup was to replace Butcher as his main parliamentary ally with the Deputy Leader of the Conservative Party, the Right Honourable Reginald Maudling.

National and international projects were consuming an increasing proportion of Poulson's attention, but the bread and butter of his business, and his corruption, remained in local government. In postwar Britain the map of local authorities had been little altered since the Victorian age, a patchwork of 'County Boroughs', 'Municipal Boroughs', 'Urban District Councils' ruling towns and cities. Outside the big cities, councils were much smaller, on average, than they are today. Many councils, particularly in regions such as the North East which were strongholds of one political party, were permanently under the control of the same group of people facing no political competition. In Felling on the south bank of the Tyne, there were twenty-one seats on the council and it was rare for more than two not to be Labour. The county of Durham itself had been continuously Labour-controlled since 1919 (and still is).

The politicians running these councils were generally honest people doing their best. But it was a situation that could have been designed as a breeding ground for corruption. Councillors are not paid, and before 1972 were not even granted reasonable expenses. The amounts of money in circulation when a town centre redevelopment was in the offing were beyond the dreams of many councillors. The lack of local political opposition meant that there was hardly any chance of being toppled or exposed. Labour councillors first elected, say, in the 1930s would grow old in office and towns would be controlled by senescent cliques of limited ability.

The more able politicians, if they chose to enter local politics in these areas, rose to controlling positions. Perhaps the greatest tragedy of the Poulson affair is the corruption of two such figures, T. Dan Smith and Andy Cunningham.

T. Dan Smith first became leader of Newcastle City Council in 1960 and acquired other local positions such as Chairman of the Northern Economic Planning Council when it was set up by the Wilson government. He believed in regional government and worked hard to foster the idea of the North East as a culturally and economically distinct area of England. He was the most radical city leader in the generally uninspiring world of local government in the 1960s, and the physical shape of Newcastle still owes much to his vision of demolishing slums and replacing them with the best housing that 'modern' styles and methods could offer, some of which is still highly regarded. He also believed in bringing art, learning and culture to his city and probably knew more about architectural history and theory than the professional Poulson. Smith's legacy to public life in the North East is still a matter of deep ambivalence.

Smith was also an innovative businessman, who had seen a trend of the future in the lobbying and public relations industry. He first became involved in the industry in 1960 with three journalists he knew, but left and formed his own company. These activities were full of conflicts of interest with his municipal leadership, including the Newcastle City Council PR account and work for building firms. Declaration of interest requirements under local government law had, as English law tends to, ignored the importance of party group meetings and caucuses among councillors. Interests had to be declared in official committees of the council, but Smith could argue in the interests of his clients to his heart's content in unofficial and private meetings. Political opponents in Newcastle could tell that something fishy was going on, but could do nothing.

Smith teamed up with Poulson in February 1962, when he was taken on as a PR consultant. The reality behind Smith's PR firm was the 'employment' of a network of 'consultants' who were councillors in areas where projects for Poulson or other Smith allies such as the building firm Crudens were proposed. It was a thinly disguised system of corruption beneath Smith's business and political life. Smith had little time for Poulson's architecture and kept his buildings out of Newcastle, although he promoted his interests enthusiastically in other areas. It was an alliance based on greed and opportunism: Smith provided Poulson with contacts in local government across Britain, and the architect paid Smith lavishly, peaking at over £30,000 (now worth £300,000) in the late 1960s.

The respect in which Dan Smith's vision and energy were held in political circles helped his business. In 1961 his firm acquired the national Labour Party as a client, in the interests of promoting the image of the party in the North and Scotland. The Labour Party cannot have been delighted with the outcome. A network of contacts and journalists went on to the Smith payroll and the pattern of their activities bore more relation to upcoming building contracts than the map of the marginal constituencies Labour had to win.

After Labour won the 1964 election Smith was a valued presence in Whitehall. George Brown brought him into the new Department of Economic Affairs and appointed him to the new Regional Planning Council. Barbara Castle became Minister of Transport in 1965 and had dealings with Smith. She now recalls:

> I think, like most people, I found Dan Smith an impressive person. What I liked about him was his enthusiasm. I was drawing up my White Papers on an integrated transport policy and meeting a lot of opposition in Tory quarters – and some quarters of the Labour Party – and it was a joy to have him say, 'Barbara, we've been waiting for this, you're on the right lines, keep it up, girl!' and so on. So it was as a pioneering spirit, a visionary, that I remember Dan Smith. It was a tremendous letdown to find out that he had been dabbling in corrupt practices.

Andy Cunningham's power in County Durham in the 1960s resembled that of a 'machine politics' boss in an American city. He was an Alderman of Felling Urban District, which he ruled as a pocket borough, and was on Durham County Council too. He also chaired the Durham Police Authority, the Northumbrian River Authority and the Newcastle Airport Authority. As well as his official posts he was Chairman of the Northern Area of the Labour Party and of the regional General and Municipal Workers' Union. This led to mindboggling conflicts of interest, none more bizarre than the fact that industrial relations at Newcastle airport were conducted from the management side by Cunningham as Chairman of the authority, and from the union side by Cunningham wearing his GMWU hat. Local investigations into his activities were hampered by fear that he would, in his Police Authority role, learn what witnesses were saying. Barnard Humphries says now:

He was a bully, but he was also respected ...When Andy Cunningham said something would happen, it happened. It was repeated to investigators on a number of occasions that he had no wish to go to Westminster to become a Member of Parliament. He sent people there.

Cunningham was recruited to the Poulson network by Smith, and his control over his various public bodies was useful in generating contracts for system-built housing, corporate headquarters and road schemes. He was paid indirectly by Poulson, in the form of holidays and a sinecure in a PR company for his wife. Poulson found him an intimidating man to deal with – 'malicious and brutal' – but of all the gang Cunningham proved the best value for money. Cunningham and Smith between them ran a thoroughly corrupt political and business network in the North East, with tentacles stretching into London and the Midlands. It was used in the interests of Poulson and, of course, Dan Smith's own companies.

There had long been suspicions that there was something rotten about the Poulson operation, and it was generally believed that there was considerable corruption within Labour Party municipal circles in the North East in the 1960s. But nothing was done for years.

The first concrete indications that Smith was at least dabbling with corrupt individuals came in 1970 and 1971, when he had a close shave over the Wandsworth affair. The leading figure in the south-west London borough was the flagrantly corrupt Sidney Sporle, who dominated the Labour group. Smith gave Sporle a 'consultancy' with his firm Open System Building, and Sporle gave Smith Wandsworth's PR contract. Wandsworth was a lucky dip of expensive construction projects in the 1960s, including a town centre redevelopment and several large housing estates. It was so blatant that Sporle was charged in 1970 over the Smith contract and accepting money corruptly in exchange for influencing contracts given in connection with the Doddington Road estate. In 1971, Sporle was convicted of being bribed by Smith but Smith was acquitted of bribing Sporle. It was a confusing situation that deterred anyone from writing about it for fear of a very complicated libel action, but it looked sordid enough for Smith to be regarded with suspicion in political circles.

The failure to investigate Poulson is not a creditable chapter in Fleet Street history. The very fact that Poulson was based in the North of England was a deterrent, requiring reporters to travel away from London and find their way in circles with which they were unfamiliar. Local government itself was generally regarded as a boring backwater, and unravelling corrupt financial arrangements required a certain amount of specialist knowledge. It fell instead to provincial journalists, television programme makers and *Private Eye* to piece the story together. Ray Fitzwalter, a Bradford journalist, picked up the trail from a local scandal involving corrupt council officers in 1969. The legal profession had cause to thank their diligence.

In the end the breakthrough came not from the Wandsworth affair, nor the evidence that Fitzwalter and *Private Eye* reporter Paul Foot had uncovered – which was ignored by the national press. It came because Poulson's business collapsed. Despite having been broadly correct in his perception that cut-price comprehensive service on contracts for local authorities would pay, and that business could be won corruptly, his companies were poorly run. He had tried to expand too rapidly into areas he knew nothing about, and faced a succession of disappointments in West Africa, the Middle East and Mexico. While chasing millions, Poulson had failed to keep track of lesser expenditures which added up. One such was the Inland Revenue, who were demanding £234,000 (now worth over £2 million) at the end of 1968. Poulson's partners staged a boardroom coup in the early hours of New Year's Day 1970. Poulson became a consultant to the firm, although the small print of the agreement left him responsible for many of the debts he had run up. He struggled on for two more years before admitting defeat.

Hearings into Poulson's failed businesses started in summer 1972 at Wakefield Crown Court. Interest in these hearings among the press spiralled as the corrupt nature of Poulson's activities became obvious. The first hearing was attended only by local journalists, but as the revelations came the national press started to take an interest. The voluminous records of his businesses were unravelled by accountants and barristers, led by Muir Hunter, trying to recover money in the interests of his creditors.

One of the barristers, David Graham, recalls that Poulson presented an unimpressive spectacle at the bankruptcy hearings:

> *Poulson was a broken man. The sadness was that as the proceedings progressed and they were spread over a period of time, he visibly deteriorated, not only physically but I suspect mentally as well. For him, bearing in mind the position he had held in the community before, this must have been absolutely devastating.*

At the second bankruptcy hearing on 3 July 1972 Dan Smith, George

Pottinger and Reginald Maudling were named as recipients of Poulson's generosity. The six Liberal MPs (including Jeremy Thorpe) tabled a motion calling for an inquiry into 'allegations of financial corruption in public life'. David Steel pressed the case: 'We have been quick in the past to crack down on politicians guilty of some sexual peccadillo. Far more corrupting in any nation's morality is the misuse by politicians or public officials of their positions for private gain.'

The accumulated evidence from the bankruptcy hearings, already in the public domain, was packaged for a mass audience by the investigative programme *World in Action*, produced by Granada Television. It was due to be screened in January 1973 when it ran into opposition from the Establishment panel which controlled what could be shown on commercial television. David Glencross was then working for the Independent Broadcasting Authority and explains:

> *Some members of the IBA were surprised that a television programme would make such damaging statements about people in public life who had not been the subject of a trial. They thought that to broadcast a programme of this kind, dealing with people with power and responsibility in local government, would frighten the horses, that it was somehow going to demoralize the nation and destroy confidence in political institutions.*

The IBA, to the fury of the journalistic profession, imposed an 'irreversible' ban on the Poulson programme despite not having read the script or seen an advance copy. The authority made the paternalist argument about confidence in political institutions but also warned that it was unfair to those accused and might prejudice any trial. The links between IBA members and Poulson, Smith and Cunningham were explored by the press. Dame Evelyn Sharp, as the senior civil servant at the Ministry of Housing and Local Government in the 1950s and 1960s, had known Poulson and Smith, and was the sole character witness at the Wandsworth trial. Sir Fred Hayday was a colleague of Andy Cunningham in the GMWU. There was no evidence of any undue influence on IBA members, but it illustrated the awkwardness of the situation when any prominent people were investigated by bodies themselves accountable to the Establishment.

Under pressure from the TV technicians' union and Granada, a revised programme appeared on 30 April 1973, although it was inevitably condemned as 'trial by television'.

Further revelations kept coming at the bankruptcy hearings, but these were less significant than the vast sums received by Dan Smith or the close involvement of Maudling in the Poulson businesses. Like Sidney Stanley, Poulson had sprayed minor gifts around in the hope of hitting someone who would do favours in return; like the 'Lynskey Tribunal' the inquiry veered occasionally into questionable territory. There were errors and trivia which the investigators subsequently regretted because of the effect on the individuals concerned and the opportunity it offered to attack the proceedings. As David Graham explains: 'We were not infallible ... with hindsight and a few more years behind me there's no doubt that we did hurt people, probably unnecessarily – take Tony Crosland.'

Crosland, Education Secretary 1965–67, had received a coffee pot as a gift from Poulson when he attended the opening of a school in Bradford, and promptly forgot about it until the bankruptcy hearings. Muir Hunter, based on a reading of the Poulson archive, alleged that it was worth £500 (now about £5,000). There was an apparently damning letter of thanks signed by Crosland with the handwritten postscript, 'I tremble to think what it cost.' The Croslands found the pot, and had it valued. It was actually worth around £40 in 1972 (now about £280), within the allowed limit for ministers receiving gifts. Susan Crosland thought the postscript reflected that 'like many who do not give or want fulsome compliments, Tony's sporadic efforts in that direction were doomed'.

The sensational nature of the evidence was an embarrassment to the legal establishment, who considered that the publicity Hunter was receiving was 'bad form', as David Graham explains:

> He was a man of immense courage acting in the best traditions of the English Bar. He was extremely forceful with his advocacy ... and the colour he was able to inject into those questions, was bound to attract public attention. All the metaphors he used were lapped up by the press, and I don't doubt that Establishment figures found this unappealing, irksome.

The closing of ranks was most apparent in the treatment of Muir Hunter, which still angers his colleagues, including David Graham:

> The pressures brought to bear on him were intolerable. He was conducting a high-profile case, the Attorney-General had taken an interest, and on top of that the Bar Council decide to institute proceedings alleging unprofessional conduct ... To do that is calculated to undermine his confidence. As it turned out, very quickly after a lot of effort by those who advised Muir Hunter the charges were dropped.

As the bankruptcy hearings wound down, police inquiries were bearing fruit. The downfall of Poulson's cronies was in the meticulous records he kept of every transaction. The policeman, Barnard Humphries, went through the files piecing the story together, and recalls:

You would have Poulson's letters arranging holidays or payments for his people on file. In another file would be letters to the local author-ity where that person was in a position of influence. All Poulson's returned cheques were there, hundreds of them. We should be thank-ful that shredding machines weren't in particular use back then. When you looked at them in isolation you began to suspect that some-thing was happening, but when you integrated them, and went to the local authorities and other bodies and took out the minutes from the committee meetings and the internal documentation you came away with the complete story, everything that happened.

Poulson and Pottinger were arrested in June 1973 and charged with corrup-tion. Pottinger was particularly vulnerable because of the stringency of the rules applying to civil servants. Andy Cunningham, unbelievably having been re-elected as Chairman of the Durham Police Authority in June 1973, was arrested next, and Dan Smith followed in October.

The Pottinger trial was a walkover, with even the defence counsel admit-ting that Poulson and Pottinger had given 'ludicrous and dishonest' answers in court. Peter Taylor for the prosecution destroyed the arrogant civil ser-vant's pretensions, joking about his receipt of clothes from the architect: 'some have greatcoats thrust upon them'. The pair were found guilty and sentenced to five years each in prison. Poulson admitted making corrupt payments in a string of other trials, although he never seemed to absorb the enormity of what he had done.

The most important trial was that of Smith and Cunningham, where both pleaded guilty and received prison sentences in April 1974. Smith co-operat-ed with the inquiry. His moral sense had, like Poulson's own, been blunted as time went by and he became more deeply involved in corrupt activities.

Though satisfactory in legal terms, the result of the criminal phase of the Poulson investigation has left a lingering suspicion that the full truth never emerged in court. Further local government corruption cases trailed on through the rest of the 1970s with less impact.

There was never a tribunal into Poulson, Smith or any related activities aimed at establishing fact as distinct from criminal responsibility. A tribunal was suggested at various points, and rejected for a host of inconsistent rea-sons which do not stand up to close inspection. At first, it was said that the problem was local and therefore outside the purview of a tribunal (although many early tribunals had been into allegations against local police forces). Then, it was said that the problems were too diffuse for the procedure to work. It was also claimed that it would jeopardize police investigations – which turned out to have no applicability for the MPs involved. There was no political will to poke into these unsavoury corners of public life. There was even less on the part of Parliament to put its own house in order.

After the main criminal trials resulting from the Poulson affair ended in April 1974, attention moved to the House of Commons where several MPs stood accused of unwise association with the corrupt architect. They were Albert Roberts, the right-wing Labour MP for Normanton in West Yorkshire since 1951; John Cordle, Conservative MP for Bournemouth East since 1959; and Reginald Maudling, who had been Conservative Chancellor from 1962 to 1964 and Home Secretary from 1970 to 1972. The ability of the House of Commons to police its own affairs was about to be put to the test. Its failure paved the way for the excesses of the 1980s.

Albert Roberts, Labour MP for Normanton, met Poulson in 1963 when the architect approached him at a dinner dance. He recalls: 'He asked if I could help him at all. I said, "It all depends." And first of all I was wanting to have this place built and I said, "Will you build me a bungalow?" And he said yes, that he'd do the architectural side of it.'

Poulson neglected to send a bill for his services in relation to the Roberts' house, which the MP named 'Cordoba' in honour of one of the first cities taken by Franco in 1936. A little later Roberts joined the Poulson organization as a consultant for £2,500 (now worth £27,500) per annum. He now says: 'It was very helpful to have this extra money coming in. I could save it, I couldn't save before; it didn't alter my style of life. I didn't think there was any purpose to [mention it to colleagues] because they had their own, quite a number had consultancies.'

Poulson was particularly interested in Roberts because of the high esteem in which he was held in Spain and Portugal, and Roberts assisted with one of the few successful prestige projects the Poulson firm was looking for, Mocamedes harbour in the Portuguese colony of Angola.

The backbench Conservative MP for Bournemouth East, John Cordle, was employed by Poulson in 1964 to advance his interests in West Africa, where a string of British colonies were gaining independence and Cordle had long-established trading relations in the area. Cordle was not particularly popular with his colleagues. He had first made his name with a sanctimonious attack on John Profumo, after the former minister had already admitted his offence and resigned. It was alleged that his displays of religious morality were hypocritical considering the MP's unsavoury private life: his marital history led none other than Poulson to describe him as a person of 'low morals'. Poulson resented Cordle's work rate as well as his morals. Cordle responded to these complaints in March 1965 by sending Poulson a letter itemizing all the ways he claimed to have used his parliamentary position to advance the architect's cause in West Africa and the UK, a catalogue of corruption so brazen that its revelation led to his departure in shame from the House in 1977. One key sentence read: 'It was largely for the benefit of Construction Promotion that I took part in a debate in the House of Commons on The Gambia and pressed for HMG to award constructional contracts to British firms.'

Conservatives thought for a while that Labour's Deputy Leader, Ted Short, was in the most precarious position. Short was the MP for Newcastle Central and a powerful figure in Labour politics in the North East. T. Dan Smith claimed in his televised confessional in April 1974 that he had paid £500 (now worth £6,000) in cash to Short, and produced what appeared to be an acknowledgement dated 1963 agreeing that the payment remain confidential. Short denied any business links with Smith and claimed that he had been paid in return for various expenses he incurred on Smith's behalf. In July 1974 a statement from a Swiss bank purporting to be a record of Short's account was circulated to several MPs and publications. It was quickly shown to be a forgery. Bizarrely, the details of the forged statement were taken from a real account held by a Communist Party member named Crookall, a retired architect living in Northampton. Short was not the only victim of forgeries; several other Labour MPs were named in a bogus DPP memorandum concerning Poulson in 1973. Nothing could be proved against Short and, following another *World in Action* exposé, attention switched to the most famous of those linked with Poulson, Reginald Maudling.

'Reggie' Maudling, as he was affectionately known, was elected Conservative MP for Barnet in 1950 and rose rapidly within the party. The 1950 intake of Conservatives included many of the most important figures in the next thirty years of the party – Iain Macleod, Edward Heath and Enoch Powell perhaps the most notable among them. Maudling shone, even in this company, as a rising star. He served on the back benches for only six months after the Conservative return to power in 1951. By 1953 he was a Treasury minister and in 1955, only five years after entering Parliament, he became a Privy Councillor as Minister of Supply. He was the main beneficiary of Macmillan's 'night of the long knives' reshuffle in 1962, being promoted to Chancellor. His rapid rise owed much to his cleverness, but perhaps even more to his position on the liberal wing of the Conservative Party. On the welfare state, Europe and social change, the political tide was flowing in his direction. Personally, he was extremely popular with people from all parties and with journalists. Andrew Roth remembers him with some fondness:

He had a lot of faults including a craving for money, not so much for himself as to indulge his wife and a sense of inferiority that he didn't have the sort of money that most senior Tories did have, and he had weaknesses like not paying his bar bill and things of that sort. Despite all these weaknesses he was a very popular man. I used to drink with him occasionally in Annie's Bar and he was a very genial, forthcoming, nice man to be with.

Many journalists found it refreshing to write about a Conservative Cabinet minister who enjoyed good food and drink and preferred the Crazy Horse Saloon to the opera when he was on business in Paris.

It started to go wrong for Maudling in 1963, when Macmillan suddenly resigned the party leadership. Maudling had ambitions for the leadership, but his moment faded; he endorsed R. A. Butler, his ideological forebear, instead. The winner, Alec Douglas-Home, kept him on as Chancellor and left him to it; famously, Douglas-Home had little interest in economics and did his sums with matchsticks. Maudling nearly managed to win the Conservatives the 1964 election by stoking up a massive consumer boom. Maudling handed the Treasury over to Jim Callaghan with the cheery benediction, 'Sorry to leave things in such a state, old cock. Best of luck.'

Maudling's income dropped suddenly from £5,000 a year to £1,750 when he ceased to be Chancellor, and he was left with the problem of sustaining for himself and his wife the standard of living to which they had become accustomed. Before he became a minister he had enjoyed a modestly successful City career, and thanks to this and inheritance he had been rich enough to become a Lloyd's Name in 1957, when membership was very restricted. It was the first time a serving member of the government had joined Lloyd's. His City connections stood him in good stead in 1964 when he, as former chancellors have increasingly done, took a job with a merchant bank. He joined Kleinwort Benson in November 1964, advising on economic matters and making introductions to people on the international financial scene. He added other directorships and by early 1965 had found jobs with salaries totalling around £18,500 (now worth about £200,000). His parliamentary colleague Jim Prior recalls:

> When we came out of government he obviously needed some directorships and he went off and got some, but he'd got some pretty unsavoury ones and it dogged him for the rest of his career ... You couldn't live on a back bench Member's salary and I don't think he expected to and I'm quite certain that Beryl, his wife, didn't expect to either.

Alec Douglas-Home never intended to serve very long as party leader. If the Conservatives had won, the Chancellor would have been in a powerful position to take over. But it was not to be. The 1965 Conservative leadership election was fought under new rules that required a ballot of MPs and, despite being the favourite, Maudling lost to a better organized campaign run by the former Chief Whip, Edward Heath. The defeat damaged Maudling's spirit. Maudling himself said, 'When one fails to realize an ambition, the ambition fades. I lost. You could sum me up as one of life's near misses. And there are no prizes for coming second.'

Once the dream of Downing Street faded, Maudling became virtually obsessed with making money. Immediately after losing office he had exercised some caution in taking directorships, but later his love of money and poor judgement attracted him to several extremely dubious operations. The journalist Terence Lancaster sums up Maudling as follows:

In his autobiography he says that one of the few distinguished actions of his life at school was when he fainted at the passing-out parade of the Officer Training Corps because he had spent the lunch hour in the tuck shop overeating. The trouble with Reggie was that he kept on looking for tuck shops for the rest of his life and he found a number of businessmen, some of them criminal, who were only too willing to serve him goodies.

After the 1966 election he joined forces with John Poulson. The Labour MP Albert Roberts approached him and invited him to get in touch with the architect. Poulson was looking for a replacement for Herbert Butcher who would work to promote the services his companies offered. Maudling, concerned at the high marginal tax rate he would face if accepting any more salary, accepted an unusual remuneration package. Maudling's actual pay was loaned back to the firm for tax purposes until profits arrived. His wife, a former dancer, had long had a dream of a 'little Glyndebourne' theatre in East Grinstead, and started the Adeline Genée Theatre Trust in honour of her ballet teacher. The project had been more expensive than anticipated and was running short of money in 1966. Poulson offered to covenant £35,000 to the Trust spread over seven years. He also gave Maudling's son a job, and Maudling himself shares in his company Construction Promotion. The total package was worth about £15,000 (now about £150,000) per annum. To the bankruptcy lawyer David Graham:

Recruiting Maudling was probably for Poulson his greatest achievement. I've often pondered the ability of Poulson to climb up the social scale and get to a position where he is able to recruit a man of Maudling's background and stature to his payroll. It was a remarkable coup and it enabled him to mix with the high and mighty. It also gave him an entrée into political and governmental circles in any part of the world that they cared to go.

Maudling's importance was in developing Poulson's international businesses. He was well known among the political élites of many countries because of his experience as Chancellor and Shadow Foreign Secretary. He could use these contacts to further Poulson's business. Given that the sort of projects and the sort of countries Poulson was considering as his markets,

Maudling's influence in Parliament might be useful in applying pressure on the government to give overseas aid funding.

Maudling's arrival was coincidentally the point at which a thriving firm tipped over into delusions of grandeur and the edifice began to collapse under the weight of Poulson's corruption and incompetence. At least with Poulson there was something of substance underneath the inflated claims; another of Maudling's sidelines had nothing at all to recommend it in a financial or moral sense.

The Real Estate Fund of America (REFA) was run by an American fraudster, Jerome Hoffman, who had been banned from dealing shares in the State of New York as part of a plea bargain in 1967. He moved his operations 'offshore' – to jurisdictions where company law was lax. In 1968 he came up with the idea of running an offshore fund based on land, which had the reputation of being a safe investment that would appreciate over time, and set about recruiting a Board which would reassure investors that it was a solid concern.

Hoffman's British legal advisers were the London firm of solicitors, Joynson-Hicks, which had impeccable Conservative connections. William Joynson-Hicks had been Home Secretary in the Conservative government of the 1920s, and his son, Lord Brentford, had been a ministerial colleague of Maudling in the 1950s. Brentford wrote to Maudling in 1968 inviting him onto the Board of REFA. He was paid for his involvement by shares in the Real Estate Management Company of America, the management company behind REFA, of which he became President.

Maudling was not the only politician to get involved with Hoffman. James G. Morton, former US Secretary of Commerce, and Robert Wagner, former Mayor of New York, were in the US contingent; Paul Henri Spaak, former Prime Minister of Belgium and NATO Secretary-General, was also on the Board. Maudling tried to interest John Poulson, but to the architect it looked too dubious to get involved with.

REFA was incorporated and nominally based in Liberia, offshoot sales and management companies were incorporated in Bermuda and an office was opened in London. It started trading in May 1969. It was not approved for investment business in Britain or the US, and drew most of its investment fund from money illegally exported by the rich of the Third World, through complex and irregular networks involving salesmen with false-bottomed suitcases and numbered Swiss bank accounts.

Fairly soon after REFA started trading, the City journalist Charles Raw started to investigate offshore property funds and discovered that Hoffman had been barred from trading in New York. Maudling was surprised and angry at the news, although he could easily have found out about Hoffman's past through his City connections. A few weeks later, as REFA came in for more examination in the British press and the BBC, Maudling resigned his

Hoffman directorships, although his letter of resignation commended it as 'a good and sound investment'. He kept his shares in REFA Management and continued to recommend the fund. In an unguarded moment he explained his involvement by the need to build up 'a little pot of money for my old age'.

Hoffman's venture collapsed in late 1970, having been unable to pay its bills in London. There was a reason that property funds were banned in Britain, and that was because they involved the classic banking error of borrowing short and lending long. In November 1970 Hoffman's business was kicked out of Bermuda. It went under when depositors tried *en masse* to reclaim their money. The DTI and the Fraud Squad investigated the matter in 1971–72, although it was only in summer 1972 that any moves were made to question REFA's illustrious British directors. Hoffman returned to the United States where he was imprisoned in 1972 for an earlier mortgage swindle.

As with Poulson, the REFA affair was not handled well by the press, with the honourable exception of a few financial experts such as Charles Raw and Michael Gillard of *Private Eye*. In 1971 *The Observer*'s business journalists tried to unravel the REFA story and explore Maudling's links with Hoffman but were the victims of an old-fashioned cover-up. Nora Beloff, a member of the privileged circle of the lobby journalists, and David Astor, the editor and scion of the Establishment, moved to suppress the investigation. The initiative came from Beloff, who wrote a note (later to become famous in a court case as the 'Ballsoff Memorandum') to Astor in support of Maudling. Instead of an investigative piece *The Observer* printed an article by Beloff defending Reggie and denouncing the questions about REFA as a 'smear campaign'.

British police investigations into REFA were under way in July 1972 when Maudling dramatically resigned as Home Secretary. He explained that he resigned because he had ministerial control over the Metropolitan Police, whose Fraud Squad were investigating Poulson; he wished to avoid a conflict of interest because he had been a director of Poulson companies. This was despite the fact that he had been ministerially responsible for the Fraud Squad investigation into REFA. This explanation was later judged by the Commons Select Committee to be 'lacking in frankness' although at the time it won him widespread sympathy.

Even before a full investigation had taken place, the Poulson affair led to the first significant admission that faith in the honour of MPs was no longer strong enough to leave regulation to the MP's individual conscience. In May 1974 the House of Commons voted to establish a public register of members' interests, a step which had been rejected as recently as 1969. It was there 'to provide information of any pecuniary interest or other material benefit which a Member may receive which might be thought to affect his conduct as a Member or influence his actions, speeches or vote in Parliament'.

In principle, this covered the spectrum of an MP's activities and interests, but as registration was self-assessed several loopholes became apparent. An interest which did not, in the MP's opinion, affect any of his or her actions within Parliament might not be declared. 'Pecuniary interests' might be diverted into funds not controlled by the MP personally, such as the Adeline Genée Trust in the Maudling case. The status of gifts in kind such as flights and hotel accommodation, or loans on preferential terms, was also vague. When an MP was working for a multi-client lobbying firm, registration of links with the lobbyist could obscure the fact that the MP's actions were on behalf of the lobbyist's clients who would not be named on the register. Additionally, as Lord Nolan commented on reviewing the rules, the 1974 rules 'tended to create a false impression that any interest is acceptable once it has been registered'.

Even in 1974 many MPs, predominantly Conservatives, opposed even self-assessed declaration of interests as unnecessary. The first register was published in 1975. Enoch Powell, now sitting for the Ulster Unionists, refused to make an entry on the grounds that it was unconstitutional to require MPs to do so, and that peer group knowledge of the integrity and outside interests of Members was sufficient to allow their arguments to be correctly assessed. After the second register in 1976 no further registers were compiled until after the 1979 election. The vagueness of the declaration requirements and the failure to keep the register up to date brought the system into discredit.

As well as the Commons taking a small step to reform itself, the government set up the Salmon Commission in 1975 to investigate standards of conduct in public life in the light of Poulson and other corruption allegations. The Salmon Report was published in 1976. It contained a series of recommendations about diverse matters, including tightening rules about hospitality and disclosure of interests in local government, bringing more types of misconduct within the scope of the corruption laws and wider police powers when investigating alleged corruption.

The report drew attention to the astonishing legal loophole that meant that Members of Parliament were not subject to the corruption laws. Technically, corruption offences involved betraying the interests of an employer or a principal for whom the offender was acting as agent, and an MP could not be shown to be in either position. The chief counsel to the Director of Public Prosecutions, John Cobb, had investigated the possibility of charging the Poulson MPs with corruption and was satisfied that there was sufficient evidence to bring charges against Cordle for the activities revealed in his letter, and Roberts and Maudling for matters relating to the Gozo hospital contract Poulson had won in Malta with their help, had they been covered by the same laws that Parliament applied to councillors and civil servants. An earlier investigation had raised the possibility that Maudling's statements had been so incomplete that there might be a case against him for perjury. The Cordle case was particularly blatant given the documentary evidence.

Maudling, it might have been argued, was in a special position because of his membership of the Privy Council, but an extremely cautious line was taken on the possibility of prosecuting. The chances of succeeding, given the special legal position of MPs, were considerably less than certain and the potential political risk large. Cobb said that it would require a 'one hundred per cent, copper-bottomed guarantee of winning' to proceed against Maudling, and considered the chances of success less than 100 per cent. Instead of facing criminal charges, Maudling was restored to the front bench as Shadow Foreign Secretary in 1975.

The Salmon Commission was disturbed by the idea that the MPs were going to get away with their activities; but the implied reference in the report was not taken up. Lord Salmon opined that Cordle's activities were so bad that they made his hair stand on end. A member of the Commission wanted to pin the Cordle letter to a noticeboard in the House of Commons. One person close to the investigation took action. Adam Raphael, then political editor of *The Observer*, who had become suspicious about Cordle's links with Poulson but was holding off in fear of a libel action, takes up the story:

> *One day – and this has very rarely happened to me in my career – a brown paper parcel arrived for me at* The Observer *containing crucial evidence, among which was a letter that John Cordle had written to Poulson. That evidence was sufficient, and we published the story, although after an interval of about three months of it being pored over by libel lawyers.*

The government initially resisted the pressure for an inquiry into the activities of the MPs, but protests were so strong that the Prime Minister James Callaghan reconsidered and a Select Committee was established to look into the cases in October 1976. The Select Committee investigation into Poulson's parliamentary allies was set up only reluctantly, and sat in private. Michael Foot as Leader of the House had responsibility for it, but, as with his criticisms of the Lynskey Tribunal, he did not like the idea of a kangaroo court sitting in judgement on allegations against MPs. As he says: 'Of course it had to be stamped out, but sometimes people don't understand how a scare, a mood can spread. In a way it's worse for innocent people to suffer in these events than it is for one or two guilty people to get through.'

Reginald Maudling, Albert Roberts and John Cordle were investigated by the Select Committee. The DPP report had found no case to answer against Ted Short and therefore the Select Committee did not inquire into his actions.

The Select Committee reported in July 1977. It decided that 'there was nothing intrinsically wrong in Mr Roberts' relationship with Mr Poulson' but that his failure to disclose his link when approaching people on behalf of Poulson was 'conduct inconsistent with the standards which this House is entitled to expect from its Members'. Roberts suffered least from the committee, although he considers that 'It was unfair. The committee were rigged. Someone went in to see the Chief Whip and he asked if certain people could go on that committee, leftists who were ready to put a knife in your back if they can.'

Roberts conceded that he may have 'transgressed in the shallow waters' but complained, as Boothby had done before him, about the lack of guidance available to MPs: 'From where do I take my standards? I have had no book on the do's and don'ts of Parliament ... I have tried to conform as far as I could. I want some ruling on what are the standards.' His complaint was justified, but MPs remained in the dark about what was expected of them. It was a missed opportunity.

John Cordle was the most harshly condemned by the committee, who considered that his conduct 'amounts to a contempt of the House'. This was strong condemnation indeed, although Cordle tried to argue that he had been vindicated. He found himself totally isolated on the Conservative benches and the disgraced MP resigned his seat in the House before the committee report was debated. John Poulson's own verdict on the pair was that he considered Roberts 'an innocent man' and that Cordle had confused private and national interests but as far as he was concerned, despite the fact that he had paid the MP nearly £6,000 (now worth £65,000), 'Cordle's help to me was non-existent' and 'I considered I was conned.'

Reginald Maudling was criticized by the committee for failing to declare his Poulson connections, and for failing to give a complete account of what he had received from the architect in his resignation letter in 1972. As for Poulson, he regarded Maudling as a 'roguish parasite' and 'as naïve as a hungry crocodile'. It was a minority view.

The Select Committee was a feeble substitute for a tribunal or a police inquiry. Even so, the House of Commons did not accept, it merely 'took note of' the Committee's findings, but the main reason for failing to accept the committee's modest condemnations was all to do with Reginald Maudling. Conservative MPs rallied round Maudling in the parliamentary debate on the committee's report. Many of them simply could not accept that Reggie had done anything wrong; others did not care. Labour MPs were uneasy for several reasons. They were keenly aware of how compromised their own party had been. There was the fear, expressed by Michael

Foot, about repeating the damage that the 'Lynskey Tribunal' had done to innocent people in 1948–49.

Maudling died suddenly in February 1979, having resisted publication of the case against him through liberal use of libel writs. Albert Roberts was re-elected in 1979 but retired from Parliament in 1983. John Cordle retired to a beautiful house in the Cathedral Close in Salisbury. The non-MPs, who had gone to prison, were less fortunate. Poulson, a sick man, served a long prison sentence and wrote his self-justificatory memoirs. Pottinger became a writer and died in January 1998. In Leyhill Prison T. Dan Smith suffered the most ignominious election defeat ever inflicted on a once mighty political figure. He ran for president of the prisoners' council and lost to a homosexual headmaster whose slogan was 'Up with the bummer, down with the briber'. When released he continued to campaign for prison reform.

*

The Poulson scandal has been incompletely absorbed by the public and politicians. It was too complicated, with three main protagonists – Poulson, Maudling and Smith – with different agendas which interlocked in a confusing way, and it required some knowledge of finance and local government to grasp. Everyone can understand a cover-up of a burglary or a male model's shot dog. Maudling's rearguard action in the courts delayed publication of books which explained it, Michael Gillard and Martin Tomkinson's *Nothing to Declare* (1980) and Ray Fitzwalter and David Taylor's *Web of Corruption* (1981), until the affair seemed like ancient history.

Many had hoped in the 1970s that the Poulson scandal would force a stern new regime on politicians. In other countries bribery scandals had resulted in wholesale reform, such as the campaign finance legislation passed in the United States. In Britain, the Register of Members' Interests was a start, but nothing was done to effect a radical change in the culture of Parliament, an omission that was to lead to increasing malpractice in the next decade. Poulson was just part of a collapse in public confidence in the standards of conduct of the political leadership. Maudling, Roberts and Cordle were far from the only political figures who had been involved in unwise business ventures.

CHAPTER 7

Sleaze in the 1970s

'Are they hunting dogs on the moors these days?'
Jeremy Thorpe, 1975

B ritish politics changed profoundly in the 1970s: the politics of sexual and financial conduct was no exception. In the early years of the decade the social and sexual revolutions – 'Sex and Drugs and Rock 'n' Roll' as Ian Dury's anthem had it – took hold in the life of ordinary people and slowly affected the way politicians were expected to behave. The restraints on media coverage of scandals collapsed, and there was a torrent of astonishing revelations starting with Poulson, progressing via a former minister who faked his own death to a party leader standing accused of a bizarre murder plot that claimed the life of a Great Dane.

The Heath government of 1970–74 was a particularly turbulent time. The government attempted to restructure industrial relations and was bitterly resisted by the trade unions. The miners went on strike twice and labour relations throughout industry were descending into chaos. States of emergency were proclaimed five times. It was as near as Britain has come to class war, and the Conservatives and Labour were lining up on opposite sides. Real war had broken out in Northern Ireland, with fatalities peaking at nearly five hundred in 1972.

The party system itself was on the point of collapse, with the Liberals and the Scottish and Welsh Nationalists making big gains in polls and by-elections, and the Labour Party disintegrating over Europe. There was a groundswell of right-wing Conservative opinion that the Heath government had betrayed the party by increasing public spending, supporting ailing industries and restricting pay increases.

Edward Heath was an unlikely figure to preside over a social revolution. His surprising election victory in 1970 was produced by disillusion with the Wilson government and a socially conservative backlash against the excesses of the 'permissive society'. Emboldened by the apparent swing in public opinion, the police and judges took a harder line on hippies and the like, resulting in the disastrous 'Oz' trial in 1971. But Reggie Maudling at the Home Office was too easy-going and liberal to want to lead a counter-revolution. He saw his role more as reconciling Tory Britain with the new social order, and pronounced himself 'appalled' at the idea of returning to Victorian ideas of personal morality. Bravely, he rejected the arguments of the pro-censorship lobby headed by Mary Whitehouse and Lord Longford and supported by most of the Conservative grassroots, dismissing their condemnation of 'sex and violence' in film and the media.

The legitimacy of the police assault on the permissive society was fatally undermined by corruption scandals affecting the Drug Squad and the Obscene Publications Squad of Scotland Yard. Drug Squad officers had been planting drugs and conniving at the import of drugs. The Obscene Publications Squad had been systematically corrupted by the big Soho pornography barons and was operating to eliminate competition rather than enforce the law – which in any case seemed to treat porn as low priority.

The confusing laws concerning prostitution were also perceived as not worth enforcing, which with social trends led to a boom in all forms of commercial sex. Call girl operations flourished just as they had done in the early 1960s, but in a much less clandestine way. By 1978 Cynthia Payne could become a folk hero for running a brothel; in 1963 Stephen Ward had been reviled for much less. Even if the Heath government had wished to crack down on the licentious climate of the early 1970s, it would have faced ridicule after a sordid episode in 1973 which showed the new contours of how sexual scandal would be treated in the press, and the inability of a political class traumatized by the Profumo affair to cope with it.

*

Anthony Lambton was, like many people who get involved in scandals and survive, an ebullient and popular figure. He had represented Berwick upon Tweed since 1950 but was still relatively young and dashing for a Tory MP. If anyone can be said to have a lust for life, he did, enjoying travel, politics, culture and the occasional paddle in the warm waters of commercial sex and drug use. While he was Minister for the Royal Air Force he was a customer of a prostitute, Norma Levy, whose husband Colin was an unsavoury character who tried to sell Lambton's story to the press. A *News of the World* reporter was hiding in a cupboard on one occasion when Norma Levy entertained the minister.

The *News of the World* eventually thought better of using the story, but bizarrely gave material they had collected to Colin Levy who then tried to sell it to other newspapers. Lambton resigned but was found out anyway. The presence of tabloid investigative reporters with a nose for sleaze and massive resources to pay witnesses for the story added a new dimension to the game between the press and the politicians. These reporters were not bound by the cosy club rules of the lobby, and were motivated solely by the need to get the story. The old networks of school tie, college or club were no longer enough to have a story suppressed. Neither could the victims among the political class appeal to proprietors to the same extent. The barons who had controlled the press between the wars and immediately after were being replaced by a new generation, with Rupert Murdoch in the vanguard. The new proprietors were more interested in having a commercially successful product than keeping in with society. Journalists were as interested as ever in what the rich and powerful were doing, and there were fewer constraints. Derek Jameson sums up nicely what was new and what was the same as ever:

> *Murdoch well understands that the best possible story for a tabloid newspaper is a sex scandal involving royalty or Cabinet ministers or whoever, in that order, so he will always back you on a story that's gonna sell newspapers. He once said to me when I was editor of the* News of the World, *'What's your idea of a good story for the* News of the World?' *and I said the old faithful, a Cabinet minister in bed with a whore. And ever after, whenever we met, he used to say to me, 'Have you found that Cabinet minister yet?'*

Lord Jellicoe also resigned as Leader of the House of Lords. He had made occasional, discreet use of an escort agency to provide sexual partners, and there were no security or criminal issues whatsoever. In the internal inquiries after the Lambton affair blew up, he volunteered this information to the Prime Minister and offered to step down. It appeared rather odd at the time when Heath accepted Jellicoe's resignation, and still does. Even though his career as a politician was over, he continued to contribute to public service and was never regarded as anything other than honourable and unlucky.

The Labour Party did not attempt to make capital out of the Lambton and Jellicoe business, and the consensus in Fleet Street was that the resignations of the ministers had been sad and unnecessary.

Lambton's alleged drug use was investigated by the police, and he pleaded guilty to possessing cannabis and amphetamines. An investigation into Lambton by the Security Commission reported that although no leak had happened there was a potential security risk if Lambton's consciousness was altered because of drug use. As with the Denning Report, sex with prostitutes was not considered a problem, but unusual forms of sex were a blackmail risk. However, a blackmail risk was not necessarily a security risk because the response of the individual involved if blackmail was ever attempted was the important consideration. It was a small but significant broadening in the official definition of acceptable sexual conduct for ministers compared to 1963.

However, the report showed that the government was just as ignorant about drugs as it had been about sex in the early 1960s. Moderate cannabis use is less likely to produce uncharacteristic behaviour than heavy drinking, which has never been regarded as a security risk (at least officially – Harold

Above: Tom Driberg, Labour MP
and promiscuous homosexual.
(Popperfoto)

Above: Labour trade minister
John Belcher arriving at the
Tribunal of Inquiry to face
allegations of corruption, 1948.
(PA News)

Right: Lord Beaverbrook: the press
baron who kept the politicians'
secrets, 1922. (Mirror Syndication
International)

Left: Christine Keeler.
(Tom Blau/Camera Press)

Below: Lord Boothby's second
marriage in 1967. (Camera Press)

Above: Harold Wilson in characteristic pose. (PA News)

Left: Marcia Falkender at work in 10 Downing Street. (Tom Blau/Camera Press)

Right: Harold Wilson and Marcia Falkender at his controversial retirement party in 1976. With them are Eric Morecombe, Wilson's sister and David Frost. (Joe Bulaitis/Camera Press)

Above: Cynthia and John Poulson opening a school, 1967.
(Mirror Syndication International)

Above: Reginald Maudling at a Conservative press conference, 1964. (Topham)

Right: Jeremy Thorpe, accused of conspiracy to murder, 1979. (PA News)

Above: Michael Brown MP enjoying the 1980s. (Grimsby Evening Telegraph)
Below: Ian Greer, lobbyist extraordinaire. (Graham Turner)

Above: Mohamed Fayed and Tiny Rowland, bitter rivals for control of Harrods, making peace, 1993. (PA News)

Right: Mohamed Fayed in exuberant form at Harrods. (M. Godwin/Camera Press)

Left: Neil and
Christine Hamilton:
'We Do Things
Together'. (Rex Features)

Below: David Mellor
and family, 1992.
(Bob Collier/Camera Press)

THISTLE COTTAGE

Right: Jonathan
Aitken unsheathing
his sword of truth,
1995. (PA News)

Above: Peter Mandelson – 'Dome Secretary' – and Tony Blair, 1998. (PA News)
Below: Peter Mandelson after his resignation, 1998. (Theodore Wood/Camera Press)

Wilson was personally worried about George Brown's carelessness with documents when drunk, as Richard Crossman's *Diaries* record). Amphetamines were at one time widely used as stimulants by politicians. For instance, in January 1957 Tony Benn was giving a lecture in East Berlin and recorded in his diary: 'I was paralysed with fear and had taken a whole Benzedrine to induce confidence ... I talked slowly and deliberately, and they were very attentive and could apparently understand what I said.' All-night sittings in the House and crisis Cabinet committee meetings were fuelled by perfectly legal speed until the dangers of amphetamine use were publicized and control over prescriptions tightened up.

The press was criticized over the Lambton affair and for creating the conditions in which Jellicoe resigned. The Press Council condemned the *News of the World* for giving the Lambton photographs to Colin Levy, and other newspapers regretted that the paper had worked with such a lowlife character.

Tabloid journalists, however, had a new line in justification for running intrusive stories about public figures. Journalists like Derek Jameson, and even the lobby correspondent James Margach of *The Sunday Times*, started to think of relations between politicians and journalists as a battle of wits or a long war, rather than a gentle game played between insiders. The idea of deference had not only collapsed but had been replaced with its opposite; that by the very act of assuming national leadership the political class were pretentiously putting themselves above the people and telling them what to do. Puncturing these illusions was therefore a valuable public service. Left-wing campaigning journalists, such as Paul Foot, were frequently accused of tarnishing the image of public figures through their investigations, but the following denunciation of the political class was actually uttered by Derek Jameson, an old Fleet Street hand:

> *They wag a reproving finger at the rest of us and try to make out that they have some kind of divine right to be leaders. It's all nonsense, of course, they're just as fallible as anybody else, and if we can pull them down off their pedestals, then I think that's a very useful role for the media to play.*

Pulling politicians down from their pedestals was not just the concern of the tabloids, but of the survivors of the satire boom of 1963 and the revolutionary movement of the late 1960s. *Private Eye* in the 1970s was also expanding into new areas. Paul Foot, who had been the driving force behind its investigative stories such as Poulson in the late 1960s and early 1970s, had gone. The 'Grovel' gossip column was under the control of Nigel Dempster and Peter McKay, cynical Fleet Street veterans who enjoyed publishing stories of the sexual escapades and drink and drug habits of the rich and famous. Even the monarchy was no longer immune – there was a stream of stories about Princess Margaret's adventures. The *Eye*'s network of informants was also growing. It seemed that public figures were now dependent on the goodwill of the magazine's editor Richard Ingrams to preserve their secrets. The *Eye*'s City correspondent Michael Gillard developed a forensic knowledge of questionable business deals, which in the early 1970s also involved politicians of all parties.

In the early 1970s, like the mid 1980s, the City of London was fashionable. After the liberalization of credit restrictions in 1971 financial institutions, underpinned by booming stock and property markets, mushroomed. Leading financial entrepreneurs, in particular Jim Slater of Slater Walker, were celebrated as the vanguard of a new dynamic and competitive spirit in British business. The Conservatives were most associated with the City boom, for the obvious reasons that they were the party of business and were in government at the time. There were also parallels between the brash new style of City business and Heath's broad project of being a kind of management consultant to the nation at large. In 1972 the Heath regime was dubbed 'the Slater Walker government' by a City commentator.

Slater Walker was the most political of the big players because Peter Walker was one of Heath's Cabinet ministers and a close political ally. Walker's rapid rise from a modest background to relative wealth at a young age symbolized the new Toryism of the Heath era, in which grammar school boys like Walker could become rich through intelligence and hard work. Heath himself, after becoming leader of the Opposition in 1965, entrusted his investment affairs to Jim Slater.

Jim Slater and Peter Walker met because they were both profiled in a series about young businessmen in the London *Evening News*. When Slater formed his own business, he invited Walker to invest in it and Slater Walker was born in July 1964. The company grew at staggering speed in the late 1960s. In 1966 it was valued by the stock market at £4 million (now worth £40 million) and made £370,000 in profit; in 1969 it was worth £135 million (now £1.2 billion) and made £10.4 million profit. It grew through takeovers and controlled a rag-bag of industrial and commercial concerns and subsidiary investment companies. It made money by restructuring the management of the companies it bought. This would, in theory, make the firms more efficient and profitable, and release inefficiently used resources that could then be sold off ('asset stripping'). But in practice Slater Walker's reputation stood so high that holdings would soar in value simply through faith in the ability of its management to extract more profit. Stock market deals, in a booming market in 1971–73, also became a more attractive investment proposition than industrial modernization. After 1970 Slater Walker, according to City journalist Charles Raw, 'was basically a machine for generating stock market profits around the world'.

When the Conservatives won the 1970 election Walker disposed of all his investments. Slater had always been the more optimistic, expansion-minded of the two and, with the more cautious Walker no longer able to put the brakes on, Slater Walker expanded too rapidly and was vulnerable when the good times came to a sudden end. The business collapsed in 1975, with losses of £42.3 million (now £200 million), a victim of the end of the City boom. Heath had already lost the leadership of the Conservative Party. Jim Slater resigned in October 1975, having suffered enormous personal losses, and the remainder of the operation was taken over by James Goldsmith. One of the fragments of the Slater Walker empire was Hanson Trust, which was to become one of the main business exponents of the 'enterprise economy' and Margaret Thatcher during the 1980s. Other Slater Walker alumni included the Rossminster group of tax avoidance consultants and Jonathan Aitken. The entanglement of Slater Walker and the Heath project had turned into a political embarrassment, but Heath's Conservative critics were also involved in rickety business enterprises.

The political and business careers of Edward Heath's critic Edward du Cann were an uneasy match. Du Cann was a successful City businessman before being elected MP for Taunton in 1956, and when he became a minister in 1962 he went further to distance himself from commercial interests than most ministers; he sold his shareholdings even though he was not obliged to. He did not return to office when the Conservatives won the 1970 election, but continued to work in the City as Chairman of Keyser Ullman, a merchant bank – one of the worst-hit when the boom went bust in 1974.

By the time Heath had been overthrown in 1975 and replaced by Margaret Thatcher, who was more to du Cann's political taste, City financial wizardry was as unfashionable as it had been fashionable only three years earlier, and du Cann remained only a senior backbencher. From 1974 to 1979 he chaired the Public Accounts Committee of the House of Commons, and from 1972 to 1984 he was Chairman of the 1922 Committee of backbench Conservative MPs.

Du Cann was also on the Board of Lonrho, the trading company run by the controversial businessman Tiny Rowland. According to biographer Tom Bower, Rowland's start in business had allegedly come from defrauding a Swiss bank in 1954 and in 1961 he acquired the London and Rhodesia Mining and Land Company. Lonrho's buccaneering activities in southern Africa involved corruption and frequent allegations of outright criminality. By the early 1970s Lonrho was regarded as a disreputable outfit, and Rowland required some respectable front men. He recruited du Cann, but his main acquisition was Duncan Sandys, Conservative MP for Streatham and former Colonial Secretary. Sandys was a figurehead Chairman of the Lonrho Board who did little besides chair meetings. He was paid £40,000 (now worth £320,000) for doing so, but he was also compensated for the loss of consultancy fees by a large lump sum paid in a tax avoidance scheme through the Cayman Islands. Meanwhile, the government lectured ordinary people on the need for pay restraint. When the Lonrho annual report was being prepared the other directors revolted against the dishonesty of Rowland and the greed of Sandys, but Sandys was able to see off his critics. Edward Heath condemned the Lonrho affair in the House of Commons as 'the unpleasant and unacceptable face of capitalism' and ordered a DTI inquiry. A rearguard political campaign to stall the inquiry did not prevent a report appearing. Lonrho returned to the front line of politics with the Harrods dispute with Mohamed Fayed later in the 1980s (see Chapter 10).

One MP fascinated by the world of banking who stepped over the line into criminality was the former Labour Cabinet minister John Stonehouse. He had been in the Cabinet as Postmaster-General in 1968–70, and appeared to be the sort of ambitious, impatient technocrat that Harold Wilson wanted to encourage in his first spell in office. Stonehouse was not widely liked among his colleagues, however, and suffered from – probably untrue – accusations of having dealings with the intelligence service of Czechoslovakia. He was not given a place in the Shadow Cabinet in 1970, or any ministerial office when Labour returned to power in March 1974. Disappointed, he decided to make money from businesses, most of which failed rapidly.

Stonehouse's main venture was British Bangladeshi Trust (BBT). He was a fervent supporter of the cause of the independence of Bangladesh, which was won in 1971, and genuinely wanted to help the troubled new country and people from Bangladesh who lived in Britain. But the BBT venture was not a success; the stock market slump of 1974 worsened the position and in November 1974 Stonehouse left his problems behind him by faking his own death on a beach in Miami and fleeing to Australia on a false passport. He was arrested a little over a month later by police looking for Lord Lucan, who had done a disappearing act a little earlier in the year.

The House of Commons was left in a peculiar position by the Stonehouse affair. It could have been even more bizarre had a writ been issued calling a by-election in his Walsall North constituency while Stonehouse was believed dead. A Select Committee was set up to consider his case, and found that, like corruption, prolonged absence was not a permitted reason to expel or discipline an MP. Stonehouse returned to Britain and from October 1975 to August 1976 sat again in Parliament as an independent and then as a member for a fringe party called the English National Party. Stonehouse advertised the fact that he had undergone a mental breakdown and that his old identity as 'Rt Hon. John Stonehouse' had to die. Parliament thought it kinder not to try to expel him for lunacy, and he resigned after he was convicted on most of the charges that faced him.

It was a strange period in parliamentary history. As well as Stonehouse, another Labour MP, John Ryman, was facing criminal charges relating to election expenses in Blyth (he was acquitted), and the three Poulson associates (Reginald Maudling, Albert Roberts and John Cordle) faced the possibility of action against them. Another MP would be charged with conspiracy to murder for his actions in 1975. It was hardly surprising that public confidence in politicians was running low.

*

Jeremy Thorpe, the Liberal leader, faced sleaze allegations across a range of activities. He came from a political family: his father had been a Conservative MP, and the young Jeremy was educated at Eton and Trinity College, Oxford. He joined the Liberal Party at the nadir of its fortunes, but managed a spectacular personal victory in North Devon in 1959, the only Liberal gain of that election. He was a showman in politics, with a talent for winning the goodwill of people he met from all across society, from the fringes of the royal family to the most remote Devon village. Thorpe had a ready wit, and landed some devastating attacks on the fading Macmillan government. He was also, for someone of such Establishment pedigree, a radical, with a strong commitment to racial equality and the abolition of the death penalty. But he was also devious and unscrupulous and loved the shallow trappings of success almost as much as Reggie Maudling.

Much as he enjoyed the high life, he was still on a backbencher's pay. He had houses in Devon and Orme Square in Bayswater and, particularly from 1973 when he married his second wife, moved in elevated social circles. His unwise financial dealings should be seen in the same kind of light as those of former Cabinet ministers – regarding a certain style of life as necessary to maintain a political and social profile.

The first Thorpe scandal to surface involved an ill-advised directorship. He joined the City boom by becoming a director of London and County Securities – a distinctly 1970s institution called a 'secondary bank' (a lending institution that was not part of the established clearing bank system). Thorpe did not bother to check its status before joining and found himself associated with a financially unstable and eventually crooked institution. He was also unwisely involved with a sinister figure, George de Chabris, a crooked businessman who left a trail of crashed-out companies in Canada and the Cayman Islands and wanted to buy a peerage. Thorpe gave him control over the National Liberal Club, which de Chabris duly looted.

Thorpe resigned his directorship of London and County shortly before the bank went bust at the end of 1973. He had not been involved in the malpractice that had been going on (including high-rate remortgaging and 'stern collection methods'), but featured in a subsequent inquiry by Department of Trade and Industry (DTI) inspectors. They cleared him but issued a strong warning that Thorpe's involvement was:

a cautionary tale for any leading politician. For unless he is properly informed of the affairs of the company he joins, he cannot make his own judgement on the propriety of its transactions; and he is liable to be reminded, as Mr Thorpe must have been, that his reputation is not only his most marketable, but his most vulnerable commodity.

By lending his name to London and County, Thorpe had allowed himself to be used to reassure investors that the secondary bank was a reputable institution, in the same way that Maudling seemed a respectable front man who helped John Poulson attract business. But Thorpe's embarrassment over his association with London and County after the publication of the critical DTI report on the morning of 29 January 1976 attracted little detailed analysis until a *New Statesman* article in July 1979. Instead, Thorpe faced a more salacious problem – that same day, a man appeared in a Barnstaple courtroom and claimed that he was being hounded because of his homosexual relationship with the Liberal leader.

Part of the reason for Thorpe's secretive and manipulative character was his obsessive need to conceal his true sexual nature. He was mainly homosexual and, like his friend Tom Driberg, had a taste for 'rough trade' and rent boys. Like Driberg, he was breaking the law when he indulged his homosexual tendencies before legalization in 1967. Despite Thorpe's efforts to maintain secrecy, word got around Westminster and the gay scene. Anthony Howard recalls that even Tom Driberg was worried about the situation, after one of his 'young men' told him that Mr Thorpe paid more for services rendered. As Driberg said, 'What's bothering me is that should I not go and tell Jeremy that this young man is going around saying that kind of thing?' Howard couldn't see how Driberg could – and indeed a well-intentioned word would not have cut much ice with Thorpe; he had taken no notice when others had warned him about the risks. However, Thorpe's biggest mistake did not involve a greedy and talkative rent boy, but a more substantial relationship with a neurotic young man called Norman Josiffe, who later changed his name to 'Scott'. It was an affair with deep emotional complications, hysterical break-ups and reconciliations, and when it ended after around three years it left a residue of bitterness and hatred. Scott blamed Thorpe for ruining his life, and Thorpe tried to wash his hands of the younger man and deny any knowledge – which only infuriated Scott still more.

Scott's life was in chaos in the years after 1965, after which he and Thorpe were not to see each other again until their quarrel reached the courtroom. Never particularly stable, he became mentally ill and reeled around in a series of relationships, with men and women, which he would inevitably wreck. He drank heavily and would tell strangers in pubs about how Jeremy Thorpe, the famous politician, was responsible for his pitiful condition.

Thorpe, by contrast, had prospered and was elected Leader of the Liberal Party in 1967. The Liberal Party in those days was a coalition between some of the most moral and correct people ever to have entered British politics and an assortment of very odd characters indeed. Out of eight other Liberal MPs elected in 1964, Thorpe unerringly chose the sleaziest of the entire lot, Peter Bessell, as his closest ally. Bessell posed as a moral Methodist, devoted to his wife, in his Cornwall constituency but spent his time in London boasting about innumerable sexual conquests. He also liked to see himself as a major businessman, but his ventures always seemed to collapse leaving confused accountants picking up the pieces.

Bessell tricked Thorpe into revealing his homosexuality, and took over the management of the Norman Scott problem. Scott's National Insurance cards, which employers had to stamp so that the bearer could obtain state benefits, had gone missing. Thorpe did not want to go on the record as having employed the young man, and instead arranged for Peter Bessell to pay a small 'retainer' every so often. Bessell also helped Scott set himself up as a male model.

Thorpe, much as he would have liked to, could not forget Scott, because he believed that his lurid tales of betrayal and gay sex would eventually reach a public audience. Thorpe worried too much; the danger he was in was rather slight. In the 1960s a purely private scandal would not have been exposed by the press, and in any case it would have been a libel risk not worth taking. There were no criminal implications worth considering. Scott had spoken to the police as early as 1962 and nothing was done, and by 1967 there was no chance at all of proceedings. Richard Ingrams of *Private Eye* comments: 'The press knew all about Thorpe and never did anything about it. I think Thorpe was obsessed by the idea that at any minute he was going to be in the *News of the World*, which led him into that bizarre conspiracy.'

Thorpe shared his fears with his two most trusted friends, Peter Bessell and David Holmes, a friend from Oxford who had been best man at his wedding in 1968. The conversation between the three in Thorpe's Commons room one night in early 1969 'would have been hailed as a work of black-comic genius if it had been enacted on stage', as *Rinkagate*, a history of the affair, put it. Bessell and Holmes were alternately horrified and amused as Thorpe expounded on how Scott might be killed and the body disposed of down a disused tin mine in Bessell's constituency. Thorpe had not thought through the issue and Holmes kept coming up with objections, including the classic response when poisoning Scott's drink was suggested: 'Wouldn't it look rather odd if Scott fell off the bar stool – stone dead?' Bessell chipped in by suggesting that the assassin could ask the landlord the way to the nearest old mineshaft. The plan for drastic action was shelved when Scott surprisingly got married, but it was revived later.

Even though the stability in Scott's life was short-lived, and he soon returned to his old ways of telling anyone who would listen about his complaints against Thorpe, the story was still contained. One dangerous moment was when Scott was interviewed by a secret Liberal Party panel of inquiry in 1971, who were unsatisfied that the evidence he produced was sufficient to justify action against the party leader. Shortly afterwards Scott poured out his story to a freelance journalist who also happened to be a South African spy, Gordon Winter. Winter did not try to sell the story immediately, keeping it in reserve for the best time to use it against Thorpe, and found to his astonishment that British intelligence already had a bulging file on Thorpe's private life and the Scott business. When Winter gave his Thorpe dossier to the *Sunday People* in February 1974 just before the general election the paper refused to print it. The Chairman of the Mirror Group, Sidney Jacobson, was a friend of Thorpe. He thought the story 'consisted of the incoherent ramblings of a man with a vendetta against Jeremy Thorpe'. Famous people attracted delusional fantasists all the time, and Scott was dismissed as just another of the 'green ink brigade'.

Even as late as 1974 the press and Thorpe's political opponents were not interested in hounding Thorpe over the Scott affair, or any of his other sexual escapades. Shortly before the February 1974 election Scott had told his usual tale to Tim Keigwin, the Conservative candidate opposing Thorpe in North Devon. Keigwin passed a statement dictated by Scott back to Conservative Central Office, considering that the national party should be aware of a story about an opposing party leader. Party officials referred the matter to the party Chairman, Lord Carrington, who thought the document 'perfectly horrible ... don't touch it with the end of a barge-pole'. Edward Heath, who was told about the allegations at the start of the election campaign, agreed that they must not be used in the election. They were not. Heath evidently did not consider them, or the contents of Thorpe's MI5 file, a barrier to offering Thorpe the office of Home Secretary shortly after the inconclusive election result, in an attempt to form a parliamentary pact with the Liberals.

In November 1974 a bundle of documents, including a file marked 'The Property of Mr Jeremy Thorpe' and containing letters involving Scott and another man, was found by two builders at Bessell's former offices in Pall Mall and handed over to the *Sunday Mirror*. Sidney Jacobson returned the documents to Thorpe, although a copy was made and kept in a Mirror Group safe.

At the end of 1974, the Thorpe story was still a sordid matter of little genuine public interest. The actions of Thorpe and his friend David Holmes turned it into something much more serious. The stakes were now much higher, because of the electoral success of the Liberals in the 1974 elections and the precarious parliamentary position which made the Liberals valued allies for either of the main parties. The hatred of Thorpe's friends for Scott also burned stronger. David Holmes believed that Thorpe's first wife's death in a 1970 car accident had been caused by inattention following a distressing phone call from Scott. Holmes was finally converted to the idea that something drastic had to be done in February 1974, when he had paid Scott £2,500 (now worth about £12,000) in exchange for documents relating to Thorpe and an undertaking that he would now shut up about the matter. Scott failed to keep his side of the bargain and Holmes started to explore what criminal connections he could find to see if someone could silence Scott more effectively. Thorpe would obtain the money to pay for the operation by diverting it from innocent political donations from the wealthy Liberal benefactor Jack Hayward.

Through two of his business contacts, George Deakin and John Le Mesurier (the latter a carpet salesman and not the actor of the same name), Holmes found an airline pilot, Andrew Newton, who was a novice hit man but willing to do anything for money. A campaign of harassment against Scott culminated in October 1975 when Newton drove Scott on to Exmoor, stopped the car and produced a gun. At this point the plan went wrong. Newton, in addition to his other deficiencies as a hit man, was afraid of dogs and Scott went everywhere with a large Great Dane called Rinka. Newton shot Rinka but, when he turned his attention to Scott, his antique pistol jammed. Newton, cursing, drove off into the night leaving a weeping male model and a dead dog in the layby. It took just forty-eight hours for the police to find Newton, largely because his car licence number had become well known locally and Scott could give a good physical description of him. The Thorpe team ended up paying £20,000 (now worth about £95,000) for an inept gunman who could not get his hands on a reliable gun, conceal his tracks or keep his mouth shut for long, and who wasted the first few days of his mission looking for Scott in Dunstable, rather than Barnstaple, because he had misheard his instructions. It was yet another poorly judged business transaction on the part of the Liberal leader.

The shooting incident was a huge blunder because it aroused suspicions among people who had previously dismissed Scott's story as paranoid ravings, and made Scott even more embittered and vengeful. Thorpe made matters worse by making a joke in bad taste about dog hunting on the moors when asked about the incident. The next time Scott appeared in court, on a benefit fraud case in January 1976, he had no hesitation about repeating his allegation that he had been persecuted because of his relationship with Jeremy Thorpe.

Thorpe responded to the threat by calling up his reserves of support in the Establishment and the Wilson circle. He boasted to political colleagues that he had the three most important pillars of state, 'Harold Wilson, Lord Goodman and MI5', on his side. He denied the allegations in a brief statement agreed with Lord Goodman, who had been his solicitor since about 1967. Harold Wilson helped him, or so it seemed, by forming the idea that Thorpe's problems were related to the plotting against him, and claimed publicly that South African interference was behind the Scott allegations. Thorpe also recruited *The Sunday Times* to his side, writing an article 'The lies of Norman Scott, by Jeremy Thorpe'. Thorpe managed to fight off the danger until May, when after the publication of some letters showing that he had been on affectionate terms with Scott – contrary to previous denials – his political support ebbed away and he resigned as Liberal leader.

Thorpe remained an active Liberal MP, and had hopes of being reinstated in due course. His resignation had been greeted with some sympathy, because it appeared that he had been forced from office because of unproven allegations about his sexuality. Some people believed that he might have been as badly traduced as another man forced from office by affectionate letters, Thomas Galbraith, who resigned over the 'Vassall affair'. Even if he was homosexual and perhaps had a fling with young Norman, argued others, to make him resign because of it would be unjust and based on prejudice against homosexuals. Andrew Newton had gone to prison; his ludicrous cover story of having been blackmailed by Scott had just about held, and he was awaiting the remainder of his payment. The line might have held if Harold Wilson had not tried to be helpful by stirring up the press. Wilson's anger at the plotting that had gone on against him led to him teaming up with investigative journalists Barrie Penrose and Roger Courtiour to try to strike back at South Africa and the far right. The first line of inquiry would be the supposed plot to frame Jeremy Thorpe because of his outspoken opposition to apartheid.

The tabloids had not been alone in adopting a more challenging investigative role in the late 1960s and 1970s. *The Sunday Times* had assembled its Insight team in the 1960s and other broadsheet newpapers were moving into investigative journalism. In 1969 *The Times* broke a story about corruption among Metropolitan Police detectives that was the first stone in an avalanche of disclosures about the extent of misconduct in the police. Broadcasters too became interested in investigations, with the establishment of Granada's *World in Action* and the BBC's *Panorama*. *World in Action*, as we have seen, played a significant part in exposing the Poulson scandal. The development of the media infrastructure to handle detailed investigations was well under way, when it received a massive boost from events in the United States.

Watergate started with a politically motivated burglary in June 1972, and a little over two years later it had forced the resignation of President Richard Nixon, the first time a president was ever to leave office other than by death, electoral defeat or retirement. Investigative journalism played a considerable part in unravelling the facts behind the Watergate burglary, the intelligence operations run by the Nixon White House and various other scandals connected to the administration. It was a triumphant vindication of what had previously been dismissed as 'paranoia'. The *Washington Post*'s reporters

Carl Bernstein and Bob Woodward ('Woodstein') were heroes, to be played by Dustin Hoffman and Robert Redford in the famous 1977 film of their book *All the President's Men*.

The search was on for a British Watergate, although the nearest equivalent – the Wilson plot – was actually an incidental part of the story that was unravelled by British investigative journalists. Leading the pack with Wilson's help were the BBC's Barrie Penrose and Roger Courtiour (nicknamed 'Pencourt'). They were adversely compared at the time to Woodstein although their role in the story is much more central than their US equivalents. The Watergate investigation was largely run by Congressional committees and a hardline judge, while in Britain baffled police officers would ask Pencourt to help them unravel the tale. The ambiguous triumph of British investigative journalism was the exposure of Jeremy Thorpe.

The BBC was an incongruous place to start such an investigation. Unlike Granada, the Corporation was unwilling to take risks and through its Board of Governors and its dependence on the government for the licence fee it was usually a tame part of the political establishment. Its founding claim to impartiality was undermined by Lord Reith's willingness to broadcast government propaganda during the General Strike. Until the 1980s an MI5 officer had an office at the BBC to vet staff. The Pencourt inquiry was hobbled by the attitude of BBC management, both to long-range investigation and to stirring up senior politicians, and their contracts did not survive the summer of 1976.

Pencourt continued with the support of a publishing deal for a book based on their results. The result, *The Pencourt File* (1978), conveys the bafflement of two reporters who had been given disconnected insights into many of the hidden currents of British public life in the 1960s and 1970s such as the Wilson plot, Thorpe, Blunt, Goodman, the activities of CIA and BOSS agents in Britain and the influence of Marcia Falkender. Their mistake was to try to fit all these pieces together into a kind of alternative history of the times. The story that made most sense as it unravelled was of Thorpe's obsession with silencing Scott. Penrose and Courtiour flew to California, where Peter Bessell was still dreaming of being a big businessman. The former Liberal MP, drawing on a long document he had written as an aide-memoire, told them the tale of how he had helped Thorpe in the 1960s, the discussions about shooting or poisoning Scott, and Holmes' admission to him that Newton had been hired to kill Scott. It slowly became clear that Newton had been hired by Holmes and his friends on behalf of Thorpe, who had diverted funds from Liberal donors to pay for the gunman.

Meanwhile, Newton had realized that his participation in this conspiracy could generate even more money than the original contract on Scott and tried to play the newspapers off against his former allies. He collected a further £12,000 from John Le Mesurier, who told Holmes that 'with Newton we had acquired an albatross round our necks far more dangerous than Scott had ever been. He was a crafty, conniving liar and was nobody's fool.' In October 1977 the London *Evening News* reported Newton's claims that he had been hired to kill Scott.

Thorpe responded with a bizarre press conference, at which a small piece of history was made. In principle, there were two entirely separate aspects to the Thorpe scandal – sexuality and criminality. But Thorpe's alleged criminal behaviour had been generated by his obsessive concern at the danger his sexuality posed to his political career. Thus, the BBC reporter Keith Graves stood up and asked Thorpe to his face whether he had ever had a homosexual relationship. It was the first time the question had been put so directly. Thorpe's lawyer told him not to answer.

The Thorpe scandal opened up a cultural divide within the press, pitting younger journalists who had been influenced by Watergate against the traditional British role of the press as part of the political establishment. The Graves question was a polarizing issue. The investigators saw it as an essential step in uncovering serious crime, although some were uneasy at the thought that it might seem homophobic; the establishment saw it as invading the privacy of a good chap, although many of them had opposed legalizing homosexuality.

The allegations of serious criminal conduct which had been made by Bessell and Newton could not be ignored although, as with Reginald Maudling, the office of the Director of Public Prosecutions was extremely nervous about proceeding against such a senior figure. When the case had been developed the office of the DPP dragged its feet as much as it could, but was eventually pressurized into charging Thorpe and his associates by the Somerset and Avon Police, whose investigating officers strongly believed that it was a worthwhile case. The police inquiries after the dog-shooting case had been reopened had been lagging behind the efforts of the press, and Penrose and Courtiour helped the police to find their way around the tangled story. It was an uncomfortable alliance for the press and the police alike, although it reflected the realities of the situation. Pencourt handed the policeman who came to see them 'the names and addresses of their sources, including the alleged conspirators, and showed him their files, which he thought were better than anything he had seen in the CID room in Bristol'. For Pencourt: 'It had become a matter of honour, verging on obsession, to prove that they had been right about Thorpe. If anyone had asked them to choose between a bestselling book and Thorpe's conviction they might well have opted for the latter.'

As well as receiving information from journalists, the police investigation appeared extremely leaky, with frequent updates on progress appearing in *Private Eye* – although the Avon and Somerset officers strenuously denied that the leaks were from them or helpful in any way. But the amount of public attention on the DPP while the decision was taken made it impossible to let the matter drop like the potential charges against Maudling. In August 1978 Thorpe was arrested, along with Holmes, Deakin and Le Mesurier, although they were given the unusual courtesy of reporting to the police station under their own steam rather than being apprehended.

In November 1978 Thorpe and his associates faced charges of conspiracy to murder, and Thorpe additionally of incitement to murder. The first stage was a committal hearing in Minehead Magistrates' Court, at which Thorpe's solicitor requested a full hearing of the prosecution case. Deakin's solicitor asked that reporting restrictions be lifted, and as a result the sensational details of the allegations against Thorpe by Bessell and Scott became public. Thorpe, protesting his innocence, lost his seat in the May 1979 election.

The Thorpe trial after the election was an anti-climax. There was little new in the prosecution case since the November committal hearing, and neither Thorpe nor Holmes entered any evidence for their defence. The defence was reliant on the skills of George Carman, Thorpe's barrister, in demolishing the credibility of Bessell and Scott, a task he largely achieved. The acquittal of Thorpe and his associates was frustrating for the assembled press, who had nearly unanimously believed that they were guilty. At first glance, the Thorpe trial was an impressive display of the power of the Establishment to protect its own. Judge Cantley's summing up showed grotesque bias in favour of Thorpe, a Privy Councillor, and against his accusers who were treated to judicial invective against their characters. The prosecution had been hobbled by the caution of the police and the evidence offered. Evidence gathered about Thorpe's financial dealings was not reflected in the charge sheet, and a gay man who had been picked up by Thorpe and made the mistake of asking him for a loan was not called to give evidence.

But the affair was the last old-fashioned cover-up the old Establishment or the Wilson circle were able to organize. The reluctance of the authorities even to charge Thorpe had been overcome by the toughness of the police but also a determined press campaign. Later in 1979 the researches of Andrew Boyle into the mysterious 'Fourth Man' of the Cambridge spy ring led Margaret Thatcher to name Anthony Blunt, who had served as Surveyor of the Queen's Pictures. Blunt's guilt had been established in 1964, but neither the public (nor the ministers of the 1964–70 Labour government) had been told about it by MI5. Hypocritically, Blunt was stripped of his knighthood after he had been exposed. It seemed that the ghosts that had haunted the Establishment during the 1960s and 1970s – the Thorpe affair, the Wilson plot and Blunt's spying – had been laid to rest by the new government. However, the new broom swept several other unsavoury matters – such as low standards of conduct among MPs – under the carpet.

CHAPTER 8

The enterprise culture 1979-92

'You need never pay for your own lunch or dinner as a Member of Parliament.'

Neil Hamilton, 1999

The election of the Thatcher government in 1979 led to radical changes which affected Parliament as well as much of society and the economy in Britain. The government broadcast its free market economic principles and many Conservative MPs were all too eager to practise what they preached. The increasing proportion of MPs who had not come from wealthy families or a career in business raced to catch up in an atmosphere where money was there to be made as rapidly as possible. This spilled over into a culture of greed and excess, made possible by the money flowing in from commercial lobbying interests and the lax climate of self-regulation that had survived the Poulson scandal.

The political class changed greatly between the 1940s and the 1990s. It became much more of a career. Previously, many MPs had a 'proper job' before entering Parliament. Conservatives tended to have been farmers or businessmen before being elected; Labour MPs often had experience of teaching, or manual working-class jobs such as mining before entering politics via the trade union movement. Such MPs came into Parliament relatively late in life, and served perhaps two or three terms as an MP without considering themselves a failure if ministerial office never came their way.

By the 1990s the idea of a political career had become established among a much larger number of MPs. In the 1992 intake there were several Conservative MPs who approached the whips impatiently asking when they would be made ministers, which would never have happened before the 1980s. The proportion of MPs who had done a 'proper job' before being elected, as opposed to working as a political researcher or doing a job such as barrister or journalist only to facilitate political ambition, fell from 80 per cent in 1951 to 41 per cent in 1992. Professional politicians are of a type socially, whichever party they belong to: they tend to be university educated – although often from a modest middle-class family – articulate and knowledgeable about at least part of the wide spectrum covered by the public policy agenda. He – or she, for greater sex equality is one of the gains from this shift – is likely, apart from being obsessed with politics, to be relatively 'normal' and devoid of either endearing or tiresome eccentricities.

The change in the social composition of the Conservative Parliamentary Party which resulted from the trend towards career politics came in several gradual shifts. The first was when the number of Conservative MPs rose from 213 in 1945 to 298 in 1950. The 'class of 1950' included several MPs from a modest or provincial grammar school background who had been inducted into the Establishment via Oxford or Cambridge. The political connection for several of them was through the Conservative Research Department, which became established during the 1950s as a route for bright young graduates to become Conservative MPs. In the late 1940s it had been under the control of Rab Butler, who was a powerful ally for Tories such as Iain Macleod, Reggie Maudling and Enoch Powell who won seats in 1950 and went on to shape the postwar Conservative Party. The younger and less wealthy members of the 1950 intake were assisted by a reform introduced in 1948 under which candidates would no longer be permitted to give more than £100 to constituency election expenses. Before 1948 constituency associations had demanded large contributions, which led to selections being skewed in favour of rich families.

However, the power of the old guard was still sufficiently strong in the early 1960s for a leading Tory to say, 'The Tory Party is run by about five people and they all treat their followers with disdain: they're mostly Etonians, and Eton is good for disdain.' The intake of 1970 was another transitional point, although the traditional 'Establishment' still dominated the parliamentary party, with 107 company directors, 40 farmers or landowners and 56 barristers making up nearly two-thirds of the 330-strong Conservative group. Some of those first elected in 1970 who went on to high office were from a set who had been to Cambridge in the early 1960s including Kenneth Clarke, John Gummer and Norman Lamont (elected at a by-election in 1972). Among the new intake, however, was Norman Tebbit, an airline pilot of working-class background who was the vanguard of the new right of the Conservative Party who were to take control in the 1980s.

The gradual changes did not go unnoticed. Cecil King quoted a lunch guest in May 1973 as saying that: 'Tory MPs show a marked deterioration from their standard of twenty years ago. They were now opportunists who sought office, not power, and their ambitions were not buttressed by principles of any kind.'

These remarks were made by John Stonehouse.

The victory of Margaret Thatcher in the Conservative Party leadership election of February 1975 led to a deliberate effort to change the composition of the Parliamentary Conservative Party. She appointed Marcus Fox as Party Vice-President in charge of the candidates' list. Fox himself had been elected MP for Shipley near Bradford in 1970, and was a prototype of the new breed of Tory MP. He had been educated at Dewsbury Grammar School and instead of going to university he went into the textile business. He was a proud, not to say professional, Yorkshireman, who recalls:

She had decided that the party needed a change in terms of the membership of the House and she certainly got one. It was one of the shocks of my life when I was called in and she said that she wanted me to be in charge of candidates. I said, 'Well, you realize what's going to happen.' She said, 'No, what?' 'What?' I said, 'You'll get more people like me.' And she said, 'That's exactly what I want.'

From January 1976 until 1979 Fox interviewed a couple of thousand hopefuls, becoming known as the 'Shipley Strangler' for the thorough weeding of the candidates' list he undertook. Fox and Thatcher believed that 'our party as it was prior to 1970 couldn't claim to be representative of the people' and set out to replace social connections with party fervour as the criterion for selection.

As well as the greater fairness to individuals that the new policy involved, it was also perceived as an electoral asset. Perhaps in the interwar period and the early 1950s the deferential attitude of voters towards the ruling class was an electoral advantage for a Conservative Party that spoke in those accents, but by the 1970s deference was a declining force. The old Establishment was increasingly regarded as effete, incompetent and responsible for Britain's decline. The Conservatives concluded that candidates who had risen through their own hard work were most likely to command the respect of voters.

To the sardonic eye of Julian Critchley, first elected a Tory MP in 1959, it was the replacement of estate owners by estate agents.

That said, the changes were not immediate or particularly dramatic. The proportion of Conservative MPs with a public school education was even a little higher in 1979 (77 per cent) than it had been in 1955 (76 per cent). The stars of the 1979 intake – Chris Patten, Stephen Dorrell, Matthew Parris and William Waldegrave, for instance – were mostly from the same sort of background as the stars of 1950. The main exception to the familiar pattern was John Major, a banker who had not been to university and had fought his way up through local government politics in London. He found the social atmosphere rather strained for people like himself.

Michael Brown, who narrowly won the gritty town of Scunthorpe, was comparatively unusual in having gone to a secondary modern school. He reckons: 'There were a lot of people who looked down their noses at the weirdos like myself who had arrived, as they would say, "by accident". There was still a lot of the old Sir Bufton Tufton image about the party.'

However, the social meaning of a university education or a minor public school had shifted over the years. Private education was now more accessible to those with marginally well-off parents, and the expansion of higher education had created a more meritocratic as well as larger body of graduates. The Conservative Party was following the lead of these other Establishment institutions.

The real change in the Parliamentary Conservative Party took place in 1983 and 1987. The landslide victory in 1983 swelled its ranks to 397 MPs, including some most unexpected winners in normally Labour seats such as the mining seat of Sherwood in Nottinghamshire and even Bridgend in South Wales. In general, the higher the proportion of Conservative candidates elected the greater the social diversity of the parliamentary party, and in 1983 this was accentuated by the efforts of Marcus Fox and the redistribution of boundaries which gave a chance to ease out some older MPs. Retirements helped make the 'class of 1987' among Conservative MPs fifty-three strong, comparatively large for an election when so few seats changed hands.

Jim Prior, a Conservative MP from 1959 to 1987, was not impressed by the new generation, as he says: 'They tended to be far more right wing and far more young men on the make without any experience of life. They came straight from the research department or being special advisers. Much tougher, less emollient, than earlier generations and I would have said nothing like such pleasant people.'

Socially, the changes were between sections of the middle class rather than a sudden influx of working-class Tories. The new Tory of 1983 or 1987 was typically the product of a minor public school and a university. However, scratching the surface reveals a significant decline in the classical élite pedigree of rich family, Eton and Oxford. The new Tories were more typically from skilled working-class or lower-middle-class families who had sent them to fee-paying schools in a spirit of upward mobility.

The broadening of the social base of the Parliamentary Conservative Party in the 1980s expanded the scope of adverse comparison within the social confines of Westminster. Reginald Maudling had been a prototype of the ambitious, upwardly mobile Conservative MP who acquired a taste for the finer things in life and had to find the means to support such a lifestyle. The expectation that a Conservative MP should have the trappings of wealth, property and success lingered on, but an ever-increasing proportion of them had no access to private means. Upward mobility had taken them through public schools, but to arrive in the Parliamentary Conservative Party was to discover yet another similar environment where the social lead was taken from the rich and privileged.

As well as comparing themselves with fellow Tories who had already made or inherited money, they were aware that friends and contemporaries were earning several times as much as them in the City or management consultancy. Their low pay was accompanied by tiresome obligations such as hanging around all evening casting votes and spending weekends at boring social events in a constituency far away from metropolitan society. There were also considerable extra expenses involved in maintaining two houses. Such MPs often became disillusioned with their lot and sick of the rhetoric of public service – a concept that was going out of political fashion anyway.

*

By the mid 1980s the victory of the right was absolute. The Conservatives enjoyed a majority of 144 in the Commons, and were confident that the Opposition, divided between Labour and the SDP–Liberal Alliance, could not get its act together to mount a serious challenge. The 1987 election result was surprisingly similar to that of 1983, the Conservatives retaining a three-figure majority and Labour suffering its second worst showing among the electorate since 1918. The Conservatives not only had political control, as in the 1950s, but the ideological tide was flowing strongly to the right. Starting with British Telecom in 1984, the large publicly owned industries were privatized. Direct tax rates were cut. Rhetoric of an 'enterprise economy' started to take hold. Other countries took steps along the path down which Thatcher was leading Britain. The culture of the House of Commons and the political class was changing too, with MPs aspiring to become entrepreneurs. Fortunately for the aspirational MPs of the 1980s, there was no shortage of people wanting to help out financially.

The familiar system of MPs having consultancies and directorships with outside firms continued, although these were now governed by the Register of Members' Interests. They grew from 541 to 974 between 1980 and 1990, with consultancies more than doubling.

The MP for Berkshire East, Andrew MacKay, was a consultant to the City merchant bankers Morgan Grenfell on political strategy. According to an internal memo from a Morgan Grenfell director that found its way to the journalist Paul Foot:

> *I do not believe we are using his considerable talents sufficiently as far as our clients are concerned, many of whom are extremely naïve as to how to work with and use their MPs to advantage. Many companies underestimate how much their MP can do for them, and many companies don't even know who their MP is.*

It was pointed out that companies do not have MPs, constituencies do.

A number of Conservative MPs in the 1980s went around looking for opportunities to make money from outside interests, badgering lobbyists for contacts and using the network of committees and groups in Westminster to further that aim. According to Corinne Souza, a lobbyist and writer:

The fact that there were no rules, no anti-corruption legislation, meant that anything went. There was a free-for-all ... we had a few Members from both the Upper House and the Lower House who were using the all-party group in order to tout for business, I found that not only distasteful but in any other country I would have thought it was corrupt as well.

John Browne, the MP for Winchester 1979–92, seemed an old-fashioned Conservative with an upright, military bearing but in reality he was as crude an operator as any in Parliament. He had been paid the enormous sum of $88,270 (£57,000) in 1982–83 to compile a report for the Saudi Arabian Monetary Agency. His research involved asking parliamentary questions, and his interest was declared in terms so vague as to be misleading. He was also on an undeclared retainer from a Lebanese firm, Selco East, which he claimed was unrelated to his parliamentary activity. These matters were brought to the attention of the Select Committee on Members' Interests in 1990 by investigative journalists and duly condemned. The House of Commons voted to suspend Browne for twenty days, and he made his situation worse by complaining about the verdict and alleging dirty tricks by the party leadership. Browne was never a popular figure. He had breached the formal rules but perhaps more importantly the informal code that, as in cricket, a gentleman walks when given 'out'. He was thrown out of the Parliamentary Conservative Party in 1991, more because of his intention to stand as an independent against the official Conservative candidate adopted in his stead than for his low standards of conduct in Parliament.

Some MPs became self-employed entrepreneurs by setting up their own lobbying firms. Marcus Fox himself was a director of Westminster Communications, a firm he formed with another MP, Keith Speed, who lost his ministerial job in the same reshuffle in 1981. Martin Smith, a lobbyist who had previously worked for the National Consumer Council, was startled to find that, as he says, 'in competing for business we were actually competing against some Members of Parliament who were running small lobbying businesses from within the Palace of Westminster'.

At the very least, such activity raised questions about the ways MPs were exercising their representative functions and the quality of service that constituency interests were getting.

As well as consultancies the 1980s saw a massive growth in the lobbying industry, and the entire public relations sector. New lobbying firms were being established, such as Ian Greer Associates and GJW, a firm set up by former aides to David Steel, Jim Callaghan and Edward Heath. Andrew Gifford, the former Liberal adviser, noticed at the time of shipbuilding nationalization in 1976 that many firms were unaware that they were directly affected. One firm that did notice and object recruited a PR firm called International News Services, which ran such a blatant campaign of hospitality, complete with entertainment barge moored near Westminster, that it proved counterproductive. Leaving Steel's office in 1979, Gifford thought, as he now says: 'There was clearly a gap in the market between private business and government and it wasn't particularly well looked after.'

Large industrial and commercial firms operating in Britain became increasingly converted to the idea of employing a political lobbyist for handling their relations with Whitehall and Westminster. By 1985, 41 of Britain's largest 180 companies employed political consultants. Heath's well-advertised disdain for the calibre of British industrial management led business to conclude that he had not understood them properly and they were anxious, as Ian Greer now says, not to repeat the experience when the Conservatives returned to power in 1979. The feeling was mutual, as Thatcher's public relations adviser Tim Bell explains:

Thatcher's government was much more open to conversations with people. It was interested in talking to business people. It was very conscious that it needed to put through legislation that was business-friendly, and the best way to find out what's friendly to business is go and ask them. And businessmen, even today, don't quite grasp that they have a right to go and talk to politicians, and they think that the government is living in a little ivory tower. So they'd much rather use people in the middle to act for them.

Companies that had previously handled such matters through Establishment networks or in-house public relations work were becoming potential clients of lobbying firms. There was also a flow of legislation in the mid 1980s privatizing publicly owned industries and throwing open business to private contractors, and a range of City and contracting concerns as well as the newly privatized management took a keen interest in the details of this legislation. Deregulation of industries rarely involved the total abolition of regulations; in some sectors, particularly the privatized industries, it involved the construction of complex regulatory systems, the details of which could be affected by lobbying activity and make millions of pounds' worth of difference to the industry. Decisions on pricing formulas in telecommunications and the utilities were being made as policy decisions involving a link between business and a government regulator, rather than being an internal government matter. New competitor firms, such as Mercury telephones and mobile phone companies, grew up and also needed to protect their interests in the policy world. Michael Brown explains the way privatization fuelled the gravy train:

Parliamentary lobbying took off in the 1980s because you had many companies in the private sector that wanted to get their hands on the spoils of the public sector, which Mrs Thatcher had made clear were going to be denationalized, so you had a large number of private companies wanting to lobby Parliament for deregulation of every state industry that was going ... It was very necessary to ensure that if you were a private company you had Members of Parliament on side being lobbied, and that was the reason for this new professional class of public affairs, public relations, lobbyists and all the rest of it.

Privatization could also involve personal benefits for MPs. The Conservative MP for Anglesey since 1979, Keith Best, dishonestly made multiple applications for British Telecom shares in 1984 using permutations of his name and various addresses. He did not stand for re-election in 1987 and was later found guilty of a criminal offence relating to the transaction.

The new class of Conservative MPs was central to the operation of the lobbyists in the 1980s. As one of them, Michael Brown, puts it:

The old school MPs on the Conservative side very much looked down their noses at this new profession of public affairs, and of course it was very easy for them to do that. They had their estates, their family money, inherited money, they had their legal qualifications as barristers and solicitors ... If you were to have a career outside politics then it should ideally be a real job, stockbroking, banking, accountancy. The world of public affairs was regarded as tacky.

Brown was exactly right. One of those old school Tory MPs was Sir Geoffrey Johnson-Smith, who had grown used to barristers and union advisers but felt, as he now explains, that it looked 'a little tacky' for conservatives to be working as political consultants for lobbying companies. It was felt that outside interests which kept an MP in touch with the 'real' world were one thing, but jobs which were essentially about acting as a mouthpiece in Parliament were another. The old school's distaste for lobbying was more at the unsubtle nature of the transaction as it was now performed than a disinterested belief in the public good. Neil Hamilton, a new right-wing MP in 1983, thinks 'their attitude was hypocritical. Lobbying was regarded as tacky by those who didn't wish themselves to be exposed for what they had been doing all those years.'

This happened when the Lloyd's insurance market sponsored a Private Bill to pre-empt official regulation which became law in 1982. The Speaker advised that MPs who were Lloyd's members should consider not voting, but twenty-one chose to do so. The Bill established a self-regulatory system and gave members of internal committees immunity from prosecution for negligence or incompetence. The protection was useful for senior figures at Lloyd's when the institution came close to collapse in the early 1990s. As Hamilton says:

> *The members of the Establishment always lobbied extremely effec-*
> *tively for themselves. Lloyd's always managed to protect itself from*
> *regulation which was, I think, largely because there were lots of mem-*
> *bers of Lloyd's in the House of Commons, and the informal networks*
> *of Establishment members prevented very necessary changes coming*
> *about in due time.*

The outrageous behaviour of certain Conservative MPs was satirized in a television comedy, *The New Statesman*, about the adventures of Alan B'Stard MP. Michael Portillo had given the writers some advice about how Parliament worked, but the unethical B'Stard was – mostly – a work of imagination. It was required viewing for some of the class of 1983; Michael Brown saw more than a certain amount of B'Stard in his colleagues, and even himself. There were a lot of ambitious young MPs in the 1980s who would do almost anything to win ministerial office or make money. Only a few could win office, because of the limited number of jobs in government, and a lot of the rest were 'bored' and felt they did not have enough to do in the Commons and might as well make some money.

This was an attitude recognized by Ian Greer, whose lobbying firm Ian Greer Associates (IGA) was the most successful lobbying firm in Britain during the 1980s boom in the industry. It had a deserved reputation as a high-class, expensive firm with extremely good contacts in the Conservative Party. Its client list included multinational corporations such as Coca-Cola, Philip Morris and Trafalgar House; privatized firms such as British Airways, British Gas and Thames Water; and foreign governments such as Canada and Kuwait. It was also the cash machine for several Conservative MPs.

Ian Greer himself had been a party agent and a member of staff at Conservative Central Office. His application to join the candidates' list in 1965 was turned down because, as he says, he was homosexual and, unlike other homosexual Tories of the time, made no effort to disguise it by acquiring a presentable wife and leading a double life. Instead of active politics he worked behind the scenes in lobbying, using his Conservative contacts, who had reached exalted levels within the party and government in the 1980s. From 1970 to 1981 he was partner in a lobbying firm, Russell Greer, before setting up on his own account as Ian Greer Associates in 1982 and building a large business from scratch in a very short time.

IGA was a class act. Douglas Smith, a rival lobbyist, remembers its best years:

Ian Greer was a magnificent organizer of social events. Cars would meet people or transport Members of Parliament to his dining room or offices and the food was excellent and the wine was splendid. He made clients feel immensely important ... if the rest of what they offered in terms of advice and experience was as good as the dining, I think he'd still be in business now.

Greer was of course not the only lobbyist to offer hospitality. According to Neil Hamilton, 'MPs are awash with hospitality, and you need never pay for your own lunch or dinner as a Member of Parliament. If your capacity to be bored is infinite, then you can eat at somebody else's expense the entire time.' The downside, as Hamilton says, is having to sing for your supper by being polite to boring clients and listening to their opinions and their special pleading.

Entertaining and impressing was very much the Ian Greer style. His offices in Catherine Place, not far from the Houses of Parliament, were lavishly, even pretentiously, decorated. His firm, like many others, sponsored receptions and parties in Westminster and at the party conferences in the autumn. The conference season was the time to pull out all the stops to impress clients with the firm's access, and the politicians with the quality of what was on offer. According to Neil Hamilton:

If you went to a Conservative conference in the early 1980s, and compared it to a conference in the early 1970s, there would have been a vast increase in the number of parties to attend, and this is largely what lobbying was about. Of course lobbyists were also able to perform formal advocacy, but by and large it was about making informal personal contacts and bonding.

Greer believed in the power of Parliament and the importance of personal contact between clients and MPs, facilitated by the smooth and popular lobbyist in the middle. He consciously swam against the tide of the conventional wisdom that Parliament was irrelevant and the real action was in quiet work in the corridors of Whitehall. His approach was disparaged by people such as Keith Lockwood, who worked for the Shandwick PR firm. Lockwood reckons that the Greer style was superficial; while it may have been entertaining for the MPs and clients, the work that got results was mundane research and briefing. However, the Greer approach interlocked with the growing love of the high life and conspicuous consumption that was prevalent among Conservative MPs in the 1980s.

As the boom developed some MPs developed a taste for freeloading at the expense of lobbying companies and their clients, to an extent that disgusted lobbyists such as Douglas Smith:

Members of Parliament of course did become greedy. In the old days you could get them to speak at things because they were really rather flattered to speak. But increasingly a number demanded money, and I think it was building on the fact that they knew others were getting the money ... the fee levels started going up. If you ask them to speak at a function or a debate you'd be paying them three or four hundred pounds whereas before you would be paying them nothing.

To Ian Greer too, the behaviour of some Members of Parliament was sheer greed. His main client, British Airways, was pestered by demands from MPs for free flights and free upgrades from economy to business or first class. Upgrades involved substantial savings for the beneficiaries, up to several thousand pounds on long-haul flights. MPs felt that BA owed them a favour because they had campaigned for privatization. Some, such as the late Member for Christchurch Robert Adley, were repeat offenders. Greer warned the Conservative Chief Whip David Waddington in 1989 that MPs were behaving in this way but refused to name the culprits. No action was taken by the whips because no individuals were identified. BA eventually stopped giving upgrades to MPs in February 1990.

The brazen behaviour of these MPs did not go unnoticed by their colleagues. Edwina Currie was among those who, as she says, 'felt slightly resentful about that. There were about twenty-odd Members who were doing quite well out of lobbying companies, particularly Ian Greer's. They would be quite triumphal, almost boastful, about it. I couldn't quite see where there was any honour in what they were getting up to.'

Some MPs also started to accept, and then demand, introduction fees for forging links between lobbyists and potential clients. The attitude of lobbyists to this practice was mixed. Douglas Smith had qualms about whether it was appropriate for an MP, as opposed to an advertising agent, to do this, and recalled that it was rare or non-existent before the 1980s: 'If you'd suggested to some of the Conservative MPs of the 1960s that their job was to procure business for a public relations consultancy the result would have been apoplexy, cardiac arrest.'

To Ian Greer it was defensible on the grounds that it stopped MPs considering that they were owed further favours at indefinite times in the future. But the unverifiable and subtle nature of what constituted an introduction made the lobbyist open to pressure from MPs, as this unsavoury tale, recounted in Greer's book, of the former Conservative MP for Wirral South demonstrates:

I would not pay an MP if I felt he had not earned a commission payment. Barry Porter was persistent in claiming that I owed him a fee after we were hired by one of his constituency companies. At one point he harangued me on the House of Commons terrace, yelling, 'Where's my commission?' I did not feel he had done anything to earn himself a commission from IGA. In the end it became so embarrassing that I bought him a case of champagne.

Michael Grylls, by contrast, gave value for money to Ian Greer. Grylls had been the MP for Surrey constituencies since 1970. He was a smooth, preening man with strong right-wing views about the economy. Grylls had one of the longest lists of directorships and consultancies of any MP. He and his wife were cheerfully blatant about mixing business and politics. Matthew Parris recalls going to a meeting in his constituency: 'Sally Grylls was there and she appeared also to be selling some kind of water purification system to people at the same time as conducting a political meeting which somewhat raised eyebrows but I'm sure it was all quite above board.'

Michael Grylls was also Chairman of the backbench Conservative Trade and Industry Committee. Backbench committees existed for all the departments of government, but the Trade and Industry Committee brought its chairman into contact with many businesses interested in public policy and gave him a platform in his dealings with ministers. Grylls' colleagues among the officers of this committee, such as Neil Hamilton and Tim Smith, were also recruited to Greer causes. Other lobbyists despaired of this backbench committee and regarded it as sewn up by IGA. As Arthur Butler says, he 'gave up trying to get my clients an opportunity to address that committee because we knew we'd be fobbed off. Greer's clients no doubt had no problems making presentations.'

Grylls was not the only Member active in committees who had commercial links with outside interests connected with the activities of that committee. Jerry Wiggin, the MP for Weston-super-Mare, was Chairman of the Select Committee on Agriculture and Food after 1987 while serving as a consultant to British Sugar. Robert McCrindle combined work on an aviation interest committee with a consultancy to British Caledonian. It was mostly up to the judgement and honour of the individual MP to keep the commercial interest separate from the activities of the committee. In 1990, however, the Select Committee on Members' Interests recommended that control over conflicts of interest be extended to the work of Select Committees, although backbench committees were not covered and, according to its Chairman: 'the House itself didn't seem interested'.

Some ministers formed their own judgements about Grylls. Edwina Currie realized that he was one of a small group of distinguished politicians who made a good living from directorships and lobbyists: 'and good luck to him. But if you're a minister and you knew that, you would take what was being said by someone like Michael with a very big pinch of salt.'

Diligent ministers would read briefings about the business connections

of delegations of MPs who lobbied them and adjust their views according-
ly. Clients often ended up getting less than they bargained for because of the
self-defeating aspect of trying to buy a good reputation. Neil Hamilton is
cynical about the lobbying transaction: 'Huge sums of money are charged
for the services which lobbyists provide to their unsuspecting clients, but
it's the biggest waste of money that you could possibly imagine.'

The real profits were made by the lobbying firms and any Members of
Parliament on their payroll. Grylls used the contacts he made in his role on the
committee to further the interests of Ian Greer Associates. Keith Lockwood
of Shandwick, whose accounts in the 1980s included British Airways and
Rank Xerox, heard Grylls telling a Xerox executive that he should sign up
to a government relations specialist and then recommending IGA. When the
Xerox man said he already had PR help from Shandwick, Grylls sounded
distinctly chilly. Grylls later, according to Lockwood, steered the British
Airways contract to IGA: 'It was very blatant and very surprising.'

Grylls was not just being a good friend to Ian Greer. He was given commission payments for finding clients for Ian Greer Associates. Grylls earned
£10,000 (10 per cent) for introducing British Airways, an extremely valuable client, to IGA. He had also been rewarded for procuring other clients.
This connection between Grylls and IGA came to light in 1989 when the
journalist Andrew Roth was preparing a volume of *Parliamentary Profiles*.
A former IGA employee told him that Grylls had been collecting commission payments, and Roth decided to put it in the profile of the MP:

*It's my policy, partly for libel reasons, to show draft profiles to MPs
before I publish them in order for them to check it for the facts. I did
this with Mickey Grylls. I sent him a copy and, as I expected, he wanted to see me as had happened the previous time. He invited me to
meet him on a Friday afternoon on the terrace of the House of
Commons and we spent about an hour and a half going through the
whole profile word by word. He passed over the reference to his relation to Ian Greer, which I greeted with a sigh of relief because I wasn't
convinced I could have got my source into a court of law to defend it.*

Roth thought that the connection was so well known around Westminster
that Grylls had forgotten that it was not public knowledge. When it was
published Grylls went to see his libel lawyers, who did not advise him to
sue Roth. Instead, he registered the payments in the Register of Members'
Interests, but in the meantime an investigation by the Select Committee on
Members' Interests had begun. It naturally discovered the claims were true
but did not recommend that Grylls be punished. It accepted that Grylls had
not registered the payments before because he considered them one-off payments rather than a continuing financial relationship, and that the rules were

sufficiently unclear for this argument to be tenable.

The Grylls case highlighted the ambivalent feelings MPs had about the register. It was accepted as a part of parliamentary life in a way it had not been in the mid 1970s; Sir Geoffrey Johnson-Smith, later Chairman of the Select Committee on Members' Interests, recalls having to exercise pressure to persuade some MPs to register at all in the early years of the system. The contents of the Register were gradually increasing in importance as far as the press, lobbyists and ministers were concerned. However, it did not take much ingenuity for an MP to arrange his or her affairs so opaquely that the entry was uninformative, and there were several sorts of financial interest that did not fall clearly within any of the categories specified on the form. MPs such as Grylls and Neil Hamilton saw no reason to volunteer more information than they thought was required. Their judgement, on matters such as commission payments, clearly differed from that of Johnson-Smith: 'Frankly, I've always thought the rules were clear.'

Michael Brown, who was himself condemned in 1997 for failing to register a commission payment made for introducing US Tobacco to IGA or declare his interest in dealings with ministers, believes that:

The problem was that there were no clear rules. MPs took the attitude, 'If the rules aren't clear, we don't have to declare it.' That has been seen to be wrong ten years down the track. The moral of the story is, if the rules aren't clear, you have to declare it. But I don't think there was any feeling of conscience at that time ... There was almost a cavalier attitude which was prevalent as a result of all that had gone on. Thatcherism had said that this is get-rich-quick Britain where anything goes, and I think Britain unregulated applied to MPs at that time.

In future, however, it was made clear that introduction payments were to be registered and eventually the practice was banned by the lobbying industry. The Grylls affair was an overture to the scandals that would envelop Ian Greer Associates in the 1990s. In addition, the failure of Grylls and Greer to explain the full dimensions of the commission payments told against them later. Greer had claimed that there were three payments, but in fact the number was considerably greater. When the matter was reinvestigated in 1997 the Commissioner for Standards, Sir Gordon Downey, found that Grylls was additionally 'on an annual, but not disclosed, retainer with the lobbying organization. I believe the concealment was deliberate.' The 1997 Select Committee found that his deception of the 1990 Select Committee amounted to a contempt of the House and that his conduct 'fell seriously below the standards the House is entitled to expect'. The charges on which Grylls was indicted were similar to those brought against John Cordle in

1977 for his activities on behalf of John Poulson, but the condemnation of Grylls was ineffective because the MP had retired at the 1997 election.

The Select Committee on Members' Interests was an inefficient regulator of the growth of lobbying and outside interests in the 1980s. Its members were themselves as inclined as any others to have consultancies and directorships and in 1989 three members had PR consultancies. The committee was chaired by Sir Geoffrey Johnson-Smith. According to Ian Greer: 'It was a committee that was pretty weak and pretty wet … Geoffrey Johnson-Smith was extremely charming, but not dynamic, not decisive. In many ways I think he could be aptly described as rather spineless.'

Johnson-Smith reckons: 'That's a bit rich coming from him. One might argue that by opening up the whole debate and having lobbyists come along, we were really opening up a can of worms. I thought the thing had got bigger and bigger and bigger, causing more and more concern and suspicion about Members of Parliament, therefore we had to do it.'

Lobbyists and politicians blamed each other for the lax climate of the 1980s. Arthur Butler, who had worked in the business for decades and knew the celebrated Commander Powell, feels that the committee was run by the friends of the people who were doing nicely and that it was very reluctant to upset the applecart. Greer also believed that it was manipulated by the party whips for political purposes:

> It is very useful for the party whips to make sure the Chairman and one or two other people on the committee are prepared to listen to you: 'Look, don't push this one too far, this could be embarrassing, this could be difficult, so I suggest you take this line.' Now of course at the end of the day it is up to the Chairman as to whether he accepts that influence.

Evidence that the whips were familiar with talking to Johnson-Smith about the committee's business was disclosed in 1996, with the publication of the 'Willetts note' written by the whip David Willetts in 1994 referring to the Chairman as 'wanting our advice'. The former Conservative MP Matthew Parris considered that it was possible that the whips had offered John Browne a kind of plea bargain in which a shorter suspension would be traded for Browne leaving quietly at the next election: 'these things happen all the time'.

The Select Committee's consideration of the wider issues involved with lobbying and the variety of interests that may or may not be liable for declaration was a meandering affair. Douglas Smith was called to give evidence on several occasions and, as he says: 'It went on and on and on discussing the issues and it reached no real conclusions whatsoever because the majority of Members did not want it to and neither did the lobbyists. It was on a long voyage out to sea with no conclusion in sight.'

Most politicians during the 1980s were not interested in reforming and regulating the system. The lobbyists, including Ian Greer, were more concerned by the issues and suggested on several occasions that registration and a professional code of conduct would be a good idea. The old-style lobbyist, Arthur Butler, was ridiculed for suggesting the registration of professional lobbyists in exchange for allowing them access to the facilities of the Palace of Westminster on an official basis. A fellow lobbyist scornfully told Butler that if he needed lessons in how to get around the Commons bars, he would gladly oblige.

A few Labour MPs also found the Select Committee a stifling environment. Bob Cryer, a left-wing MP who served on the committee, was proud to be a troublemaker. He regarded the fact that other members of the committee had commercial interests meant that they were compromised and unable to deal with the situation. He was particularly incensed at the fact that Sir Marcus Fox controlled the Committee of Selection which governed the allocation of MPs to Select Committees, while running Westminster Communications. Dale Campbell-Savours was also impatient with the way the committee operated, but with the exception of the investigation of John Browne in 1990 it ambled at a slow pace and took an indulgent view of the unfortunate Members who came within its purview. The wilful vagueness of some MPs in choosing what to declare led to a revision of the 1975 rule to clarify the phrase requiring registration of any material benefits 'which might be thought to affect his actions, speeches or vote in Parliament'. The new version, proposed in early 1992 and enacted in 1994, replaced this with 'which might *reasonably be thought by others* to influence his actions, speeches or votes in Parliament'.

*

The lobbying boom of the 1980s and the unethical conduct which was associated with it is largely a Conservative story. The first Register of Members' Interests of the 1992–97 Parliament was published in January 1993 and showed that 60 per cent of backbench Tories had paid consultancies with outside firms, compared with less than 10 per cent of the Parliamentary Labour Party. Half of backbench Tories were company directors; only twelve Labour MPs were similarly employed. Labour and Alliance MPs were massively outnumbered and lacked political influence; their opinions had next to no effect on public policy and were therefore of no interest to the clients of lobbying firms. Before 1987 Ian Greer Associates had virtually ignored the Opposition parties but, realizing that Labour in particular was recovering from its nadir of 1983, Greer moved to build relations with Labour and Liberal MPs. He gave donations to the constituency campaigns of people he personally admired, such as Chris Smith and Alan Beith, and established a Labour presence on the Board of IGA through Baroness

Turner. Most lobbying firms hedged their bets by inviting at least token Opposition representatives to sponsored events and having some pro-Labour employees, but the overwhelming direction of the efforts of lobbyists was towards the Conservative government.

There were also cultural reasons for the lack of involvement of Opposition MPs in the business. They resisted the political shift to the right that had generated a lot of the activity, particularly that involving privatized companies, and held fast to the ideological position that public service should be an end in itself rather than an opportunity to make money. In the Labour Party it had become much easier to deselect sitting MPs, and this gave an incentive for MPs to maintain ideological purity and a high standard of constituency service. The two Militant-supporting Labour MPs Dave Nellist and Terry Fields promised to be 'workers' MPs on workers' wages' and gave away the difference between their parliamentary salary and the average earnings of a skilled worker. They took no outside earnings. This austere example was not followed by other MPs, but the culture of the Parliamentary Labour Party was certainly not dominated by wealth and high living. Labour sleaze in the 1980s amounted to little more than a few MPs demanding upgrades from British Airways – according to Ian Greer this behaviour was sometimes accompanied by hypocritical comments about class barriers – and the grotesque figure of Robert Maxwell.

Labour's uneasy alliance with Maxwell is all too explicable. The party was in a desperate condition in the mid 1980s and, other than the Mirror Group papers, had no reliable supporters in the press. Even *The Guardian* was more interested in the Liberal–SDP Alliance than Labour. The populist right-wing politics of *The Sun* was perceived as a major advantage for the Conservatives, and if Labour lost the *Mirror*, its hopes of communicating its message to the electorate would be very slim. Maxwell had to be appeased because of his power. He was also very welcome as one of the few wealthy individuals who supported the Labour Party, both as a symbol that business success was not incompatible with British socialism and for the large donations to party funds he was able to make. Despite this, Neil Kinnock supped with a long spoon. Maxwell was never recommended for a peerage. The full scale of Maxwell's fraudulent dealings was only revealed after his death in 1991.

One crooked businessman who commanded a certain amount of fear and respect from controlling newspapers (as figures as dubious as Beaverbrook and Cecil King had in the past) did not – in any way – balance the culture that had developed among some Conservative MPs. Lobbying, consultancy and the greedy fringe were firmly established by the early 1990s. In the closing period of the 1987–92 Parliament, according to Douglas Smith:

The turning point was when the Conservatives in the 1990s were coming up to what could be an electoral defeat, and then of course a number of Conservative members started getting greedier and greedier because they perhaps saw the end of their careers looming and indeed one or two ministers left government in order to become consultants and make money before the election.

The surprising Conservative victory of 1992 seemed at first to indicate that this state of affairs could continue indefinitely. Several former Conservative MPs who had lost their seats returned as lobbyists. By the mid 1990s there was also an unprecedented number of former ministers on the government back benches. In political terms this caused trouble for the government: former ministers often had disappointed ambitions and compared their successors unfavourably to themselves. The profusion of former ministers also meant that increasing numbers of MPs had faced the sudden drop in earnings that had been disastrous for Reggie Maudling and people like him. It is unsurprising that company directorships and links with lobbyists multiplied in this climate.

The influence of Ian Greer Associates was also at its highest in the afterglow of the 1992 election. Ian Greer had supported John Major in the 1990 leadership contest, and lent him a car to help with a photo-opportunity. Greer also paid the £5,000 bill for the publication of his collected election speeches in 1992. The tenth birthday party of Ian Greer Associates at the National Portrait Gallery in February 1992 was a glittering occasion, with four Cabinet ministers plus the Prime Minister in attendance as well as a host of illustrious clients.

Five years later the firm would be out of business, the government would be disintegrating and Conservative MPs would be deprived of many of their lucrative outside interests. To add insult to injury, sex wasn't what it used to be either.

CHAPTER 9

'Family values'
1979-97

'Victorian values – those were the values when our country became great, not only internationally, but at home.'

Margaret Thatcher, 1983

The Conservative victory of 1979 was greeted with joy and relief by moral campaigners: it was hailed as the turning of the tide of permissiveness and the revival of moral leadership from government. The previous Conservative administration had enlarged the state's role in the economy and allowed liberal attitudes to sex and censorship to flourish. A truly Conservative government, it was argued, should roll back the permissive tide just as it should roll back the expansion of the state in the economy. The prophet of Thatcherism, Keith Joseph, had coupled his endorsement of monetarist economics in 1974 with an apocalyptic vision of social degeneration wrought by the breakdown of old-fashioned morality. In the pre-election period in 1978 and 1979 Thatcher herself flirted with the moral lobby, telling Mary Whitehouse that she would fight pornography and that sex education should be based on Christian principles. Whitehouse warned that if Labour was re-elected in 1979 'we shall see a steady deterioration in moral standards'.

Safely in power, the government actually did little to satisfy the moral lobby. Homosexuality was decriminalized in Scotland in 1980 (thanks to Robin Cook and Lord Boothby) and in Northern Ireland in 1982. Modest moves on licensing and regulating the window displays in sex shops, and a video classification system followed, rather than a crackdown on pornography. The Conservative government fought all the way to the House of Lords against Victoria Gillick's attempt to restrict the access of under-16s to contraception in 1984. The moral lobby had support in government, principally from Norman Tebbit, but its agenda was not for the most part translated into government legislation. Groups such as Mary Whitehouse's National Viewers' and Listeners' Association worked with sympathetic MPs such as Graham Bright and Winston Churchill to promote Private Members' Bills on issues such as 'sex and violence' on television. Sometimes the groups sponsored showings of controversial films at the House of Commons; these events were often well attended by MPs anxious to see in person just how disgusting all this filth really was.

There was a great internal debate within the Conservative right on the relationship between liberal economics and liberal social attitudes. A private-sector economy was advocated not only on the grounds of greater economic efficiency but also because state intervention was held to be a threat to personal freedom. Some on the right, such as Michael Brown and Alan Duncan, felt that the proposition that the government should stay out of the boardroom, but still take an interest in what went on in the bedroom, was inconsistent. Their answer was to embrace libertarianism, and argue that government regulation of private life was just as much an invasion of personal freedom as economic regulation.

Thatcherism was not a libertarian form of Conservatism; although most libertarian Conservatives considered themselves Thatcherite the bulk of her supporters remained fairly traditional on social and sexual issues. The government itself regarded the moralizing right as an outside pressure group to be balanced against others and bought off where necessary with gestures that were as cheap as possible. Thatcher's home secretaries, like Heath's, were broadly liberal figures. Douglas Hurd and Willie Whitelaw showed bravery similar to that of Maudling in confronting the massed ranks of the party conference demanding moral lectures, hanging and flogging (except between consenting adults). Similarly, health and education policy were only affected at the margins by the social conservatives.

It was just as well that the government did not decide to start a moral crusade, because by the early 1980s Conservative MPs were privately enjoying the benefits of the permissive society that some of their colleagues condemned. Extra-marital affairs were probably as widespread as they have ever been, in society in general and among the rank and file of Conservative MPs. Very few of these MPs' relationships ever came to public attention. An MP openly socializing with his mistress in the bars of the Palace of Westminster would naturally meet many lobby journalists and MPs from opposing political parties, but the rules of discretion and friendship would stop anything reaching the public in recognizable form. The more mischievous journalists would write coded references which were intelligible only to those already in the know, as a joke and a reminder of how much politicians depend on the ability of political journalists not to tell tales. The only time that silence about an MP's private activities in Westminster was broken concerned the eccentric left-wing MP for Leith, Ron Brown, in 1988. On the day that the Labour whip was withdrawn, another MP told newspapers about an incident in the showers involving Brown and his secretary.

The Conservatives also benefited from the very close relationship between the press and the Thatcher government, cemented by a scattering of honours and the defeat of the Fleet Street unions. The senior managers of the papers were wholehearted believers in the Thatcher political project, and she took care to keep them in touch. The links between the press and the Tories helped to deflect scandals. Michael Dobbs was Conservative Chief of Staff in 1987 and part of his job involved working with the press: 'We established two-way communication between the media and Central Office. We got quite a lot of early warning of storms brewing because many of these stories develop over a long period of time.'

Advance warning was useful because newspapers usually needed to do some work to get enough proof to print the story, and if a politician changed his habits for a while the threat would go away. There was often a long lead time between someone being gossiped about and that person being set up to establish proof about his activities, in which there was the opportunity to stop or hinder the investigation. In one case, Michael Dobbs learned that a Conservative politician was under threat and took the step of 'explaining what was being said about him and making sure that he added no fuel to the fire – that he was sensible and behaved himself. But above all that he didn't say anything and wasn't badgered into making a full and frank confession to the press.'

At election times there was heightened interest in the private lives of political figures on the part of the tabloid press. This partly reflected the internal politics of newspapers, when the investigation specialists who normally spent their time on showbusiness exposés were diverted into stories about the politicians who were suddenly the centre of attention. In general, though, trouble only happened when someone involved in the relationship chose to speak out or outside agencies became involved.

Such is the vanity and folly of Members of Parliament that they sometimes volunteer information about their sex lives to press conferences. Geoffrey Dickens, the Conservative MP for Huddersfield West, did so in March 1981, telling reporters that he was leaving his wife for a woman he had met at a tea dance. When this strange press conference ended he asked the journalists to wait while he telephoned his wife, who had not been previously informed about his decision. Two weeks later Dickens called another press conference to announce that he was going back to his wife. This behaviour was probably a misguided attempt to ensure that his campaign of naming paedophiles under parliamentary privilege was not derailed by tabloid exposure of his own private life. On the Labour side, MP George Galloway told a startled news conference in 1987, called to rebut claims about his financial arrangements, that 'I actually had sexual intercourse with some of the people' at a conference in Greece concerning the Horn of Africa.

*

The 1970s also saw a change in the role of women in politics, reflecting the successes of the women's movement and the changes in society that were taking place. Labour intellectuals had always had at least a notional commitment to sex equality, but the Conservatives had stressed traditional family values of a male breadwinner and a woman keeping house and children. The election of Margaret Thatcher as party leader in 1975 was a visible but misleading indication that the Conservatives were recognizing that social change was taking place. It was misleading because, for all Marcus Fox's efforts to broaden the class base of the party, little was done to encourage women to participate in politics and for the most part women retained the traditional role of holding constituency party office and working as secretaries.

Secretarial work, a traditional pattern of employment for women, was a pathway into the enclosed world of Westminster, which to this day is a male-dominated environment. Some Labour women, such as Jo Richardson (secretary for Labour MPs and Tom Driberg's successor as MP for Barking) and Marcia Williams had used the knowledge and contacts gained from routine secretarial work to move into active politics, but it was not so usual in the Conservative Party. Sara Keays, therefore, was something of a pioneer. She was interested in politics from an early age and worked for several Conservative MPs in the early 1970s in research and secretarial jobs, including Cecil Parkinson from June 1971. A little after this, she and Parkinson began an affair.

'MP and secretary have affair' has always been a cliché of an adulterous relationship between a man of some power and public reputation and a woman with illusions or ambitions. The relationship between Keays and Parkinson involved stronger feelings than most such dalliances, and was also conducted relatively discreetly by Westminster standards.

Keays worked for Parkinson until 1979, when she found a job at the European Commission in Brussels. She and Parkinson tried to end the relationship but could not make their resolution stick, and instead Parkinson offered to marry her in late 1979. However, the next year Parkinson decided that he could not leave his wife and told Keays that they could not marry. In 1982 she decided that she finally had to get her proper political career started, and applied for the Bermondsey constituency where she lived. She did not get the chance to drink from that particular poisoned chalice – Bermondsey Tories were thin on the ground and the by-election in the seat in February 1983 was a vicious affair – but she joined the list of approved candidates and seemed to stand a reasonable chance of a seat.

Parkinson had long since moved on from the political foothills Keays was climbing. He was appointed to the Thatcher Cabinet in 1981 as Paymaster-General and in 1982 became Conservative Party Chairman, a post he occupied when the party won its greatest postwar victory, in June 1983. But his triumph was marred by the knowledge that he had made Sara Keays pregnant and she was intending to have the child.

Parkinson's adultery was not considered reason enough for his dismissal.

He eventually admitted to Thatcher on election day 1983 that he had been having an affair with Keays. According to Thatcher, 'this gave me pause. But I did not immediately decide that it was an insuperable obstacle to his becoming Foreign Secretary.' She only decided that he could not be appointed Foreign Secretary when Keays's father wrote to her telling her that his daughter was pregnant by Parkinson. Instead, Parkinson was appointed to be Secretary of State for Trade and Industry, 'a less senior and less sensitive post'. Until September 1983 he combined this with the post of Conservative Party Chairman.

The pregnancy was becoming the currency of Westminster and Fleet Street gossip by summer 1983, and at the start of the Conservative Party conference in Blackpool, Parkinson issued a statement admitting the affair and the pregnancy, and saying that he would not divorce but would of course make provision for the Keays family. Parkinson's resignation at the end of the conference was the result of Keays' unwillingness to play the traditional game by keeping her counsel. She was angry with Parkinson's behaviour, which she considered selfish, and with the sympathy he had been shown during the conference week. She decided instead to tell her story in an interview to *The Times*, and Parkinson resigned under the impact of the adverse publicity.

Parkinson was restored to the Cabinet in 1987–90, and had a surprising Indian summer of his political career in 1997–98 when he was made Conservative Party Chairman again.

Ironically, Parkinson had been punished for breaking promises he made to his mistress and staying with his wife. MPs such as Nigel Lawson, who broke marital vows by leaving their wife and marrying the mistress, excited little comment. Margaret Thatcher had no desire to stigmatize divorce, having herself married a divorced man, and her Cabinet after Parkinson's resignation in October 1983 contained a majority of divorced ministers. Thatcher generally averted her eyes from the sexual peccadilloes of her colleagues, having a rather proper view that it was a private matter and not to be broadcast by an intrusive media – or indeed, in the case of people coming out as gay, by the individual concerned. This did not amount to a pledge to defend anyone who was caught out by tabloid disclosures.

Most ministers, in reflective moments, knew that the pressure of a political career was itself damaging to marital stability. Human relationships have never been as simple as the sloganizing about family values maintained. The party leadership was left with the difficult task of steering a path between moralizing – and risking accusations of hypocrisy – and abandoning an ideological theme that struck a deep chord with the party membership and the press.

The issue of homosexuality aroused even more contradictions than infidelity and divorce. If Thatcher herself had any distaste for homosexuality it did not interfere with ministerial appointments; several members of her Cabinets were homosexuals. There was a considerable number of gay MPs in the party, including Michael Brown. Brown recalls that 'there was a very friendly tolerance, providing you made clear your disposition to the Chief Whip immediately. There was a desire to maintain the conspiracy of silence, which most of the newspapers were prepared to engage in as well.'

Matthew Parris, a Conservative MP from 1979 to 1986, came as close as any Tory in the 1980s to coming out. He made a brief heartfelt speech during the debate on gay law in Northern Ireland in which he declared that he felt 'deeply, strongly and personally' about the issue. On another occasion he showed the Chief Whip, Michael Jopling, a speech which came close to admitting his sexuality: 'He told me he didn't believe in God but hadn't ever found it necessary to inform his wife, his family, his constituency association and certainly not the press. He then poured me a whisky and left it at that.' The conspiracy of silence was enforced without the word 'homosexual' crossing anyone's lips.

Homosexuality was also a fact of life in the younger echelons of the party. By the early 1980s the Conservative Research Department, based at Old Queen Street, was reputed to be a hotbed of exotic gay sexuality. Michael Gove, in his biography of Michael Portillo, described the louche climate of the CRD in the late 1970s: 'The influence of those desk officers who were gay permeated the atmosphere of the place. One contemporary of Portillo's remembers raucous talk about buggery after hours in which even the most vigorously heterosexual would join.' The CRD had much in common with the homosexual milieu of the high Tories of Cambridge from which Portillo had recently graduated.

However, libertarianism and good old-fashioned decadence were minority strands within the broad coalition of Thatcherism. Her electoral appeal was widely reputed to be based on an appeal to the materialism of skilled working-class formerly Labour voters ('C2s' in market research jargon), who had aspirations to own their own homes and build a good standard of living. In the 1980s the Conservatives continued to gain ground in places such as Stevenage and Basildon where many of these voters lived. The Thatcherite C2s also tended to be strongly traditional in their attitudes to sexual morality, in particular to homosexuality. Although much of this sociological analysis was very crude (for instance, C2s are concentrated in safe Labour seats like Wigan as well as the new towns) there was enough to it, and it was so widely believed, that it affected the attitudes of politicians and the media.

The newspaper of the Thatcherite aspiring working class was *The Sun*. The Murdoch paper was a crucial supporter of the right-wing economics and nationalism of the Thatcher government. It was also strongly hostile to homosexuals, with repeated slurs in its news and editorial coverage and even in cartoons. The editor, Kelvin MacKenzie, personally disliked gays and had a rich fund of abusive names for them, although headlines were restricted to the relatively tame 'poofter' and 'queer'. Most of the rest of the Conservative press shared the opinions of *The Sun*, although they were usually written in more restrained language.

The Labour candidate in the Bermondsey by-election in 1983, Peter Tatchell, was hounded over his homosexuality by the tabloid press and supporters of a so-called 'Real Labour' candidate opposing him. He lost the election on a massive swing, although the victorious Liberal Simon Hughes was himself a supporter of gay rights.

'Gay MP' stories were firmly established as good tabloid stories by the 1980s, although the MPs exposed were still the relatively unfortunate who had talkative partners or brushes with the police. Labour MP Allan Roberts appeared in the *News of the World* in 1981 after a visit to a sado-masochistic gay club in Berlin but survived the bad publicity. A Conservative MP, Keith Hampson, was arrested in a gay strip club in Soho after a police *agent provocateur* claimed to have been groped. Hampson fought the charges in a highly publicized trial and, after the jury failed to agree a verdict, he was declared not guilty. The exposure of these police practices caused disquiet because it seemed neither fair play nor an effective use of police resources for 'pretty police' to stand around in gay bars waiting for someone to make a pass at them. The Conservative whips tried to protect their charges as far as possible from press exposure when any potential trouble arose, but also warned them, as Michael Brown says, that they should not go to 'funny clubs' or cruise in public places.

The case of Harvey Proctor illustrates the hostility between the press and Conservative homosexuals in the 1980s. He had gained Basildon in 1979 and had extreme right-wing views on immigration and race issues that many of his constituents shared. In 1983 the seat was divided by the Boundary Commission and he was selected for the safer half, now named Billericay. Disaster hit in 1986 when the *People* published allegations by rent boys that Proctor enjoyed spanking young men, and turned over their evidence to the police. Proctor was arrested in April 1987 and pleaded guilty to four charges of 'gross indecency' and resigned renomination for the seat just before the June 1987 election.

The public interest dimension to the exposure of Proctor is not easy to detect. He had tried to establish that his sexual partners were of the age of consent (then twenty-one for homosexuals) and they were all willing and experienced. He did not meet them in public toilets but in the privacy of his flat. Neither had he been hypocritical by voting or speaking against gay rights. Proctor was given support by sixteen colleagues on the Conservative benches who invested money in a shirt shop he founded after leaving the Commons. Had his views on other matters been more palatable he might have gained more general sympathy; as Matthew Parris says, he was regarded as dangerously right-wing and was not part of the parliamentary 'club'. Even so, had he been exposed in a more tolerant climate than the 1980s the story would not have received such notoriety.

Coverage of AIDS had worsened the situation. In spring 1985 panic broke out in the British press about the disease, and the government was faced with the need to control the spread of the HIV virus and simultaneously to dispel the scares that had been circulating about how the disease could be transmitted.

The Conservatives were split between the moral right and much of the press on one hand, and health policy recommendations on the other. Some Conservative backbenchers, such as Geoffrey Dickens, thought that reversing the 1967 Act legalizing homosexuality was the answer. The Conservative Family Campaign's response to AIDS was a programme of national testing, isolation of those suffering from the disease, criminalizing homosexuality and, most astonishingly of all, removing funding from the Terrence Higgins Trust (which cared for and supported people with AIDS) and the Family Planning Association (which promoted the use of condoms). Instead, funding should go to promoting family values and 'offering Christian counselling to persuade homosexuals to desist'.

This manifesto and the more moderately phrased ideas of church leaders were rejected by Norman Fowler, then Secretary of State for Health and Social Security. The urgency of the situation was such that a moral message was impracticable; Fowler and the DHSS decided to encourage the use of condoms. Looking in the other direction when sexual issues arose was no longer possible, and health ministers received a crash course in some of the more exotic manifestations of human sexuality. John Patten had to be told what 'fisting' entailed; he could probably have requested a Research Department briefing note on the practice.

In the mid 1980s press hostility to gays reached a height not seen since the witch hunts of the 1950s. It was part of a political attack on the 'loony left' of the Labour Party in control of town halls in London, designed to suggest that Labour was the party of racial and sexual minorities rather than 'normal' people.

The left in the early 1980s, particularly in London, had become interested in the politics of the personal, including the sexual. Campaigns such as the women's movement and gay liberation had taken place outside the party structure in the 1970s, but by the 1980s sections of the Labour Party were following this path. Discrimination against women and homosexuals was seen as part of the more general oppressive nature of society. Just as the working class at the turn of the century had liberated itself through union activity, women were urged to cast off servility and homosexuals cast off the shame that society demanded they feel. The pioneer was the Greater

London Council (GLC) under Ken Livingstone from 1981 to 1986. Grants were given to organizations representing women and minorities and the council's own employment policies were overhauled to reflect the new priority given to equality. Other London boroughs followed, particularly after the 1986 local elections.

The GLC had two advantages in its pursuit of equality. One was the ability of Ken Livingstone and a skilled public relations department to present the policies in an appealing way. The other was that the GLC was not an education authority. New left authorities such as Ealing and Haringey did not have these advantages and the 'loony left' was born. It was at first a press campaign. The education angle was an opportunity to accuse the local authorities of exposing pupils to 'homosexual propaganda' and the alleged risks of gays in the teaching profession. But it was too rewarding a campaign for the Conservatives, under Norman Tebbit's chairmanship, to ignore. A delegate was cheered by the 1985 Conservative conference for commenting 'If you want a queer for a neighbour, vote Labour.' It was an echo of an ugly slogan used against racial minorities in 1964. Posters appeared at the 1987 election of a book called *Young, Gay and Proud* under the slogan 'Is this Labour's idea of a comprehensive education?' By the time of the Greenwich by-election in February 1987 the Labour leadership realized that the 'lesbian and gay rights issue is costing us dear, particularly among the pensioners'. Against the national trend of a small swing to Labour, the party lost three seats to the Conservatives in London in the June 1987 election. It appeared that Labour's identification with gay rights was an easy target for the Conservatives.

The main legal result of the loony left campaign was Clause 28 of the Local Government Act 1988, which outlawed the 'promotion of homosexuality' by education authorities. Part of the clause was prompted specifically by a tabloid furore about a teaching aid called *Jenny Lives with Eric and Martin* designed to help teachers describe the increasingly complicated situation of families in the 1980s. The clause forbade the depiction of 'pretended family relationships' between homosexuals. The clause was important not so much for its actual content, but as an official act of stigmatizing gays. Only three Conservative MPs rebelled against it, including Michael Brown who was aware that there would have been a huge effort to 'out' him if he took any other line.

The 1987 election and the clause polarized the parties on the issue of gay rights. Labour and the Liberal/SDP Alliance put equal rights and protection from discrimination on an official party footing. Labour had an openly gay MP, Chris Smith, in a marginal seat in London. Smith 'came out' in 1984, becoming only the second homosexual MP voluntarily to admit the fact (the first was Maureen Colquhoun, Labour MP for Northampton North 1974–79).

The Conservatives, despite the gay presence among their MPs and their officials, seemed virtually united against conceding legal equality and had a militant fringe which favoured putting homosexuals in prison. Clause 28 was a high point of the campaign, but throughout the 1980s Conservative rhetoric if not policy emphasized traditional morality and family values.

In retrospect the collapse of a Conservative campaign with moralizing overtones (Back to Basics) after a vigorous attack from the press had been on the cards for some years. Alongside the increasingly moralistic speeches of Conservative ministers in the late 1980s there was a rash – there is no better word – of 'kiss and tell' stories in the tabloid press. The rules of 'bonk journalism' as it was more accurately described required a moderately famous person, although a vicar or an army officer would do if necessary, and a talkative former lover or prostitute to tell tales on him (the male pronoun is used advisedly). The account would be spiced up with details, true or false, of superhuman feats of sexual endurance, or imaginative uses of foodstuffs, or whatever else would amuse newspaper readers. Bonk stories would be worth at least a few thousand to the source, often enough to make a substantial difference to their lives.

The first phase came to a halt in December 1988 when *The Sun*, having been sold a pack of lies about Elton John, paid out £1 million in a libel settlement. Politicians generally got away quite lightly from this gold rush, which was totally outside the control of the Westminster journalistic fraternity. The only significant brush with this sort of manufactured scandal was the Pamella Bordes affair of 1989 when a call girl was found to have been employed by a right-wing Tory MP as a Commons researcher. There was less to the tale than met the eye, and Bordes probably had more newspaper editors than MPs among her admirers. However, the 'bonk journalism' boom had created its own infrastructure of journalists and publicists which could be turned, when the time came, on politicians.

Bonk journalism was regarded by some MPs, even those with no personal stake in the matter, as a gross infringement of privacy with no public interest, and prompted the issue of whether the existing system of self-regulation and the libel laws was doing enough to protect the privacy of public figures, or even ordinary people. Conservative MP Bill Cash suggested a Privacy Bill in 1988, and in April 1989 the government set up the Calcutt Inquiry into the conduct of the press. The Calcutt Report in 1990 recommended the press to replace the toothless Press Council with a more powerful Press Complaints Commission (PCC) to make self-regulation work within eighteen months, or else statutory regulation should be considered. The hint was taken, the PCC established and a code of conduct drawn up, but self-regulation remained under review.

The temptation to use private matters for political purposes was very great in the run-up to the 1992 election. Labour was narrowly ahead in many opinion polls in 1991 and early 1992 and all parties were looking for any extra advantage they could find. The Conservatives in particular had started to paddle in very dangerous waters.

The first victim of the 1992 sleaze season was Paddy Ashdown, the Liberal Democrat leader from 1988 to 1999. A burglar broke into the offices of Ashdown's solicitors and stole a document prepared in 1990 in which Ashdown described an affair he and his secretary, Tricia Howard, had conducted a few years earlier. Ashdown had been concerned about being named in Howard's divorce proceedings and had placed his account on private record. A Brighton criminal, Simon Berkowitz, hawked the document to the tabloids, who would not use it because of the criminal way it had been acquired but felt free to make enquiries of Tricia Howard. Ashdown stalled publication of the story in England through injunctions but could not control the Scottish media. He decided that the best approach was to admit what had happened before rumours got out of hand, and called a press conference on 8 February 1992. Ashdown stoutly defended his right to privacy. He suffered a certain amount of ridicule, none as on target as *The Sun*'s headline 'It's Paddy Pantsdown!', but in general his candour was respected and he survived the fuss unscathed.

The Ashdown affair had been exposed in a sordid fashion by a criminal, but there were worrying political aspects to the way the story was propagated. Berkowitz had been a Conservative activist, and there were suspicions that Conservative Central Office had been involved in spreading rumours about Ashdown's sex life. There were confident predictions that the election campaign would be the closest fought and dirtiest in memory, or at least since 1974.

The implicit bargain between the parties about privacy came under most strain on the night of Saturday 4 April 1992. The media strategists of the two main parties waited nervously for the first editions of the Sunday tabloids, as rumours had circulated that day that the dirt might fly. It was reliably reported that a Conservative-supporting Sunday tabloid had a homosexual story about a senior Labour figure, but had been threatened into silence by a Labour tabloid with similar allegations about a Cabinet minister. Neither story saw print, to the relief of the individuals involved and probably both parties. The Conservatives went on to win the election.

Press regulation, including a second Calcutt committee, was given to the new Department of National Heritage created after the 1992 election. The Secretary of State, David Mellor, warned that journalists who invaded people's privacy were 'drinking in the last chance saloon'. Mellor was himself not persuaded by the case for a privacy law, but was arguing that the pressures might grow too great to resist. But Mellor's downfall paradoxically made a privacy law impossible.

The married minister had been having an affair with an actress, Antonia de Sancha, which was exposed in the *People* newspaper on 19 July 1992. A flimsy public interest defence was put on the story by Mellor's comment that he was too tired from having sex with de Sancha to concentrate on a speech he was making. His ministerial speeches were not noticeably poorer than those made by his colleagues, and this line was not taken seriously. John Major gave Mellor a display of support by making a public appearance with him at a reception and briefing the press to the effect that Mellor's affair was a private matter and nothing whatsoever to do with his ministerial job.

Mellor's defence was also made through a cringemaking photo opportunity with his family. Matthew Parris wondered at the contradictions of the 'civilized nature of his opinions combined with an extraordinary insensitivity of his human relationships'. To hostile observers like the publicist Max Clifford it was simply nauseating. Mellor's father-in-law voiced what was to be a common objection to having ministers with complicated private lives in government: 'If he'll cheat on our girl he'll cheat on the country.' The argument ran that dishonesty and unreliability are indivisible qualities that are found throughout a person's character like lettering in a stick of rock.

There is not really a debate on whether this is true; it is a proposition one either accepts or does not, and there is little that argument can do to change minds. In applying the doctrine to the case of David Mellor, it was being carried further than it had ever been before. Even at the time of the Profumo affair it was accepted only by a minority. Mellor's affair, however, did not bring him down, and over the summer of 1992 he seemed to recover from the setback.

In September 1992 the story returned to haunt Mellor, with de Sancha's story as mediated by Max Clifford appearing in *The Sun*. The first phase of the publicity had been unpleasant for de Sancha as well as Mellor and she had been introduced to the publicist to see if she could salvage something from the affair. More than in July, Mellor became a laughing stock as tales of toe-sucking and the minister scoring in a Chelsea shirt were told and retold. The details were, to put it kindly, variations on a theme of truth rather than strictly to be believed.

Then disaster struck at a libel hearing in the case of Mona Bauwens. Bauwens, the daughter of a leading member of the Palestine National Council, was a friend of Mellor who had lent his family a villa in Spain in summer 1990. George Carman, appearing for the defence of the *People*, which had published the story, compared Mellor's acceptance of such hospitality at a time when Palestinian leaders were internationally isolated for failing to condemn Iraq's invasion of Kuwait to the behaviour of an ostrich which 'puts its head in the sand and thereby exposes his thinking parts'.

The cumulative damage to Mellor eroded his support within the

Parliamentary Conservative Party. His abrasive personal manner, and his outspoken criticism of Israel's treatment of the Palestinians, had made enemies, and the collapse of the government's economic policy on 16 September 1992 ('Black Wednesday') left Tory MPs divided and fractious. Mellor learned that Marcus Fox, as Chairman of the backbench 1922 committee, was about to report to John Major that the game was up, and duly quit.

Mellor, as with most ministerial resignations, did not resign because of anything in particular he had done but because he had lost the confidence of enough of his fellow MPs. The Conservative Party was in such a poor state for nearly all of the 1992–97 Parliament that the slightest whiff of press interest in someone's private life seemed to be enough to cause a fatal slippage of support. The press had decisively won the first battle in the war between the Tories and the media from 1992 to 1997.

It was no longer in the commercial interest of the press to push out Conservative propaganda that was increasingly striking a grating note with readers. The considerable number of Thatcherite irreconcilables scattered throughout the media delighted in attacking the government from the right on its policies over Europe, Ireland and taxation, and pouring scorn on John Major. Many journalists were bored with the same old faces in government. The climate had changed, and even minor slip-ups like the Chancellor's late payment of his credit card bill were seized upon as a chance to take a swing at the government. There had been nothing like it since the vendetta against Harold Wilson in 1974–76.

The failure to give a clear steer to the press was, according to Michael Dobbs (who had returned to Central Office in 1994), a symptom of a more general failure of will and direction that the Conservatives suffered in the 1990s: 'Once you begin to lose faith in your own ideals, or lose track through exhaustion, then everything else begins to unravel. The Conservative Party lost faith in itself and what it believed, and once that happened everything got worse.'

The government's main attempt to reconnect with the Conservative faith was a disaster. The Conservatives limped into their October 1993 conference after a year of divisive and tedious votes on the Maastricht Treaty. A new theme was needed to bind the party's wounds and recapture the imagination of the voters who had been alienated since Black Wednesday. Major's Downing Street Policy Unit had been unable to produce a single organizing theme to the next stage of the government's activities and Major was increasingly drawn to the attractions of staking out a traditional Conservative position. This involved such old conference floor favourites as traditional teaching methods, 'toughness' on crime and the dangers of 'dependency' and 'welfare scroungers'. A debate had already taken place within the Major retinue about where 'personal morality' fitted in, with muddled results. Major himself was never much of a moralizer; his well-received 'Back to Basics' speech contained a line disavowing the idea that it was for governments to make people good. However, enough of a prescriptive line on how people should behave remained to give the speech a moralizing flavour.

The moral dimension was increased by the atmosphere in which Major made his call to get Back to Basics. The Cabinet right had been greeted with delight on the conference floor and in fringe meetings as they called for a return to traditional values. Single-parent families were criticized by Michael Howard as leading to social breakdown, and foreigners crudely mocked by Peter Lilley. Tim Collins, the party's director of communications, briefed the press about Major's own speech in a fashion that led to headlines about a 'war on permissiveness' and 'making liberalism a dirty word like socialism'. Matthew Parris attended the infamous briefing as a journalist:

Immediately Tim got questions on morality. And surprisingly Tim Collins said, 'Yes, you can read it in that way. It is about personal morality. It's about families.' He made it clear that it was personal morality that the Prime Minister was talking about just as much as structures of government.

The press, including Parris, were astounded that the Conservatives had not considered the consequences, although there was a delay before Back to Basics blew up in the government's face. Strangely, that very conference was enlivened by revelations about the private life of Steven Norris, the junior Transport Minister. His marriage had broken up and the tabloid press gleefully went on a hunt for Norris mistresses. The generally accepted total was five, which led to ribald comments about the minister's sexual prowess and timetabling skills, although the relationships had not actually all taken place at the same time.

Norris recalled a few years later that it was almost exclusively a tabloid story, with only two small items in broadsheets and no coverage on the main BBC or ITN bulletins. Most of the media thought that the minister and the mistresses was not a proper story, and the fact that one of the famous five was Sheila Gunn, a parliamentary journalist for *The Times*, no doubt helped at this end of the market. Norris noted with amusement that one of the pieces was written by Julie Kirkbride, a journalist for *The Daily Telegraph* who was a close friend of one Tory MP, Stephen Milligan, and later married another, Andrew MacKay. It was a bit too incestuous for comfort. Norris survived as a minister, mainly because his private life reflected his public image. As Matthew Parris says: 'Many of the people who got away with it, like Tom Driberg and Alan Clark as well as Steven Norris, do so by a certain candour, a publicly acknowledged roguishness. They haven't waved their finger at us. We can feel we've already been taken into their confidence, we haven't been betrayed.'

Central Office believed that Back to Basics had struck a chord with the voters and were enthusiastic about campaigning on it. There were certain attractions to painting Labour as the party of the 1960s – tower blocks, progressive education, drugs, pornography and family breakdown. 'Back to Basics means expecting and respecting personal morality' wrote the Downing Street Policy Unit.

The Conservative whips, by contrast, had an uneasy, sick feeling that it was a fiasco in the making. It was an excuse for the press to hunt down erring Tory MPs, and they knew that there was no shortage of potentially embarrassing stories that could now see the light of day. Exposure could be easily justified on the grounds that the targets had been hypocritical in allying themselves with such a campaign. Back to Basics was a product of the professionalization of politics which had taken place in the last twenty years. Specialization in media relations, opinion polling or communication strategy had resulted in knowledge of human nature falling outside the policy process and being ignored.

The first blow came on Boxing Day 1993 when a junior environment minister, Tim Yeo, was exposed in the *News of the World* as the father of a child by a London Conservative activist, Julia Stent. The source of the story was not Stent, Yeo's wife or even Yeo himself, who all regarded it as private; it was not 'kiss and tell' but a newspaper investigation of a politician's private life.

Tim Yeo was on record as having regretted the incidence of single-parent families, although his record was generally on the tolerant side of the Conservative Party. Having created a single-parent family, he was open to criticism for belonging to a 'Back to Basics' government. He was labelled a hypocrite in some newspapers and some Conservatives agreed.

Some members of John Major's Downing Street staff, in hindsight, thought the only way of saving the government's credibility was to have sacked Yeo as soon as the allegations were publicized. But the Chief Whip and the Prime Minister decided to defend Yeo when they first heard that the *News of the World* had the story. Not unreasonably, they thought that if Ashdown and Norris had been able to ride out stories about their private lives it should be possible for Yeo to stay on and the story to fade away over the Christmas holiday. Yeo went on a family holiday to the Seychelles, but his decision was unfortunately seen as arrogant and lost him some support. He was openly attacked by the populist right-wing Tory MP for Welwyn-Hatfield, David Evans, who said that the morality of 'people bonking their way around London' could not be excused.

The struggle to save Yeo was fatally undermined by a revolt within his constituency, Suffolk South. On 4 January 1994 he failed to receive the unqualified support of his constituency association officers for remaining a minister, and some local activists wanted him to resign the seat as well. On 5 January he resigned, having been informed that the constituency revolt had lost him the Prime Minister's support.

As with Mellor, the irresolution of the Prime Minister was more damaging than any particular decisions he made. Major had appeared to take the extraordinary step of delegating the final say over ministerial appointments to a small committee of local Tory activists, whose views did not even represent the Suffolk South executive committee. Conservative constituency party officers have a bad reputation in political folklore, such as the Michael Dobbs novel *Goodfellowe MP*, as consisting of the most prim and joyless elements of small town society, a view that was confirmed when the spotlight shone on Suffolk South. The fall of Yeo confirmed that, whatever Major's intentions, he had lost control over who could sit in the government to the newspapers and the most intolerant parts of his own party. Major denied that he had intended Back to Basics had anything to do with 'personal morality' – a curious aspect of the Back to Basics period was the equation of sexual behaviour with 'personal morality' – but the damage had been done. It was open season.

Stories about two obscure backbench Tory MPs, David Ashby and Gary Waller, followed. Ashby had particularly good reason to feel aggrieved. Thanks to indiscreet comments from his wife and a mix-up over hotel accommodation in France he was portrayed as a homosexual. He denied that this was the case, and even if it had been Ashby had been outspokenly liberal about homosexuality and not a hypocrite. He took out a libel action against *The Sunday Times* and lost. He did not contest his highly marginal seat at the 1997 election. Despite the farcical aspects of Ashby's troubles, he paid a heavy financial, personal and political price for briefly amusing the nation and was deeply hurt by the affair. Waller, not married but in a long-term relationship, had a child by his mistress but for a short time joined a dating agency as well. As scandals go, it was very small beer.

Although there was little in individual cases like these, it added up to a frenzied atmosphere in January 1994. Rumours circulated but were never proved or printed – in the mainstream media – about the sexuality of Cabinet ministers, including Michael Portillo. This torrid period established 'sleaze' as a factor in British politics. It was a convenient expression, covering a multitude of sins from sexual exuberance to outright financial corruption. In the public mind it established a thread running through all the damaging stories about the conduct of Conservative politicians. 'Sleaze' was later officially defined by Lord Nolan as 'a pervasive atmosphere ... in which sexual, financial and governmental misconduct were indifferently linked'. It was a useful word for the media. Its lack of precision meant that it could not attract libel writs the way the word 'corrupt' could, and it was pleasantly onomatopoeic. Jeremy Hanley, Conservative Party Chairman 1994–95, recalls: 'A BBC radio correspondent told me how there was a bet going on between all the reporters as to who could say the word the longest. They would talk about the Tory party and sleeeaaaze. It eventually went into two or three syllables.'

The cumulative effect of the cascade of sleaze in early 1994 was to send the Conservatives spiralling down in the polls again, as the electorate gained the impression that the Conservatives were enjoying themselves while giving lectures to the rest of the population. The Parliamentary Conservative Party's morale plunged and divisions broke out between moralizers and MPs despairing at the damage that Back to Basics had caused.

There were some individual tragedies caught up in the Back to Basics campaign. In January Lord Caithness resigned as Minister for Aviation and Shipping after his wife's suicide over his relationship with another woman. In February Stephen Milligan, the MP for Eastleigh, who was one of John Major's most loyal supporters in the 1992 intake of Conservative MPs and had a promising future, was found dead on his kitchen table, dressed only in stockings with a cord around his neck. Back to Basics did not long survive Milligan, and the theme had been dropped by the end of February. It lived on only in the person of 'Baxter Basics', a cartoon strip in *Viz* magazine about a sleazy MP.

The campaign was a searing experience for the ministers and Tory *apparatchiks* who had sought to politicize morality. Major himself fought shy of any further actions that could be construed as moralizing during the remainder of his time as Prime Minister, worrying about even the slightest family values component to any of his speeches or policies.

The end of the Back to Basics campaign had not strengthened the position of Conservative ministers whose private lives were exposed in the newspapers: according to a Tory adviser involved in the process 'eventually we ended up with a rather ruthless regime in which it became clear that defending ministers was a mug's game and it was better that they quit quickly'. This was a dangerous doctrine, because it seemed that unorthodox sexual behaviour was now officially a disqualification from ministerial office.

Michael Brown fell victim to the new regime in May 1994, when his relationship with a twenty-year-old man was publicized. Brown's sexuality had never been much of a secret at Westminster, and he had tentatively suggested when he was appointed a government whip in 1993 that he might come out. The suggestion was not well received by the Chief Whip or the Prime Minister. Brown's resignation was particularly ironic because his relationship would not have been a problem within a few months. In February 1994 the Commons decided to reduce the age of consent for gay men to eighteen. An amendment to reduce it to sixteen, proposed by Edwina Currie, was narrowly defeated.

Brown spoke openly about his sexuality later in 1994, becoming the first 'out' gay Tory MP. The roof did not fall in, but nobody joined him either. Although John Major had voted for eighteen rather than sixteen, he had called off the Tory campaign against homosexuals several years previously. Major's personal attitude to gays had been positive from an early age and his attitudes towards the social recognition of gay partnerships were far more liberal than was the norm for the Conservative Party. He abolished discriminatory security clearances for gays and welcomed the distinguished actor Sir Ian McKellen to Downing Street in 1991 to talk about gay issues.

The remainder of ministerial resignations over sexual conduct were for heterosexual adventures. Resignations over purely private affairs followed in the cases of Robert Hughes in March 1995, Richard Spring in April 1995 and Rod Richards in June 1996. Hughes had an extra-marital affair with a female constituent. One of Spring's partners in a three-in-a-bed session, delightfully enough a Sunday school teacher called Odette Nightingale, told the *News of the World* about the MP's sense of fun and his indiscreet gossip about ministers. He resigned, despite being unmarried. Rod Richards, an aggressively right-wing Tory, had been having an extra-marital affair.

As the 1997 election approached, the publicist Max Clifford waged a private campaign against the Conservatives. Clifford had emerged in the late 1980s as an agent for people wishing to sell their stories, including the sexual partners of famous people. His first venture into the political world was Pamella Bordes in 1989; in 1992 he represented Antonia de Sancha and sold imaginative stories about her sexual activities with Mellor. After Mellor, Clifford became known as the person to go to for any 'other halves' discontented with the behaviour of a Tory politician. Clifford was bitterly opposed to the Conservatives' policies on the National Health Service which he blamed for increasing his daughter's suffering from rheumatoid arthritis.

Clifford's weapon was sleaze. The climate of the last months of the Major government was so hostile to the Conservatives that Clifford's campaign struck a popular chord. As he says: 'I tried to do everything I could to get the word "sleaze" tied into the word "Conservative" and it worked.'

Clifford's first target was Jerry Hayes, the colourful Tory MP for Harlow. Clifford's client, a young Conservative called Paul Stone, alleged that he had conducted an affair with Hayes while under age. Hayes denied the allegations, and received considerable support as he was a consistent supporter of gay rights and an amiable man with many friends in the House. He lost his seat in 1997 although the swing against him was not unusually large. Although Clifford promised more revelations, and some Conservatives feared that Labour and Clifford had co-ordinated a stream of new scandals to be released over the weeks of the election campaign, only a trickle followed.

The first bombshell of the campaign involved a minor figure, the backbench MP for Beckenham Piers Merchant. Merchant had posed as a defender of family values but was photographed with a seventeen-year-old Soho nightclub hostess, Anna Cox, who had apparently developed an interest in grassroots Conservative politics in the London suburbs. *The Sun*'s photographers caught Merchant and Cox kissing in a park. Cox had, according to Max Clifford, contacted the publicist and told her story. The morning the story broke, John Gummer attempted to talk about the environment, with an image of some woodland as a backdrop to the Central Office press conference. He was faced with ribald jokes by journalists along the lines of 'Where's Piers Merchant?'

Merchant weathered the storm and secured the backing of his constituency association after telling them that Cox had some ideas for regenerating the Young Conservatives. Despite a huge swing to Labour, Merchant held his Beckenham seat in the May 1997 election. He then did something incredibly stupid. He resumed contact with Anna Cox, claiming that they were 'researching a book on tabloid intrusion', and spent the week of the 1997 Conservative conference with her in York and Darlington. The *Sunday Mirror* had been watching them, thanks to surveillance equipment loaned by a former friend of the pair. The paper splashed a story on 12 October about their 'four nights of passionate sex' – surely a better way to spend a week than among the despondent Tory faithful. Merchant resigned from Parliament two days later. A spokesman for the new Tory leader William Hague said that while the party was being more relaxed about sexual indiscretions, Hague would not tolerate hypocrisy or behaviour which brought the party into disrepute. The Tory leadership made no effort to dissuade Merchant from resigning. The book on tabloid intrusion has yet to appear.

*

'Back to Basics' and the sexual antics of the Tories during the last years of the long Conservative government were generally regarded as an amusing sideshow. Sex always sells newspapers, but it played only a minor part in the Conservative defeat of 1997. Public opinion distinguished between sex and the more serious financial irregularity and even corruption that was the 'cash for questions' scandal.

CHAPTER 10

Cash for questions 1987-97

'The press knocked on my immediate neighbour's door and said, "What does it feel like to live next door to a lobbyist?" as though one was a child molester or a serial killer.'

Ian Greer, 1999

Ian Greer Associates, quintessential lobbyists of the 1980s, acquired their most notorious client in October 1985: Mohamed Fayed. This contract would bring disaster to the lobbying firm and disgrace to the MPs involved – principally Tim Smith and Neil Hamilton – when the full story was told in 1994–97. It would fatally undermine public trust in the integrity of the Conservative Party, and end parliamentary self-regulation.

*

Mohamed Fayed is not a member of an old-established Egyptian family, despite his claims to the contrary. He and his brother Ali were in fact self-made businessmen who had built up a fortune in trade in the 1970s. He had always had a sentimental admiration for Britain and a desire to be British. In 1985 he had come close to achieving his dream by acquiring the House of Fraser retail group, which included one of the symbols of the British Establishment, the Knightsbridge department store Harrods.

The battle to take control of House of Fraser had been bitter, and the defeated bidder 'Tiny' Rowland was still not reconciled to losing. Fayed was under public attack in the pages of *The Observer*, which Rowland owned, and in Parliament. According to Michael Cole, who served as Fayed's spokesman from 1988 until 1998:

Rowland unleashed a campaign against Mohamed which turned into a very vicious personal vendetta. And it so happened that the Chairman of Lonrho was Sir Edward du Cann, one of the grandest of the Tory grandees. He was a man of great influence and there were very many MPs in the party who owed him – he'd been their mentor. Du Cann had no difficulty in finding plenty of friends who were prepared to attack Mohamed on a more or less daily basis through Questions and Early Day Motions.

Du Cann had succeeded Duncan Sandys as Chairman of Lonrho in 1984, a position which attracted a spectacular salary for less than onerous duties. His role at Lonrho was well known in Parliament and declared in the Register of Members' Interests, and in reality the Lonrho forces were not as well connected to the British Establishment as Fayed imagined. The company was still regarded with suspicion because of the 1970s scandal and the whiff of sulphur and brimstone that surrounded everything Tiny Rowland did. Du Cann's insistence on the importance of British ownership of important national business interests also did not chime with the free market values of the Thatcher government. Norman Tebbit, the Trade Secretary who allowed the Fayed takeover, thought it was none of the government's business who owned department stores – it was a matter for the shareholders.

Fayed, however, felt isolated and outgunned by the connections Rowland and du Cann were able to deploy against him. His own resources in Parliament amounted to a parliamentary adviser to House of Fraser, Sir Peter Hordern. Hordern was a gentlemanly Conservative MP who had never asked a parliamentary question on behalf of his employer. Nor did he make any effort to conceal the fact that he was linked with the company.

Fayed was impatient with the lack of an aggressive response to the Lonrho forces. He was pointed towards Ian Greer by Lord King, who had hired IGA for British Airways business. In a meeting at Fayed's residence, 60 Park Lane – close to where Sidney 'the Spider' Stanley had operated in the 1940s – Greer agreed to take on the contract for £25,000 (now worth £43,000) per annum. He would inform Fayed of parliamentary developments and attempt to make sure that his case was made. Fayed claims, but Greer denies, that the lobbyist told him that you had to rent an MP like a London taxi to speak on your behalf. As Michael Cole says:

Mohamed is a businessman. He's very familiar with the concept that professional men require their fees be they architects, lawyers, whatever, so it wasn't such a terrible shock when it was explained to him that these MPs would need to be recompensed for their parliamentary efforts on his behalf.

Fayed shared Greer's fascination with Parliament. Perhaps because Hordern refused to do it, Fayed set great store by having his MPs ask parliamentary questions on his behalf. Greer had doubts about whether this was an effective way of wielding influence, but Fayed believed in creating as much noise as possible in the House of Commons and never felt he was getting value for money. They had other differences. The fastidious Greer found Fayed's language crude and his attitude to those who worked on his behalf verging on bullying. In return, according to Michael Cole: 'I don't think [Fayed] ever had any respect for Greer. He regarded him as a necessary evil because he had to use any means that was available. He disapproved of his sexual proclivities and did not want me to see him or have anything to do with him.'

Fayed demanded that Greer organize 'processions in the Parliaments' on his behalf. Greer knew that would be counterproductive and instead assembled a more discreet lobby to rebut the Lonrho attack. Tiny Rowland was not a popular figure among Conservatives because of *The Observer*'s allegations about Mark Thatcher. The group consisted of Neil Hamilton, Tim Smith, Michael Grylls, Sir Andrew Bowden and Sir Peter Hordern. Hordern led delegations as he was the official consultant to House of Fraser, but was less involved in the parliamentary campaign and was cleared of misconduct. Bowden, like Grylls, was a Greer crony of long standing, but his participation in the campaign in 1987 was relatively brief. The campaign involved parliamentary questions, letters to and meetings with ministers. It also involved donations to the 1987 election campaign funds of several Members of Parliament.

Neil Hamilton was Greer's most famous recruit to the Fayed cause, and one of the most egregious and extreme products of the 1983 election, winning the safe Conservative seat of Tatton in Cheshire. As a student in Aberystwyth he had engaged in juvenile right-wing posturing, such as naming the student paper 'Feudal Times and Reactionary Herald', and his basic political position had not evolved greatly by the time he entered Parliament. He rather proudly states that:

My political opinions have hardly changed in the thirty-five years that I've been thinking and debating about politics. I've found the rational underpinnings of my youthful prejudices and I've spent my life advocating largely the same kinds of policies that I supported when I was a schoolboy.

Hamilton was on the hard right of the Conservative Party, opposing trade unions, anti-apartheid protest, and any regulation of the economy. He became known in Parliament for his harshly partisan attitude and was one of the attack dogs of the Conservative Party when debates got rough. As well as wild rancour, Hamilton had a sharp sense of humour. He won the *Spectator* 'Parliamentary Wit of the Year' award in 1990 and engagingly said that he thought an award for being a shining wit must be a spoonerism.

Neil Hamilton's wife Christine, who doubled as his Commons secretary, was a formidable character. She had once had parliamentary ambitions, and would surely have managed to browbeat any selection committee into choosing her, but decided not to pursue a conventional political career. She was instead, according to Hamilton's friend Michael Brown, a 'driving force behind his political career'. Their motto was 'We Do Things

Together' – Neil was one of the most uxorious men in Parliament. She managed most aspects of her husband's life, perhaps fortunately for him, as he admits: 'I think she's got better judgement than I have. I don't think we'd have got into quite so many scrapes if I'd always done as I was told.'

In 1986 Hamilton won a libel action against the BBC for a *Panorama* programme 'Maggie's Militant Tendency' about extreme right-wing infiltration of the Tory party, and his victory 'gave him a sense of invincibility' according to Michael Brown. In the late 1980s he was prospering politically and financially. Until he was appointed a government whip in 1990 his outside interests were generating a steady and large income, and providing opportunities to exercise his taste for high living at the expense of others.

Hamilton had the reputation of being an accomplished freeloader as an MP. Charles Lewington, a journalist in the 1980s and Conservative Director of Communications 1995–97 under John Major, recalls his reputation in the 1980s:

> *It didn't come as any great surprise when Neil Hamilton was metaphorically caught with his hands in the till. There had always been a lot of rumours about his lavish lifestyle and penchant for hospitality, shared with Christine. When you look at the bill he ran up over dinner in the Ritz there would be very few Conservative MPs who would enjoy someone's hospitality to that extent.*

The Hamiltons' week-long stay at the Paris Ritz in September 1987 courtesy of Mohamed Fayed has become notorious as a defining moment of 1980s excess. As well as a room in the luxurious hotel, the pair made free with the contents of the mini-bar, restaurant dining and the services of the hotel's staff for shopping and driving. The cost of the accommodation if paid for would have been £1,482, and for the various extras £2,120 (now worth about £5,400 in total). The extremely high cost of the extras led Fayed to complain that Hamilton was abusing his hospitality. On returning to Britain, Hamilton 'talked freely' about his exploits in the Paris Ritz. Greer considered that Hamilton's habit of recounting such stories was foolish and open to the charge that he was taking Fayed's hospitality for granted. According to the Hamiltons, such hospitality was not unusual in the 1980s and it is only the leak of the bill which brought them notoriety.

The relationship between Hamilton and Fayed, despite the Ritz episode, was not without warmth. Hamilton rather liked Fayed, finding him engaging and humorous company. He was intrigued by the opulence of the Fayed residence in Park Lane and amused by his habit of handing out minor gifts like bottles of whisky and Harrods ties: 'I've got one. I don't wear it any more.' Fayed was a less gracious recipient of gifts. Hamilton gave him a pair of gold-plated House of Commons cufflinks in 1988 but this gesture was scorned by the tycoon: 'A pair of rubbish cufflinks! They're all fuggers, these politicians.'

Tim Smith was another soldier enlisted in the Greer army. Smith was as grey as Hamilton was colourful. He won the Beaconsfield by-election against Tony Blair in 1982, having previously been an MP after a freak by-election victory in Ashfield in 1977. He was an accountant from central casting – tall, dour, dull, and an ally of Michael Grylls on the backbench Trade and Industry Committee. Even before the scale of his involvement with Fayed was revealed he was known as a more than usually assiduous collector of consultancies. He used parliamentary questions on behalf of one of his clients, Price Waterhouse, to ascertain information about government management consultancy contracts. This was a registered interest which Smith was prepared to defend as within the rules. His link with House of Fraser was only registered, and then for a short time, in 1989, after he had been attacked in a press release issued by Tiny Rowland which more or less directly accused him of corruption. His late registration was regarded by the Commissioner for Standards in 1997 'as a disingenuous attempt at concealment. On any view this was a totally unacceptable form of registration.'

As well as working through Ian Greer, Fayed made private arrangements with Tim Smith, whom he considered particularly aggressive in pressing the House of Fraser case in Parliament. Smith would collect cash pay-offs in brown envelopes from Fayed in his office at Park Lane, or occasionally sent by courier to his home, during a period between May 1987 and around January 1989. Although the transactions have been admitted, the amounts involved are curiously imprecise. Fayed placed them at around £10,000 and *The Guardian* relied on a figure of £6,000 in its libel defence. Smith admitted to the Cabinet Secretary Robin Butler in 1994 that it could have been as much as £25,000 but in his evidence to the Downey inquiry he gave the figure as 'about £18,000' (now worth about £27,000). Fayed was clearly underestimating, not exaggerating, Smith's misconduct.

Smith admitted receiving cash when questioned by Robin Butler in October 1994, but denied that he had acted corruptly. Smith claimed that the payments were related to advising Fayed rather than his own parliamentary work for House of Fraser. This was dismissed by the Downey Report and the Select Committee who found that the payments had been for 'lobbying services' and by any standards operating since the 1941 Boothby case a clear contempt of the House.

The Guardian also named Neil Hamilton as having received bribes from Fayed between 1987 and 1989. According to Fayed, Hamilton took more money than Smith for his parliamentary services. £28,000 (now worth £42,000) was Fayed's figure in 1994, but he has not been consistent about how much he paid the MP. Fayed said that Hamilton would appear regularly at his Park Lane offices and collect brown envelopes stuffed with cash. Hamilton, unlike Smith, vehemently denied receiving cash for questions and fought the charges for five years until in December 1999 a libel jury in effect ruled that he had indeed been corrupt.

The Sun called the 1999 libel case 'Liar v Liar', with some justice. Fayed's credibility had been rubbished by the DTI report on Harrods, and both Sir Gordon Downey and the trial judge, Mr Justice Morland, warned against accepting his uncorroborated word, even when it sounded plausible. Much of his evidence to the libel trial consisted of frankly implausible ranting, alleging all sorts of iniquities on the part of the royal family and Hamilton alike. Hamilton, for his part, was also an unsatisfactory witness. Downey found that 'It is difficult to escape the conclusion that, as the inquiry has progressed and more and more has been discovered, Mr Hamilton's credibility has suffered increasingly serious damage.' The Select Committee and the libel jury apparently considered Hamilton a more polished and devious liar than Fayed, who came across as a fantasist.

The balance of evidence, as Downey in 1997, the Commons Select Committee on Standards and Privileges in 1997, and the civil courts in 1999 all agreed, was against Hamilton. Fayed's claims were corroborated by former employees, whose integrity Downey and the jury saw no reason to doubt. Hamilton's other activities also gave credibility to Fayed's allegations: the parliamentary inquiry found several cases where he had flouted the rules. Perhaps the decisive blow to his libel case was the discovery by Fayed's legal team that Hamilton had demanded £10,000 from the Mobil Oil Company for an abortive Finance Bill amendment in 1989, and subsequently misled Downey about the matter.

Downey found the case against Hamilton 'compelling' and the libel jury believed that the allegation that Hamilton had behaved corruptly was 'highly convincing', and there the matter rests. Hamilton still protests his innocence, but his gamble in trying to reverse the result of the parliamentary inquiry through the civil courts decisively failed.

Brown envelopes stuffed with cash – crude bribery – was a private arrangement between Smith (and equally, it now seems, Hamilton) and Fayed. Ian Greer had more sophisticated ways of buying influence which could be disguised among more legitimate transactions. It is normal practice for lobbying organizations to give assistance in the form of loaning staff to constituency campaigns and party headquarters during election campaigns. This took place during the 1997 election campaign as well. IGA also created an election fund for donations. The pool of money came from two clients, £11,250 from the DHL courier firm and £18,000 from Fayed's personal funds. It was distributed to a selection of MPs and candidates. Small donations were parcelled out to various friends of Ian Greer, which were mostly below 25 per cent of their election expenses and therefore did not have to be registered. A couple of cases were more complicated. Greer's own MP, Norman Lamont, had received £2,000 in 1987 and a further £5,000 from DHL in 1992, but the money went into a general 'fighting fund' account which did not only pay out at election time. It was therefore unclear whether it counted as sponsorship and had to be registered, but in the view of the Downey Report 'such an arrangement defeats the spirit of the registration requirements' and the rules should be reviewed to stop such large donations being obscured.

The donations caused embarrassment to the MPs involved when they became known, but their recipients did not break any rules; with the exception of Andrew Bowden, MP for Brighton Kemptown since 1970. The largest Ian Greer donation in 1987 was to Bowden's constituency, to the tune of £5,319. It came to rather more than the total declared election expenses in the constituency and was more than double the next largest Greer payment. It was supposedly linked to office equipment, but in fact Bowden's agent doubted whether the Kemptown Tories needed such a large amount. The Downey Report concluded that it had been 'intended as a reward for lobbying and Sir Andrew probably knew it came originally from Mr Fayed'.

Grylls was in a different position which has still not been adequately explained. He was accustomed to receiving commission payments for introducing clients to IGA, and was on the payroll of the Unitary Tax Campaign (UTC) as an adviser. The UTC was a premier-division client for IGA – a lobby which united many of Britain's biggest businesses to campaign to change the way some US states taxed their worldwide earnings.

Grylls also received payments described by Ian Greer as 'top-ups' to compensate him for his excessive work for the UTC. The UTC could not shed any light on why the workload on Grylls was considered excessive and did not share Greer's recollection of the UTC not having enough money to pay Grylls at a higher rate in a regular fashion. The payments coincided with Grylls engaging in lobbying activities on behalf of House of Fraser, a fact described as 'unfortunate' by Greer and regarded by Downey as raising the possibility, but not being proof, that the top-up funds had originated with Fayed. The matter has not been resolved, and the case against Grylls not proved, and the records kept by Grylls were so vague that it was impossible even to tell how much he had taken in the so-called 'top-ups'.

The aim of the Fayed–Greer campaign was to pressure the government into inquiring into Lonrho's business, holding off criticism of Harrods management, and criticizing the conduct of the Department of Trade and Industry (DTI) investigation into the Harrods takeover which began in 1987.

The campaign was less than a total success, although it did not allow Tiny Rowland's version to go unchallenged and publication of the DTI report was delayed. Rowland probably did his own cause more harm by printing an extraordinary midweek edition of *The Observer* in March 1989 given over to a leaked copy of the draft DTI report which condemned Fayed. Its contents were less noticed than the Lonrho manipulation of a once proudly independent newspaper, but they were still enough to make any amount of lobbying on behalf of Fayed ineffective. The lobbying contract between House of Fraser and IGA ended in November 1989 and was replaced by a £500 per month monitoring service, with a cheque for £13,333 plus VAT for various still-mysterious services in early 1990.

The official DTI report into Fayed's career and the Harrods battle was published in March 1990. It was harsh reading for Fayed, who was denounced as a man whose evidence was not to be believed unless it was well corroborated, and that his statements about his past business career and his assets at the time of the House of Fraser battle had been false. It stopped short, though, of taking Harrods away from him or criticizing his management since the takeover.

Fayed was deeply unhappy with the DTI conclusions; he strongly believed that it was an unjust slur on his good name and he was determined to have it challenged in any court he could. Fayed had not given up all hope of having the report set aside through political channels and was delighted when his old ally Neil Hamilton was made a minister at the Department of Trade and Industry after the 1992 election.

In Texas it is said that an honest politician is one who, once he is bought, stays bought. Mohamed Fayed's grievance against Neil Hamilton would be understood in Texas. When Hamilton was made a DTI minister Fayed wrote him an ill-considered letter congratulating him and inviting him back to Harrods for lunch. Hamilton, as he recalls, was 'advised not to make any reply in case it compromised the government in some shape or form in defending the action which Fayed had taken out'. He also distanced himself from anything to do with House of Fraser while at the DTI.

Hamilton's conduct as a minister was correct in this instance, but *The Guardian* alleged that he had shown partiality to other Ian Greer clients while in office; this was strongly denied by Hamilton. Ministerial conduct fell outside the remit of the parliamentary investigations into the cash for questions affair and the truth or otherwise of these allegations remains unproved. However, Fayed's delight at having an ally in the department that mattered most to him was replaced by rage. His ally had deserted him and got involved in serious politics rather than having fun freeloading. By Hamilton's account, it is ironic that 'if I had been prepared to take decisions in Fayed's interest, which I had the power to do, we would never have heard of cash for questions. It's because I acted honestly and uncorruptly that I've been accused of corruption.'

Before his disaffection, Fayed had also donated lavish amounts to the Tory Party and this was the first thread that came loose from the House of Fraser lobbying network. In summer 1993 *The Guardian* and *The Sunday*

Times were investigating the perennially secretive finances of the Conservative Party. Large donations from foreign sources had bolstered the party's rickety bank balance before the 1992 election, and the editor of *The Guardian*, Peter Preston, was told that Fayed had information which could be helpful. He was eager to hear it because *The Guardian* had got into trouble for a report, which it could not substantiate, that a member of the Saudi royal family had given an enormous donation to the Tories. Tim Smith was of interest to Preston because of his activities as a Tory Vice-chairman for finance, but instead of detail about the Saudis, Preston heard that Smith and Neil Hamilton had been paid thousands of pounds for their parliamentary services on behalf of Fayed. *The Guardian*'s investigation into Ian Greer and the Tory MPs began.

The Guardian printed a rather opaque article about 'the power and prestige of Ian Greer' in October 1993 which hinted at more than could be delivered. Investigators from *The Sunday Times* and the television programme *The Cook Report* tried to run sting operations to expose the methods of Ian Greer, but their efforts in early 1994 were rumbled by the lobbyist. A barrier to standing up any of the stories circulating about corruption was the ban imposed by Fayed on naming him as a source. Without him at that time there was no story. *The Sunday Times* found a way round this problem, and ironically the first casualties of cash for questions had nothing at all to do with Greer or Fayed.

Tales of MPs being willing to accept cash for asking parliamentary questions had been floating around since the 1980s. An academic article had suggested some MPs operated a tariff of £150 per question in 1985, but when Andrew Neil, editor of *The Sunday Times*, heard of the allegations against MPs he was amazed. He asked Insight journalist Jonathan Calvert to contact a random sample of ten Labour and ten Conservative MPs to see if any of them would accept money to ask questions on behalf of a bogus company. Two Conservatives, David Tredinnick and Graham Riddick, took the bait, but all Labour and most Tory MPs rejected the suggestion as improper. 'Cash for questions' went public on 10 July 1994. Both MPs were suspended from their jobs as PPSs to ministers.

The political class was nearly as outraged by *The Sunday Times*' sting operation as the revelation that two Conservative MPs would accept money from an unknown company in return for using their parliamentary position. The Privileges Committee reported in April 1995 that the MPs had behaved in a way that 'fell below the standards which the House is entitled to expect from its Members' and the House of Commons agreed with the recommendation that Tredinnick should be suspended for four weeks and Riddick for two. The MPs were fined £1,800 and £900 respectively. Riddick's more lenient treatment was because he had eventually returned the cheque. But the Committee also criticized *The Sunday Times* as having fallen 'substantially below the standards to be expected of legitimate investigative journalism'. The body which more normally comments on the conduct of journalists, the Press Complaints Commission, upheld the sting as a legitimate inquiry. It is hard to know how else this pattern of behaviour, surely a legitimate subject of public concern, could have been exposed without entrapment.

The Tredinnick–Riddick operation was a sideshow from the main sequence of events, which moved rapidly behind the scenes in September and October 1994. In September the European Court of Human Rights ruled against Fayed's attempt to have the DTI report set aside. He had finally exhausted all conceivable legal avenues – 'Had there been an intergalactic court of appeal Mohamed would have gone there,' said Michael Cole – and he decided to take his chances in the court of public opinion. Fayed told Peter Preston that he could use the material on the Tories and Greer.

The story had seeped out widely by this time because Fayed's outbursts had not been confined to *The Guardian*'s journalists, but the Conservative Party leadership first heard of it, apparently, at the end of September through the *Sunday Express*'s editor Brian Hitchen. Hitchen had misunderstood Fayed's intentions as being to blackmail the government into disowning the DTI report, and gave John Major a garbled account of the conversation and the allegations against Conservative MPs. An ineffective and dilatory investigation was set in uncertain motion, conducted by Sir Robin Butler, at Major's request. It was, to say the least, a strange use of the time of the senior civil servant. However, Tim Smith confessed and there seemed to be at least circumstantial evidence against Hamilton. Both remained in government while the investigation was under way, even after Smith had confessed, while the government wondered what to do. It was certainly a contrast to the prompt suspension of John Belcher when allegations were made against him in 1948, and the low-key Butler inquiry bore no comparison to the Lynskey Tribunal.

On 20 October *The Guardian* went public with the allegations against Hamilton and Smith, to the effect that both men had taken cash and that Hamilton had enjoyed an undeclared stay at the Paris Ritz. Smith resigned as a Junior Northern Ireland minister the same day, but Hamilton tried to fight it out. Michael Heseltine, his boss at the DTI, asked him privately whether he had a financial relationship with Ian Greer, and Hamilton denied it despite having accepted commission payments for introducing firms to IGA. Hamilton claims that he thought Heseltine was asking about any general consultancy contract with Greer through which money from Fayed might have reached him. This defence cut little ice with Sir Gordon Downey or the 1997 Select Committee, who agreed that Hamilton had 'deliberately misled' Heseltine.

Hamilton's lack of candour with Heseltine weakened his position, as did a public comment. While visiting a school he was given a biscuit, which he accepted and joked that he would of course declare it in the Register of Members' Interests: 'It was a spontaneous gesture. We all thought it was a joke, and the world has divided into two: boring old farts who thought it was outrageous that I should be making fun of such serious allegations on the one hand, and the others who thought it was a jolly good joke.'

John Major and the Cabinet did not find Hamilton amusing. Even less funny was his reference to John Major's libel action against the *New Statesman*, during which Major had remained in office. Hamilton resisted the doctrine that set in after Back to Basics which dictated that accused ministers resigned without a fuss and it was understood that they might be restored when the air had cleared. Major had never liked Neil Hamilton, and the fact that he had been adopted by the right as a *cause célèbre* – and remarked on a matter the Prime Minister was understandably sensitive about – only made things worse.

On 25 October Hamilton was relieved of his ministerial office. Later that day John Major announced to the House of Commons that a committee was to be established chaired by a judge, Lord Nolan, to investigate standards of conduct in public life. Its remit was similar to that of the Salmon Commission in 1975–76 in that it was to produce recommendations as to future practice rather than investigate past events. Its membership included nominees from the senior ranks of the political parties and the political scientist Anthony King who had written on standards of conduct from an academic standpoint.

The lobbying business was discredited by the allegations – which initially overstated Greer's role. Greer's reputation was damaged, as he recalls: 'The press knocked on my immediate neighbour's door and said, "What does it feel like to live next door to a lobbyist?" as though one was a child molester or a serial killer.'

Revelations kept coming until the end of October, including the mystery over who had paid a hotel bill in Fayed's Paris Ritz for Jonathan Aitken in 1993 while he was Minister for Defence Procurement. In the long term this puzzling detail unravelled to produce one of the more shocking examples of political misconduct in the 1990s. Further revelations, including that a Tory MP had continued to practise part-time as a dentist, did not carry the momentum of the Hamilton, Smith and Aitken cases and the saga then appeared to become quiescent.

The Ritz allegation against Hamilton was investigated by the Select Committee on Members' Interests; the cash for questions allegations were ruled out as *sub judice* because of Hamilton's libel action against *The Guardian*. It was a less than effective investigation. Extraordinarily, a government whip, Andrew Mitchell, had been installed on the Select Committee. Another whip, David Willetts, spoke informally to the Chairman, Sir Geoffrey Johnson-Smith, about how the matter might be downplayed. When the committee reported, it ruled that Hamilton had been 'imprudent' not to declare the stay, but recommended no action against him and accepted his plea that the rules had not been entirely clear at the time. The vote in the committee was on strict party lines.

The Nolan Committee reported for the first time on 11 May 1995. It diagnosed a pervasive climate of slackness in parliamentary conduct. Its recommendations were truly shocking to Conservative MPs. While upholding the right of MPs to have paid employment unrelated to their work in Parliament, it recommended banning MPs from maintaining 'any direct or active connections' with multi-client lobbying firms. It also said that the amounts received in connection with outside interests should be declared in £5,000 bands, that control over interests should be extended to all aspects of parliamentary business including committees, that the law on bribery be reviewed, and that it should all be consolidated in a new Code of Conduct.

The most radical change was the introduction of an outside commissioner to monitor parliamentary standards and investigate cases in which MPs had been alleged to have transgressed. John Major responded to the report by agreeing with the broad thrust of the proposals, but many of his backbenchers were in open revolt against Nolan. This became clear when a Commons debate took place on 18 May. It was an unedifying spectacle, as MPs dressed up their self-interest in the language of defending the dignity of Parliament. It was rendered even more ludicrous by the activities of Jerry Wiggin MP, who had tried to pass off one of his amendments to a Bill under the name of another MP, Sebastian Coe. Wiggin was a paid consultant to a lobby which favoured the amendment.

At the end of the Nolan debate the government announced that a committee of senior backbenchers would be set up to see how the proposals might be implemented. The Opposition feared that the government would use this committee to delay and water down the recommendations of the Nolan Committee. The report and the debate had put the Parliamentary Conservative Party in a sour mood with Nolan and Major, who was blamed for setting up the committee and for being a 'boy scout' about the report. It contributed to a drastic erosion of support for Major. A month later he resigned the party leadership and dared his critics to challenge him.

The Select Committee came back to haunt Major and derail his attempt to restore his authority in November 1995. Its report had attempted to rewrite part of the Nolan recommendations and rejected full disclosure of outside earnings, replacing disclosure with an outright ban on 'paid advocacy'. Paid interests that did not amount to direct advocacy would neither be banned nor the amounts involved be publicly disclosed. The government backed the unhappy compromise – the Leader of the House Tony Newton had indeed used his casting vote to put it in the Select Committee report –

but it was a calamitous mistake. Public opinion demanded 'Nolan in full' and saw the government's failure to back disclosure of earnings as a capitulation to sleazy backbenchers. It was impossible, despite strenuous whipping on a nominal free vote, for the government even to convince its backbenchers to vote down the disclosure rule. Twenty-three voted for it with Labour and twenty-nine abstained and disclosure was approved by a majority of fifty-one on 6 November. For Emma Nicholson, the backbench Conservative MP for Torridge and West Devon, the greed and panic of her colleagues during the vote was the last straw: she was so repelled that she left the Conservative Party, joining the Liberal Democrats in December 1995, reducing the government's majority to a perilous five. Softness on sleaze was the worst possible issue for the government to be defeated on in a high-profile vote.

The attempt at a compromise banning paid advocacy backfired. Few MPs could stand up to defend the practice and this recommendation was approved by an even bigger majority. The idea of hiring an MP as a mouthpiece was widely regarded as repugnant and an infringment of what had always been expected of parliamentarians. The advocacy rule was not without its complications, however, because the ever-widening definition of payment threatened to drag in most MPs with a detailed knowledge of the subject. Should an MP who had been on a fact-finding trip paid for by a foreign government really be disqualified from speaking and voting on the relevant matter? The government would have done better by sticking to the letter of the Nolan Report.

As Corinne Souza says:

> Had the Select Committee on Members' Interests been doing its job in the 1980s none of this would have happened. Of course, it's absolutely outrageous to charge for parliamentary questions and much more besides. The Select Committee refused to do its job. Every single matter raised by The Guardian has been made time and time again with the Select Committee and jolly good for Nolan who came along and effectively said in polite language that the Select Committee is defunct.

Sir Geoffrey Johnson-Smith, who chaired the committee, conceded that it was an unsatisfactory instrument for investigating complicated sagas such as the Fayed–Greer–Hamilton affair: 'We didn't have the confidence, we didn't have the staff, we didn't have the procedures which could deal very thoroughly with these sorts of cases.'

The investigation, when it came, strained the resources even of the new system. Downey and the parliamentary Select Committee found the investigation 'analogous in some ways to that of a tribunal of inquiry' and despite the flaws in the procedure revealed by the 'Lynskey Tribunal' in 1948 it might have been more satisfactory if such a judicial, rather than parliamentary, mechanism had been used.

Hamilton and Greer attempted to test the matter in the courts through a libel action. The case was an extraordinary one. It was halted in 1995 because of the rules of parliamentary privilege, and could only be restarted in summer 1996 because Hamilton and his allies had amended the 1689 Bill of Rights to allow it to go ahead. It never did, because the case collapsed suddenly after differences opened up between Greer and Hamilton as they approached court. Greer was increasingly worried about how Hamilton's casual attitude to registering interests and his champagne lifestyle would play in court; Hamilton was 'incandescent with rage' about Greer's inaccurate statements to the 1990 Select Committee on his payments to Grylls. The end of the libel action brought doom to Neil Hamilton, denounced the next day in a headline in *The Guardian* as 'A Liar and a Cheat'. It finished off what was left of Ian Greer's lobbying business. As well as the cash for questions allegations various other matters which cast a discreditable light on recent parliamentary history were revealed and investigated.

Ian Greer Associates made most of its money from blue-chip British and foreign companies, and made much of its pro bono work for the African National Congress. It also represented some less proud causes. In early 1992 it did its best to polish the image of the brutal Serbian regime and prevent British action on the atrocities in former Yugoslavia. It also attempted to promote a highly carcinogenic new tobacco product.

US Tobacco had devised a new way of using tobacco – a pouch resembling a teabag to be placed in the mouth and sucked. It was to be sold under the name of 'Skoal Bandits' and the American firm was interested in producing and selling the product in Britain. Neil Hamilton and Michael Brown argued that Skoal Bandits should be allowed in Britain, on the libertarian grounds that people who wished to consume the product should not be stopped from doing so. Health ministers and civil servants were appalled at the idea, because the product caused terrible mouth cancers which would lead to individual misery and huge cost to the National Health Service. Edwina Currie, a health minister 1986–88, met a delegation lobbying for Skoal Bandits to be allowed, and recalls:

The meeting was fairly acrimonious. I had asked the hospitals for pictures of people with conditions caused by Skoal Bandits and they sent some from Scandinavia ... horrible, people with their face missing and teeth showing through. I listened to the representations and then took the photos out of the brown envelope. I showed them round and the others all went slightly green – but Neil Hamilton shoved them back in the envelope and said, 'I don't think this is relevant.'

Skoal Bandits were banned in Britain in 1989. Hamilton and Brown had not been frank with the ministers when they lobbied for the tobacco bags to be permitted. Both had received unregistered commission payments amounting to £6,000 each (now worth about £10,000) for introducing US Tobacco to Ian Greer Associates, and Hamilton also had three days in the Essex House Hotel in New York courtesy of UST in October 1989. The Downey Report established that Hamilton 'persistently and deliberately failed to declare his interests' in dealings with ministers on Skoal Bandits as well as House of Fraser. Hamilton claimed that he was not clear about whether such payments should be registered, but Downey was unimpressed and pointed out that the Registrar had issued a reminder that MPs were obliged to register single payments. Combined with failure to register introduction payments from National Nuclear Corporation and a consultancy fee from Strategy Network International, Hamilton's pattern of omissions was condemned by the Select Committee in 1997 as 'a casualness bordering on indifference or contempt towards the rules of the House on disclosure of interests'.

The committee went out of its way to point out that this pattern was enough by itself, regardless of the alleged cash for questions, to justify a substantial suspension from the House.

The 'Willetts note' had unusually put the machinations of the whips on paper and thus made it subject to legal rules of discovery. Willetts had not long been in the whips' office and as one of the more intellectual MPs had the habit of writing things down. Friends also thought that Willetts had tried too hard to appear devious, believing that it was expected of whips. The content of the note plainly indicates that the whips were taking a keen partisan interest in the proceedings of the supposedly quasi-judicial Privileges Committee. Cynics said that this was precisely why parties employed whips, but it further advertised the shortcomings of self-regulation of parliamentary standards. Willetts himself was hauled before the reconstituted Committee on Standards and Privileges, where he was brutally questioned by a fellow Tory, Quentin Davies, about the meaning of his note. His attempts to argue about the definition of 'want' were dismissed by the committee as 'dissembling' and he resigned in December 1996 as soon as he was criticized.

As the election approached, cash for questions tainted the image of the entire Conservative Party. Even sympathetic observers like Matthew Parris were surprised by what had been revealed: 'the extent, the depth, the naked vulgarity of what was happening', and felt let down: 'I instinctively took their side against the media. It came as a shock to realize that more and more of what the media was saying was palpably true and fewer and fewer of the defences of my old friends and colleagues were sustainable.'

The feelings expressed by Parris, a non-judgmental Conservative insider, were magnified among the electorate in general. The Tories carried the reputation of standing for low ethical standards into the election, where it was a fatal handicap.

The last act of the sleaze drama was the 1997 election campaign. The full Downey Report was near completion when the election was called; his findings are dated 27 March 1997 but were received by the Select Committee on Standards and Privileges on 1 July 1997, after the election. Receipt of the full report had been made impossible by the early 'prorogation' of parliament by John Major when the election was called on 17 March. Parliament was prorogued on 21 March at the cost of several pieces of legislation and the Downey Report, although Parliament was not technically dissolved until 8 April. The reason for this unusual state of affairs was mostly political. The Conservative leadership thought a long campaign would expose Labour divisions, while the longer MPs sat in Westminster the more attention was drawn to Tory problems. Major denied, to widespread disbelief, that the Downey Report was part of the calculation. The long wait for dissolution brought the outgoing MPs into the new financial year, allowing defeated Members to claim pensions and severance pay based on the new, substantially increased, parliamentary salaries. It was an appropriate end to the inglorious Parliament of 1992–97.

MPs who had done nothing except receive campaign contributions from Ian Greer were cleared of misconduct in an interim report on 19 March 1997, although the Commissioner recommended that the rules on registration of campaign contributions be reviewed. In the case of the Conservative MPs their acceptance of such payments sat uneasily with criticism of the Labour Party for the system of trade union sponsorship – which at least was open and on the record. Of these Conservative MPs twelve were defeated in the election and three retired. None survived, although this was a reflection more of the size of the national swing against the Tories rather than any personal unpopularity of MPs associated with Greer.

Allegations remained outstanding against three people standing for the Conservatives in the election, namely Neil Hamilton, Tim Smith and Michael Brown. *The Guardian* stepped in by publishing details on 21 March from the transcripts of oral evidence taken by Downey outlining the case against Smith and Hamilton. Downey was angry with this action because it seemed in breach of natural justice and gave the MPs the opportunity to claim that they were prejudged by the media.

At this point Conservative Central Office devoutly hoped that the accused pair would be standing down; it would perhaps have been better for the national party if the Downey Report had been published. Any pressure had to be exercised indirectly because the party had no powers to override the decisions of the local associations in Beaconsfield and Tatton. Neil Hamilton was oblivious to the feelings of the party high command: 'At no stage was I asked, nor indeed was my constituency asked, by the Prime

Minister, Central Office or anybody else in the party not to have me as a candidate in the general election.'

A few days later, Tim Smith stepped down as a candidate. Neil Hamilton doggedly refused to do so. His brazen behaviour left Major 'speechless' with impotent fury and embarrassment. Labour and Liberal Democrat parties united to back an independent candidate, the former BBC correspondent Martin Bell, against Hamilton in Tatton, which boundary changes had made the fifth safest Conservative seat in the country. The bizarre Tatton campaign cast a lurid light over the rest of the Conservative campaign. Some tabloid reporters tried to make an issue of Bell's past marital difficulties, but this carried no conviction and proved irrelevant. Hamilton's conduct looked so disreputable, according to the Tories' jaded Director of Communications Charles Lewington, that 'anyone standing next to Neil Hamilton on the hustings would have come across as being a fine upstanding member of society'.

Martin Bell crushed Neil Hamilton by 11,077 votes. It was the worst slump in the Conservative vote anywhere in Britain and the first victory by a new independent candidate since 1945. In his victory speech to his constituents Bell said: 'I believe you have lit a beacon which will shed light in some dark corners and illuminate the Mother of Parliaments itself. It is a strong signal that will be heeded.'

In other constituencies Conservative MPs touched by sleaze did badly. Michael Brown and Graham Riddick were defeated, as was Jonathan Aitken. David Tredinnick narrowly survived. Olga Maitland, who had been rebuked by the Speaker for passing off government-sponsored wrecking tactics on a disabled rights bill as her own, was swept away.

The Downey Report on Fayed's MPs was published in July 1997. The new Commons Select Committee on Standards and Privileges later considered the report, but it was rather a futile exercise because Hamilton, Brown and Bowden were defeated and Smith and Grylls had not stood for re-election. The committee did not have the power to punish former MPs and was reduced to stating what it would have recommended had the guilty MPs still been in the House. Hamilton had his disastrous day in court when his libel action against Fayed was heard at the end of 1999. The case, in all its preposterous and colourful detail, effectively concluded the cash for questions affair. Fayed's credibility was damaged, but Hamilton's was destroyed, and the Conservative Party once again found itself cursing Hamilton's futile quest to save his reputation as 'Tory sleaze' dominated the headlines.

Cash for questions would have been a significant scandal in any circumstances. It struck such a popular chord because it seemed to symbolize a general pattern of arrogant, unethical and greedy behaviour among Conservatives, but it was probably not even the biggest scandal of the declining years of the Conservative government.

CHAPTER 11

The culture of sleaze 1992-97

'If it falls to me to start a fight to cut out the cancer of bent and twisted journalism in our country with the simple sword of truth and the trusty shield of British fair play, so be it.'

Jonathan Aitken, 1995

Cash for questions and Back to Basics were far from the only scandals of the declining years of the 1979–97 Conservative government. Notably, there were the arms to Iraq scandal, culminating in the Scott Report of 1996, and the Pergau Dam affair of 1994. While these two matters fall rather outside the scope of this book – having more in common with the 'abuse of power' cases referred to in the introduction – they did much to confirm the image of the Conservative government as dishonest and disreputable.

While safeguards against parliamentary misconduct were put in place after Nolan, the issue of ministerial accountability and integrity remained, unsatisfactorily, self-regulated. This system was discredited by the scandal surrounding one of John Major's Cabinet ministers, the scale of which only became apparent after the 1997 election.

Some of the appointments in Major's reshuffle after the general election of 1992 were so bizarre that they were either jokes, or became jokes shortly afterwards. David Mellor was the 'Minister of Fun'. The bulky Nicholas Soames, whose sexual performance was once immortally compared by a former girlfriend to having a wardrobe fall on top of you with the key sticking out, was Minister of Food. Neil Hamilton took charge of business ethics. And Jonathan Aitken became Minister of State for Defence Procurement.

If Jonathan Aitken had to be given a job in government – and his undoubted talents gave him a strong case – this was the last job on earth he should have been given. Adam Raphael, who had investigated arms dealing with Saudi Arabia, thinks: 'It was an absurd appointment, and very dangerous because of his previous and continuing Saudi connections. It was unfitting, it was unsuitable and it was unnecessary and I'm afraid it showed John Major's lack of judgement.'

Aitken had become a rich man through his association with Prince Muhammad, the son of King Fahd of Saudi Arabia, and his business manager Said Ayas. In the mid 1970s Aitken was working for Ramzi Sanbar, an 'agent' based in London associated with the Prince. Ken Williams, the Poulson associate, moved into Saudi Arabia slightly ahead of the rush generated by the 1973–74 oil crisis. He was familiar with the way business worked in the Middle East, as he says:

Anybody who wants to do business in Saudi Arabia must have an agent. You've got to have somebody who works for you in the country, it doesn't matter what you're selling, you have an agent. Then you can either allow the agent to sell the stuff direct himself, or if it's a project the agent negotiates the project for you.

The quadrupling of the oil price in 1973–74 produced an enormous increase in the revenues Saudi Arabia was receiving from its principal export, and a gold rush among Western contractors eager to build a modern country, complete with highways, tower blocks, hospitals, hotels and telephones, more or less from scratch. The agency system meant that the body commissioning the project would pay many times what a comparable project would cost in the West. The agent would take a share, and large amounts would also disappear into the pockets of people whose influence might otherwise hinder the project. According to Williams:

Commission means that the agent has to pay certain people who are involved. The people can be politicians and members of the royal family. Funnily enough the royal family hasn't got any money otherwise because the state doesn't pay them. Armaments is dead easy, people want arms. You sell something which is worth a million pounds to them for two million and there's another million to divide between them.

Prince Muhammad was one of the main players in the commission game and became a very wealthy man in the late 1970s. Aitken, as a London contact, shared in his good fortune with gifts such as a Jaguar car in 1976. The extent of Aitken's gains from the relationship are not known; despite conducting complicated business such as the purchase of a jet aircraft in 1977, Aitken claimed not to have been rewarded. In 1978 the Prince decided to make Aitken his main London functionary, replacing Sanbar with a firm under Aitken's chairmanship called Al-Bilad. The firm was a contact point and commission collector for British firms bidding for Saudi contracts. Again, it is not clear how much money Aitken made out of the arrangement – although he was able to afford a succession of extremely expensive houses in the early 1980s.

Business links between Britain and Saudi Arabia became more sensitive in the 1980s with the massive al-Yamamah arms deals, particularly the secretive Yamamah 2 signed in 1988 and worth something of the order of $100 billion. The scale of arms purchases by Saudi Arabia is out of all proportion with the size of the country's armed forces and proved militarily ineffective in the 1990–91 Gulf War. The amount of commission that is skimmed off a deal of this size is astronomical.

Before he made his Arab connections Aitken was already well known as a versatile journalist and a popular, unstuffy man about town. He scandalized respectable Tory opinion by endorsing the legalization of cannabis as a signatory to a famous advertisement in *The Times* in 1967. He celebrated his friends and, indirectly, himself in his 1967 book *Young Meteors* which described a generation of dynamic and successful young people. Some of the meteors, like David Steel, turned out to be durable stars; others dazzled and faded away. Aitken himself was more of a meteorite, who crashed and burned leaving a battered grey lump. As well as the bright young things of London, he covered serious stories like the Six Day War in 1967 and the Biafran secession from Nigeria. His efforts on the latter story earned him a trial under the Official Secrets Act in 1971, at which he was acquitted. The official secrets prosecution cost him the Conservative nomination for the safe seat of Thirsk and Malton in the 1970 election, but he entered the Commons as MP for Thanet East in February 1974.

While he was raking in money from his connection with Prince Muhammad and Said Ayas, Aitken was enjoying himself in high society. He had a string of girlfriends and was considered one of the most eligible bachelors in Britain until he married in 1979. Marriage did not cramp his style all that much, and he had an affair with Soraya Khashoggi (Sandra Daly, who can also claim Winston Churchill as a former partner) which produced a child. Aitken was a cheerful throwback to the world of his great-uncle Max Beaverbrook – or even the lusty and corrupt eighteenth century – grabbing as much sex and as much money as he could.

Like Beaverbrook, Jonathan Aitken could command loyalty and affection in the most surprising places, for instance his left-wing Commons 'pair' Diane Abbott. He was the centre of a social circle around his Conservative Philosophy Group. Unlike many Conservative salons, Aitken's gatherings were generally regarded as interesting and worth while in their own right rather than a step on a career ladder. Matthew Parris rather admires this aspect of him:

> *Jonathan Aitken didn't appear to be in the business of peddling power or influence. He was an interesting, open, sympathetic, thoughtful person, whom to meet was fun in itself. He could introduce you to a great many other people like that. He was terrifically hospitable and a very good listener.*

Despite being one of the more obviously talented members of his generation, and his generally right-wing approach to economics and Europe, Aitken was consistently denied ministerial office during Mrs Thatcher's governments. It was puzzling enough for friends and the press to speculate about why Thatcher did not want him. The most common answer was that he had made the mistake of dumping Carol Thatcher in a particularly cruel way. Another was *lèse-majesté*: in 1975 he had quipped that Thatcher was so ignorant of Middle Eastern affairs that she probably thought Sinai was the plural of sinus. This was unlikely, as Thatcher was thick-skinned enough to keep Richard Needham in her government in 1990, even after he had been overheard saying, 'I wish the old cow would resign.' Anthony Howard thinks the Carol Thatcher story is:

> *strictly for the birds ... I think the real thing was that the Prime Minister thought that nobody got that much money unless there was something to be explained. Mrs Thatcher had a pretty shrewd idea about Aitken's dabblings. Despite her indulgent view of Mark Thatcher, she thought this was unacceptable in a prospective member of her government.*

In 1992 it seemed that Aitken's career was back on track, but it was only a matter of time before his past, his connections and his dishonesty would catch up with him. In reality John Major had done him no favours by appointing him to such a sensitive job because it made his business dealings a legitimate subject of press and public interest.

Aitken's downfall started with an incidental detail provided to *The Guardian* by Mohamed Fayed in his battle against the Conservative government. Fayed produced evidence that Jonathan Aitken had stayed at the Paris Ritz on 19 September 1993 and that the bill was paid by an unknown woman. Aitken claimed that there was no mystery and the woman was in fact his wife Lolicia. In reality the woman was a member of Prince Muhammad's Paris entourage and the bill was paid by Said Ayas or the Prince.

The reason for Aitken's rushed visit to the Paris Ritz, and his years of deceit after the event, remained mysterious even after his downfall, but his conduct left the whiff of large-scale corruption. Michael Cole recalls Mohamed Fayed telling him that:

> *Jonathan Aitken, who he knew to be minister in charge of defence procurement, was sitting with two characters Mohamed knew to be key figures in Saudi business and industry also with arms interests. He said to me it was like seeing the Attorney-General sitting with Al Capone.*

In March 1999 *The Guardian* finally published a more explicit account of the Paris meeting: the paper alleged that he had been secretly meeting his patron, Prince Muhammad, to co-ordinate a plan for British arms sales to Saudi Arabia. Aitken was trying to ensure that the sale was organized so that the Prince and his allies would receive the commission payments. Aitken has offered no convincing alternative version of events: a story floated by his 'friends' that he was doing secret MI6 work was dismissed as fiction.

Aitken's elevation to the Cabinet in July 1994 as Chief Secretary to the Treasury brought his record under closer scrutiny than before; his strange and persistent denials about the Paris Ritz meeting only stirring the curiosity of *The Guardian*'s team. In September 1994 he was 'investigated' in relation to the Fayed allegations by Robin Butler at the request of John Major. Butler was a professional and competent Cabinet Secretary, but he was not cut out for work as a private detective. He later admitted that such a murky business was beyond his powers: 'It's not right for a Cabinet Secretary to get into this.' Butler took Aitken's denials at face value and gave him a clean bill of health.

Next, Aitken's directorship of an arms firm called BMARC came under scrutiny in *The Independent*. BMARC had concluded a disreputable arms deal called 'Project LISI' which was purportedly to supply weapons to Singapore. The real client was Iran, against whom there was an arms embargo. Aitken had not known about the deal, but was open to the charge that he had been less than energetic in his duties as a company director. The matter was inconclusively investigated by Customs at the request of Michael Heseltine, then in charge of the DTI, and by a parliamentary committee.

Aitken came under further attack in April 1995 when allegations surfaced that his experience in procurement was not restricted to the Ministry of Defence weapons budget. It was said that he had attempted to obtain prostitutes to entertain Saudi visitors at a health spa, Inglewood, which he managed on behalf of Arab investors in Berkshire. More seriously, journalists had started to probe Aitken's business links with Saudi Arabia and Prince Muhammad. Allegations about all these matters, plus a comic camel wandering around sand dunes near Liverpool, were screened in a Granada television documentary called *Jonathan of Arabia*.

Hours before the *Jonathan of Arabia* programme was broadcast Aitken summoned a press conference at Conservative Central Office and treated the assembled journalists to a breathtaking display of arrogance, pomposity and deceit:

> If it falls to me to start a fight to cut out the cancer of bent and twisted journalism in our country with the simple sword of truth and the trusty shield of British fair play, so be it. I am ready for the fight.

Some Conservative MPs, angered by the constant battering they had been getting from the media since 1992, were delighted that battle had been joined: Neil Hamilton thought it was 'splendid'. The Party Chairman, Jeremy Hanley, who allowed him the use of Central Office says he 'felt that he was doing what many of us would like to have done in the same set of circumstances had we been able to afford it'.

Others, including his friends, were concerned that the 'sword of truth' speech had gone over the top. Alan Clark's reaction was of 'mild distaste ... I thought it was ludicrous to be so demonstrative and to use these extraordinarily trite expressions'.

Less friendly colleagues such as Edwina Currie felt that his record might not withstand close inspection: 'There was the feeling he was in the pay of a bunch of rather shady Arabs and possibly some of his activities were not entirely in this country's interests.'

Aitken instructed his lawyers to fire off libel writs against Granada and *The Guardian*. In July 1995 he left the government because his legal actions were consuming too much time, and he was also embarrassed by revelations about his sex life. His sudden prominence had awakened fond and not so fond memories in Paula Strudwick, who had been Aitken's mistress in the early 1980s. She had been a prostitute specializing in sado-masochism, although Aitken claimed not to have known that she was more than just an enthusiastic amateur. Stories about the beatings Aitken had enjoyed at the hands – and canes – of Strudwick were spilled across the *Sunday Mirror* the weekend after his resignation.

Aitken's legal actions rolled on, and he was so confident of victory that he rejected an offer to settle made by *The Guardian* shortly before the May 1997 election. Aitken was one of the most surprising casualties of the rout of the Conservatives, although it was not a personal vote against him. Thanet had long been a safe Conservative area, but the decline of British seaside resorts had hit the far corner of Kent extremely hard and Aitken was defeated by 2,878 votes by Labour candidate Stephen Ladyman. Aitken remained confident that he would win the libel action against his accusers and recover from his electoral setback.

Aitken started off the libel action ebulliently. The judge had ruled that it would go ahead without a jury, and in addition quickly ruled in Aitken's favour on one of the counts. It seemed that *The Guardian* was heading for disaster until investigators pieced together the evidence from a defunct Swiss hotel, a car hire firm, American Express and British Airways passenger lists that proved incontrovertibly that Lolicia Aitken had not been to Paris that weekend. Aitken's account of what had happened, and the statements of his family, were proved to have been untrue.

The sudden collapse of the libel action in June 1997 left Aitken exposed as a liar, who had arranged false testimony at terrible risk to his own daughter. His marriage broke down at the same time as his attempt to shore up his reputation by defrauding *The Guardian* out of libel damages. At the end of June 1997 Aitken resigned from the Privy Council, joining the inglorious company of John Stonehouse and John Profumo as the only three such resignations since 1945. A police investigation began into Aitken's false testimony and he was charged on five criminal counts in 1998.

Aitken pleaded guilty to two charges of perjury and perverting the course of justice in January 1999. He admitted having told lies about the Ritz bill and getting his wife and daughter to lend support to his false testimony. He told *The Express*'s reporter Gerard Greaves 'for that I plead guilty in law, and morally as well. Thankfully I've made my peace with my family members and the Almighty. I've learned my lessons. I hope I never tell any lies again. Sometimes you become a prisoner of your own lie. Ultimately I have no excuses.' Aitken was resigned to going to prison, finding solace in the fact that he had already experienced the discomfort and forced proximity to others that constituted an Eton education in the 1950s. Aitken was sentenced to eighteen months in prison on 8 June 1999 and was condemned by the judge for his 'calculated perjury' and his 'gross and inexcusable breach of trust'. He was sent to Belmarsh prison in London, and transferred to Standford Hill open prison on 29 June where he was visited by Michael Howard. Aitken had declared bankruptcy, and the trustees seized and sold as much of his property as they could to repay his creditors. Suspicion lingered that his Swiss divorce, and bankruptcy, were devices to evade payment.

*

The exposure of the Aitken scandal was an offshoot of the talks between Fayed and the then editor of *The Guardian* Peter Preston, which was in turn an offshoot of an inquiry into the Conservative Party's finances. Tory fundraising has been one of the murkiest corners of British political life since the days of the sale of honours just after the First World War. In the 1920s and 1930s various slush funds existed, and in 1948 the 'river companies' were established to launder funds from sources unwilling to be identified in their accounts as party donors, or barred, as trusts were, from political donations. Until 1992 a group called British United Industrialists (BUI) also served as a conduit to disguise political donations by large firms, and an account called 'Free Enterprise' held at a private bank in London was used for this purpose too.

The 1987 election was extremely expensive, particularly because of a massive advertising blitz during the last week of the campaign caused by Conservative jitters about the threat from Labour on 'wobbly Thursday'. During the chairmanship of Kenneth Baker the party also extended and refurbished Central Office at considerable expense. By 1991 the Conservative Party was £12 million in debt and it was spending much more than it was generating in income.

Senior Conservatives were aware by the early 1990s that the way the party was funded would not stand up to close inspection. The recession of 1990–92 caused more problems; it made the task of convincing the electorate that the Conservatives deserved another term in government much harder. The recession also dried up the funds available from British business to fight an election campaign, both because companies needed to economize and because they found it harder to justify to shareholders. In the 1980s about half the Conservatives' income came from corporate sources, but by 1997 only a fifth did so.

Longer-term trends were also affecting the party's income. In the 1950s Conservative Party membership was well over two million. By the early 1990s the highest serious estimates put it at around half a million, most of whom were of retirement age. Broad-based fundraising by small donations and thousands of 'bring and buy' sales across the country was withering away.

The shortfall was increasingly met by massive donations from private individuals. According to Cecil Parkinson there was a 'huge blitz of one-off, big donations' after the 1992 election. The party tapped its wealthy supporters again in the run-up to the 1997 election. A considerable number of these individuals were foreign tycoons. Over the 1992–97 period the Conservatives accepted £16.2 million in foreign donations, nearly 10 per cent of the party's total declared earnings, while Labour did not accept any.

The risks of depending on large donations from individuals were obvious. Michael Dobbs knew that 'it was bound to lead to tears ... As soon as you start relying on a handful of wealthy individuals you've lost control over your reputation and effectively your independence. It relies very much upon instinct to decide which donor is a good egg and which has problems attached to them.'

Several of these individuals did indeed prove embarrassing, including Fayed. According to Michael Cole: 'Mohamed gave a quarter of a million pounds to the Conservative Party ... he has always felt it was the worst money he ever spent.'

Harsh words indeed from the man who bought Fulham Football Club.

Two large-scale Conservative donors, Asil Nadir of Polly Peck and Octav Botnar of Nissan UK, were later exposed as crooked businessmen. Nadir gave the party at least £440,000 directly and through a channel called the Industrial Fund during the late 1980s. In 1993 Nadir jumped bail and fled to the unrecognized Turkish Republic of Northern Cyprus. It has been alleged that the donations to the Conservative Party had been made improperly from company funds, but the party has resisted all calls to return the cash to Polly Peck's creditors.

Hong Kong business interests contributed some of the largest sums: Li Ka-Shing contributed £1 million and Tung Chi-hwa, who became Chief Executive of Hong Kong after the handover to China, gave a substantial sum; £1.5 million was donated by C. K. Ma, owner of the Oriental Press

Group and member of a family whose fortune was suspected of being based on drug trafficking. Ma wrote to the Conservatives complaining that 'certain undertakings' had been broken and demanded a return of £1 million of the contribution. The Conservatives refused until it could be proved to have been from an illegal source.

Another foreign donor was John Latsis, a Greek shipping tycoon who was an associate of the Colonels' Fascist regime which ruled Greece from 1967 to 1974, who gave at least £2 million to the Tories. The Latsis donation is the largest ever known. Several large-scale donors to the Conservative Party benefited from an anomalous tax loophole by which foreign residents only paid tax on earnings generated in Britain, a loophole which was upheld by the Major government.

The most serious allegations concerned interests associated with foreign governments. In 1996 *The Sunday Times* alleged that money had been reaching the Conservatives from businesses associated with the criminal Bosnian Serb regime of Radovan Karadzic. Unwelcome attention was drawn to the activities of a pro-Serb Tory prospective candidate, John Kennedy, who ran a small lobbying firm and had escorted Karadzic around London. No doubt to the relief of the Tory leadership, Kennedy was trounced in the marginal seat of Halesowen when the election came. Earlier, *The Guardian* had made allegations about a massive Saudi donation to the Conservatives. While that charge could not be justified, the interpenetration of Saudi royalty, business interests and arms dealing is so great that there is no way of telling quite what links, if any, there are between these activities and the British Tories. The party seems to have made little effort to investigate the truth behind the allegations of links with Serbia and Saudi Arabia, so the matter remains murky.

The secrecy of Conservative finances meant that such stories, well-founded or not, multiplied and could not easily be proved or disproved. It also meant that suspicion about whether the donors were getting anything in return for their cash could neither be dispelled nor substantiated. Since the early 1980s the trade union-funded journal *Labour Research* had been drawing attention to the strong statistical correlation between firms donating money to the Conservatives and honours given to senior members of their Boards, but the confidentiality given to individual donors meant that there was no way of checking whether they were being rewarded in some way. The Conservatives always denied that there was a trade in honours, and undoubtedly there was nothing so crude as an explicit deal, or a Lloyd George honours-selling menu of prices and options. It was, as many British Establishment systems are, more subtle. But by 1993 the former Chairman of the Political Honours Scrutiny Committee Lord Shackleton thought that 'it is highly likely that ... secret donations are bypassing the scrutiny system and that honours are in effect being bought'.

The Conservatives were well aware that sleaze associated with party funding had tarnished the image of the party with the electorate. Alistair McAlpine, Treasurer during the fat years of the 1980s, later wrote: 'If the money I took was in any way likely to lose the party votes and so put the winning of elections in jeopardy, then far better to send that money away.' This rule was admittedly easier to follow when blue-chip British companies were queuing up to give money to the Tories, but after the defeat of May 1997 the party realized that it had to clean up its finances. In July 1997 the new Conservative leader William Hague announced that the party would no longer accept foreign donations, and in the party's 1998 accounts published in November the identity of donors giving over £5,000 was disclosed for the first time. There were only 33 in the nine months between July 1997 and March 1998, compared to 127 for Labour. Only two public companies gave money to the Tories, one of which also gave money to the Labour Party. In summer 1999 the party Treasurer, Michael Ashcroft, was the subject of serious allegations about his business activities in Belize.

One of the most successful – though controversial – Tory fundraisers since the 1980s has been Jeffrey, now Lord, Archer. McAlpine tended to think that he was a liability for the Conservative Party, but there was little anyone could do to get rid of the irrepressible novelist. McAlpine recalled Margaret Thatcher saying that while Archer often got his party and himself into awkward scrapes, he always got out of them. His career has been so littered with embarrassing incidents and allegations that it is difficult to know where to start. At the age of twenty-nine he was elected MP for Louth in Lincolnshire in a by-election in 1969 although he was already a controversial figure. His Commons career ended with the October 1974 election because he was on the brink of bankruptcy. He was reduced to this state thanks to a foolish investment in a firm called Aquablast which turned out to be fraudulent: Archer admitted to being the victim of 'my own stupidity, and my own greed, and my own arrogance'.

Archer's career revived from this low point. He turned his hand to writing thrillers and became extraordinarily successful, and returned to political favour during the mid 1980s. His ambition and ability to recover from setbacks chimed with the celebration of entrepreneurial values and he was made Deputy Chairman of the Conservative Party in 1985, a showman to balance the lugubrious Chairman, Norman Tebbit. In 1986, however, he made another foolish error by sending a friend, Michael Stacpoole, to Victoria station with a brown envelope stuffed with cash for Monica Coghlan, a prostitute. Archer intended her to use it to escape from tabloid reporters, but the *News of the World* was watching the transaction. Archer resigned as soon as the story broke, to the relief of Conservative Central Office, and the odd incident seemed to pass off without party political consequences. The following year Archer obtained £500,000 in libel damages from the *Star* for its allegation that he had used Coghlan's professional services. It was one of the classic libel cases of our times: the judge asked the jury of Mary Archer, 'Is she not fragrant?' and the expression 'fragrant witness' is still used occasionally. However, Archer's tactics during the case may have had a more pungent odour. He is alleged to have persuaded a friend, Ted Francis, to swear a false alibi statement and the veracity of another person who claimed to have dined with Archer at the crucial time has been called into question. His private life was more complicated than the marital bliss which the trial judge claimed to discern. But these facts remained hidden as Archer resumed his political career. He ingratiated himself with John Major, and was controversially awarded a peerage in 1992. He had ambitions in 1994 to become Conservative Chairman or possibly a National Heritage minister, but these were destroyed by the Anglia shares affair. Archer had purchased shares in the regional television company on behalf of a friend, at a time when takeover speculation was rife and his wife, Mary Archer, was on the Board of the company. DTI inspectors examined the transaction, and unusually the Department announced that it was investigating Archer. In the end no further action was taken, and Archer resumed political activity with his campaign to become the first directly-elected Mayor of London. He won the Conservative nomination, but was forced out in November 1999 after Ted Francis claimed that Archer had asked him to lie during the 1987 libel case. This time the Conservative Party was severely embarrassed. William Hague had called Archer 'a candidate of probity and integrity' only the previous month, and the party's much vaunted Ethics Committee had not been convened to look into any of the allegations against Archer.

Back to Basics, cash for questions, the Scott Report, the Aitken case and the scandals over party funding amounted to a formidable catalogue of sleaze afflicting the Conservative government in the 1990s, but that was not the end of it. Another skeleton in the closet dating back to the 1980s emerged at the same time as the collapse of Back to Basics in early 1994 in the form of the Westminster City Council gerrymandering scandal.

The Conservative administration under Dame Shirley Porter had panicked after the 1986 local elections reduced their majority to four, and had adopted a strategy to change the social composition of the wards they needed to hold and regain from Labour. Unlike central government, local authorities are subject to a stern regime by which councillors are personally accountable for mistaken and illegal decisions. The Westminster case was investigated by the District Auditor, who concluded that the strategy was motivated by gerrymandering, 'a disgraceful and improper purpose', and that the councillors and officials involved would have to repay (be 'surcharged for') the £27 million the policy had cost. A parallel investigation found that the council had improperly placed tenants in two tower blocks riddled with asbestos. At the time of writing in 1999 the District Auditor is appealing against a court judgment in Porter's favour.

Local authority scandals happen all the time, and are not confined to the few Conservative-controlled councils. By the mid 1990s there were very few Conservative councils left; Labour had been in control of its strongholds continuously since the early 1970s and of most large cities for the past fifteen years or more. It was not surprising that some of the problems exposed by the Poulson scandal had started to recur at local level in Labour councils such as Doncaster and Lambeth. The difference in the Westminster case was that the Tory leadership there was closely linked to the national leadership. Michael Portillo headed the Conservative London campaign and, even after the District Auditor's report, proudly endorsed the Westminster Conservatives. Barry Legg, one of the councillors condemned by the District Auditor in 1994, was Conservative MP for marginal Milton Keynes SW. Legg was subsequently removed from the list of miscreants to be surcharged, but was swept away in the 1997 landslide.

During the 1980s and 1990s the powers of local authorities had been reduced and the role of 'quangos' increased. A quango is a Quasi-Autonomous National Government Organization, consisting of a Board appointed by the minister from the relevant department. Quangos, because of the unaccountability and secrecy in which they worked, were a hotbed of low-level sleaze. During the early 1990s, under the guise of introducing more 'business experience' to the Boards, appointments became politicized and quangos increasingly staffed by allies and members of, and donors to, the Conservative Party. Baroness Denton, a health minister responsible for appointments to NHS quangos, admitted that 'I can't remember knowingly appointing a Labour supporter.'

In 1995 the first Nolan Report recognized that there was public concern about 'jobs for the boys' in quangos and recommended that 'formal and impartial assessment of candidates is vital'. Nolan also recommended that strict standards of conduct be imposed on quango members in the light of scandals such as the West Midlands Regional Health Authority (RHA) and the Wessex RHA, which wasted millions of pounds of taxpayers' money through gross incompetence.

The unprecedented flow of sleaze revelations in 1994 damaged the Conservatives for the rest of the Parliament. Because of his high profile, Neil Hamilton seemed to be a lightning conductor for public anger at the entire range of malpractice which had gone on under the Tory government. A sense had developed that the Conservatives represented the entire self-serving world of secretive quangos, boardroom 'fat cats' awarding each other massive salaries, and selling weapons to whatever vile regime wanted them. Labour played successfully on public disenchantment with the Conservatives and their values, and were rewarded by the biggest landslide victory the party had ever enjoyed. It was up to 'New Labour' to prove that it could do better.

CHAPTER 12

New Labour, new sleaze? 1997-

'There are seventeen people that count, and to say that I am intimate with all of them is the understatement of the century.'
Derek Draper, lobbyist, 1998

There is an old adage that Labour MPs fall victim to financial scandals and Tories to sexual scandals, but the pattern tends to be disproved by the record since 1945. Reggie Maudling and Neil Hamilton's troubles were not sexual, and although Tom Driberg's finances were always precarious he was mainly a sex scandal waiting to happen. However, even if the saying has not been generally true it seems to apply to the government's handling of problems since 1997. New Labour has so far been successful at fending off criticism over the sex lives of ministers but has run into a succession of minor problems over financial matters.

The idea of a standard of public sexual morality was finished off with the election of 1997. As early as 1988 the Chancery Division of the High Court ruled that there was 'no generally accepted code of sexual morality ... no common view that sexual conduct of any kind between consenting adults was grossly immoral'. Labour, old and new, broadly agreed, and some Conservatives envied the clarity that could be imposed after the change of government. According to Charles Lewington, the Conservative Director of Communications 1995–97: 'It was one of the more sensible things that Tony Blair did. He established early on that he was not going to stand in moral judgement over the personal lives of his colleagues.' John Major's instincts had been similar, but his party was so divided and confused about 'morality' that even if his leadership had been more securely based he would have had difficulty enforcing them. Labour's longer tradition of social tolerance helped the leadership to stand firm. But in September 1999 Blair confused the issue by talking of a 'moral crusade' which reminded some commentators of Back to Basics.

The most drastic redefinition of 'acceptable' sexual conduct in political circles during the late 1990s has been in respect of homosexuality. In a relatively short space of time it has become accepted and even unremarkable. Gay Labour MPs who choose not to comment publicly on their sexuality now do so out of personal choice rather than fear of damaging their political career. Chris Smith had been the only openly gay MP when he came out in 1984. His re-election in 1987 and with a vastly increased majority in 1992 was put down to a relatively sophisticated electorate in his constituency of Islington South and Finsbury and did not encourage other MPs to follow him. The 1997 election changed all that. In Exeter Ben Bradshaw overcame a fierce campaign against him, including attacks on his sexuality, with a similar change of votes to that in similar seats. It was only the second time Labour had ever won Exeter. In Enfield Southgate, an affluent London suburb, Stephen Twigg obtained an exceptionally high swing to oust Michael Portillo. Homosexuality did not seem to matter much to the voters, and after the election several other Labour MPs decided to come out. There were no significant protests in the press or from Opposition politicians when Chris Smith was made the first openly gay Cabinet minister, appointed Secretary of State for Culture, Media and Sport in May 1997; even ten years ago a certain amount of prejudiced comment would have been expected. Homosexuality within the sort of stable relationship enjoyed by Chris Smith and his partner, for instance, was unremarkable and could now even be celebrated by the *Daily Mail*.

Homosexuality returned to the agenda in October 1998 when the Welsh Secretary Ron Davies was the victim of a crime in south London. Like many senior politicians, Davies was overworked and lonely. On the evening of 26 October, by his account, he went for a walk on Clapham Common, to think and to wind down from the pressures of the day. Nobody knows precisely what the real story was, but Clapham Common is a noted cruising area for anonymous gay sex. According to one version, Davies did not even get out of his car. At some point, he invited a local criminal into his car and they went to a rundown estate in Brixton. Davies was robbed by the criminal and two of his associates, who stole his wallet, mobile phone and car. Only when they examined the loot did they discover that they had robbed a Cabinet minister.

Davies spoke to the police in Brixton, somewhat later, in a shocked and disoriented condition. He was an extremely poor witness, whose story was full of gaps and contradictions. Davies was only a little clearer when he spoke to Tony Blair next morning, and the Prime Minister and his staff realized that if Davies clung on to office it could only lead to a wearying press campaign to uncover the full story. The bad luck and bad judgement of Ron Davies cost him his Cabinet post, and the prospect of leading the Labour group in the new Welsh Assembly which he had successfully steered through a difficult referendum and the House of Commons. The obvious faults with his account of the events in Clapham made it plainly unsatisfactory for Davies to remain in Cabinet: 'a grievous error of judgement' in Davies' own words.

Davies told the House of Commons that 'we are what we are, the product of our genes and our experiences'. He later explained what he meant. In June 1999, after a tabloid story, he declared that 'I am, and have been for some time, bisexual.' Then he admitted that he was having therapy for compulsive risk-taking which he blamed on a 'troubled, violent and emotionally dysfunctional' childhood, and announced that he was having a divorce. He resigned from his chairmanship of the Economic Committee of the Welsh Assembly he had worked so hard to establish. Emotional instability and risk-taking are not unusual in politicians, but Davies faced problems which made it impossible for him to continue in office.

The discussion of sexuality after the Clapham Common incident had an unexpected outcome. The gay Conservative columnist, Matthew Parris, named Peter Mandelson as a homosexual during a live discussion on *Newsnight* on 3 November 1998. Jeremy Paxman made the mistake of asking him to elucidate a reference to the number of gay Cabinet ministers and Parris mischievously complied.

Parris defended his action: 'The only reason I said what I did about Peter is that he is out, he's completely out, and he's been out for a very long time.' Within the social circle inhabited by the political class, including Parris, this was perfectly true, although Mandelson preferred to keep his sexuality private as far as the world in general was concerned. Parris, a few months later, admitted the difference between what is known at Westminster and what is public in the full sense:

It was a category mistake. Privately he is completely open and everyone in Westminster talks about it as if it was no secret at all. It had been mentioned in the papers and on the radio – I thought this was now in the category of public knowledge, rather than Establishment, political class knowledge. It was a blunder.

Mandelson's sexuality was (marginally) a matter of public record since a 1987 *News of the World* story printed shortly before the general election told of 'My Love for Gay Labour Boss'. Mandelson was then Labour's Director of Communications. He was also the target of an autumn 1998 story in Fayed's *Punch* magazine which contained allegations about his social life on a visit to Rio de Janeiro. William Hague referred to the claims by calling him 'Lord Mandelson of Rio' in a Commons speech. It was an ill-advised and potentially dangerous slur.

Hague's cheap joke made him look almost as ridiculous as the BBC, who had rushed to Mandelson's defence by imposing a blanket edict against references to Mandelson's sexuality the day after the *Newsnight* incident. Mandelson himself had been a broadcaster before working for the Labour Party and his colleagues from the early 1980s were by the late 1990s some of the most senior figures in the Corporation. As a public body run by a sub-committee of the Establishment, the BBC is extremely sensitive and as a bureaucracy it has an internal culture of memos and directives. When Stephen Milligan's body was found in February 1994, the awkward euphemism 'unusual sexual circumstances' was used before a memo was circulated allowing mention of women's clothing, a plastic bag and bondage 'but on no account mention fruit'. In 1998 the Mandelson edict was mocked to destruction on the satirical TV show *Have I Got News for You* and it did seem to reflect a vanished world where the views of a small, politically connected hierarchy could determine what people could know.

Another Cabinet minister, Nick Brown, was 'outed' the following weekend, on the night of 7 November. Brown had joined the Cabinet as the Agriculture Minister in the 1998 reshuffle, having previously been a well-regarded Chief Whip and an Opposition Treasury spokesman. He had been told that an ex-lover had gone to the *News of the World* making false claims about their relationship, and decided, in co-operation with the Downing Street press office, to pre-empt the story. Brown announced that he was gay but emphatically denied ever having paid for sex. The *News of the World*, for whom Brown expressed no bitterness, said that they would not have used the story anyway because it seemed 'fanciful'. Brown's reason for not coming out had been kindness to his family; he was relaxed about the consequences for his political career although understandably sad that he had not been able to take the step at a time of his choosing.

Michael Brown, the gay Conservative who came out in 1994, thought: 'Nick Brown handled the circumstances brilliantly. If challenged by a newspaper asking, "Are you gay?" and you answer, "Yes," it's a twenty-four-hour story and that's the end of it. But the Ron Davies situation was inevitably going to cause a mass of difficulties.'

After Brown's private life became public, *The Sun* asked if a gay mafia was running Britain, and made the unappealing offer to gay MPs of a telephone number to call if they wanted to come out. The idea of a gay mafia, according to Peter Chippindale and Chris Horrie in *Stick It up Your Punter!*, probably reflected Rupert Murdoch's own belief that 'they were a dangerous mafia which would take over an organization once let in. Murdoch had come up against the gay network in New York and Hollywood, and found that, like the British Establishment, it was another club he was excluded from.' But it was a grossly misleading analysis of internal Labour Party politics. Ron Davies, Nick Brown, Peter Mandelson and Chris Smith do not form a cohesive group and in fact owe allegiance to several different ideological and personal currents within the government.

Times had changed since the 1980s, when scurrilous campaigns and rude language against homosexuals was commonplace in Fleet Street. *The Sun*'s provocative speculation was regarded as being in bad taste and within days the paper was making peace with homosexuals and the Labour government.

It had been unsure of its ground politically over Mandelson, because it had gone out of its way to praise his record at the Department of Trade and Industry, and retracted its raising of the 'gay mafia' allegation. The editor, David Yelland, said that the paper was 'no longer in the business of destroying closet gays' lives' and would not print stories unless they really were in the public interest.

The Conservative Party seemed to realize that it too had to change. William Hague and Michael Portillo both spoke to Conference meetings about the need to appear more inclusive and welcoming. Hague's record as a supporter of gay rights, including an equal age of consent and even raising the possibility of giving legal recognition to gay partnerships, is among the strongest in the Conservative Party. Portillo spoke personally in an interview in summer 1999, declaring that 'I had some homosexual experiences as a young man', but rubbished some of the more outlandish rumours that had dogged his career. He returned to the Commons in November 1999 as the successor to the old roué Alan Clark as MP for Kensington and Chelsea.

However, the party's attitude to homosexuality is still shot through with contradictions between startling private tolerance in the party hierarchy to blatantly homophobic activists in some areas. Michael Brown, who lost his seat in 1997, thinks that: 'The Conservative Party just cannot cope with this issue. They have still to address the prejudice in their constituencies. That is why the Conservative Party constantly gets itself into a terrible mess.'

The Conservatives endured another terrible mess when Labour decided to repeal the anti-homosexual 'Clause 28' in 1999. The Tory leadership decided to impose a three-line whip to retain the Clause, a decision denounced by all its remaining London mayoral candidates and the sacked Tory spokesman on London, Shaun Woodward MP. Woodward defected to Labour in December 1999, blaming Tory extremism and homophobia. A smaller proportion of Tory MPs voted in favour of reducing the age of consent in 1998 and 1999 than in 1994. The Tories limped into 2000 still fundamentally divided and uncertain on gay issues.

*

The public understanding shown to political figures involved in marital trouble which developed in the 1970s and 1980s has continued. Separation, divorce and remarriage are now considered unremarkable, although 'Cabinet minister has mistress' is still a story which interests tabloid newspapers. In summer 1997 Robin Cook was the first member of the government to be the subject of this classic tabloid story. Cook's relationship with Gaynor Regan was well known in political circles, and had not been considered relevant when Tony Blair appointed him Foreign Secretary. But the danger of tabloid disclosure led Cook to act hastily, on the advice of Downing Street, to separate from his wife Margaret.

In 1998 Margaret Cook was told that nothing she wrote about her personal relationship with Robin Cook would cost her ex-husband his job, and published *A Slight and Delicate Creature* in January 1999. The press, not unnaturally, highlighted the parts of the book which dealt with episodes Robin Cook would not remember with pride. Ludicrously, the Shadow Foreign Secretary Michael Howard, and the newspaper columnist Melanie Phillips, called for Cook's resignation but hardly anyone agreed. The support shown to Cook by his colleagues contrasts with the pressure on Cecil Parkinson when Sara Keays made public disclosures about their relationship in October 1983.

New Labour, therefore, knows roughly what it thinks about sexual morality. Homosexuality is regarded as equal and respectable, and not in any way as lacking in morality. Transgressions, homosexual or heterosexual, from the ideal of a stable partnership are regarded with toleration rather than approval as long as the person's public work is not affected. There are probably limits. Ron Davies was obliged to resign because of the stupidity of what he had done and the unreliability of his statements afterwards, rather than for his sexual preferences. Casual and promiscuous gay sex such as cruising in public parks, however, are probably still beyond the pale if they lead to trouble. Tom Driberg's exploits would still be scandalous if a politician of today was to replicate them: compulsive cottaging and a steady stream of rent boys would not be smiled upon, and might still be enough to lead to resignation. A modern Ian Harvey might face calls for resignation from his ministerial office, but his right to remain an MP and be reinstated within a couple of years if he did resign would not be challenged.

New Labour's relative clarity about sex is in contrast to its confused relationship with business. For most of the century, Labour has been at least nominally opposed to the power of private business, although in practice a more pragmatic attitude has ruled. Labour has also historically been the political manifestation of the trade union movement, which exists to represent workers' interests and has therefore been in repeated conflict with employers.

But the apparent grand conflict between Labour and industry has not been a universal pattern, just as the representatives of unions and management spend more time in agreement, helping production to flow smoothly, than in conflict. Labour has always recognized, even in its most radical periods, the right of sections of private industry to exist. However, Labour's conception of the best way of organizing business has in the past involved a greater role for government intervention than business itself would demand. The party's belief in a more equal society, the redistribution of power and wealth, is more directly inimical to the personal interests of the class of people running British business. The fact that much of the traditional business élite shares a common educational and social background with the Conservatives has created a strong bond.

In general, Labour and business have each felt misunderstood by the other. The exceptions are of considerable interest. All too often, the party has reacted to the slightest flicker of business interest or support with unconsidered delight, and been exposed to attack as a result because of the sharp practice of its allies and the naïvety of the party's approach. Sidney Stanley's machinations were assisted by the enthusiasm of the Labour Party to encourage business links, and crooked businessmen such as Joe Kagan and Eric Miller were able to gain access to Harold Wilson and the Labour Party organization because of the need to find allies in the business community, and not turn away recruits without good reason.

The sort of businessmen who generally became involved with Labour politics for much of the postwar period were themselves outsiders, snubbed by the traditional business establishment through snobbery or anti-semitism. Eric Miller, for instance, was desperately unhappy and insecure and his property firm's money gave him the chance to win friends and move in influential circles. Arnold Goodman's money enabled him to do favours for people he wanted as friends – he was never paid for his work on the many public bodies he served and even neglected to bill some of his legal clients. The fact of their outsider status and political connection with the Labour Party meant that they could not rely on the old boy network to cover up any of their misdeeds, as could their Conservative equivalents. In the 1980s it was still advisable to count the spoons when 'socialist millionaires' such as Robert Maxwell came to dinner.

Throughout history, Labour's links with business have been controversial and New Labour's promises to have an even closer relationship with business were opening the way to more problems. Considering the puritanical climate in which the party took office in May 1997, and the acceptance by New Labour of much of the Thatcherite approach to business, the risks were obvious.

New Labour's 1997 manifesto made far-reaching promises about raising standards: 'We will clean up politics ... The Conservatives are afflicted by sleaze and prosper from secret funds from foreign supporters. There is unquestionably a national crisis of confidence in our political system, to which Labour will respond in a measured and sensible way.'

At the 1996 Labour conference Tony Blair had promised that Labour would be 'tough on sleaze and tough on the causes of sleaze'; at the same conference John Prescott lambasted John Major for clinging on to Neil Hamilton – 'the immoral majority' of one which was propping up the government. On taking office, Blair promised that the government would be whiter than white – in retrospect a hostage to fortune in the same way as Major's Back to Basics campaign. Labour could hardly have promised less without the assault on Tory sleaze seeming mere verbiage. To a greater extent than generally realized, the Parliament elected in 1997 has made good on the promise to cut down on sleaze.

Extending the corruption laws to MPs was already under consideration in the last months of the Major government, after the Nolan Committee suggested that it should be reviewed along with the totality of the law relating to bribery. The Law Commission published proposals on bribery law in March 1997 and in June 1997 the new Home Secretary Jack Straw announced that government legislation would cover the whole area of corruption of public and private bodies. A new offence of misuse of public office would be created. Straw also announced that, once the relevant parliamentary committees had reported, bribery of MPs would be brought under the law. Draft proposals were expected to be published in late 1999.

The government also expressed interest in tougher restrictions on ministers. In July 1997 new, stricter guidelines were introduced for the financial affairs of ministers, including for the first time a code of conduct for ministers taking out legal actions for defamation, specifying that they should consult government legal officers and then their own solicitors. This particular clause was a response to the complaints about the Treasury paying some of Norman Lamont's legal bills during his efforts to evict a sex therapist from his Notting Hill basement. After the issues raised by the Aitken case and the ineffectiveness of the Cabinet Secretary's investigation, the government considered bringing ministers within the net of some sort of commissioner for ethics who could give advice privately or conduct public investigations. How this might be implemented is still under consideration.

The cesspit of political funding was referred to the Committee on Standards in Public Life, now under the chairmanship of Sir Patrick Neill rather than Lord Nolan. The report, published in October 1998, was – like the first Nolan Report in May 1995 – well written for an official document and surprisingly radical. It recommended full public disclosure of all political donations exceeding £5,000, a ban on foreign donations and a £20 million cap on national campaign spending. It also recommended the end of blind trusts and wider scrutiny of honours which might be perceived to be linked with political donations. While state funding was not recommended, tax relief on political donations of under £500 was approved. The government announced that it would implement the Neill recommendations.

The Labour government started off with a stern, even brutal, approach to the misdeeds of its own backbenchers. The case of Robert Wareing, Labour MP for Liverpool West Derby, was unusual in that the Labour Chief Whip, Nick Brown, was the complainant against one of his own backbenchers. Brown first wrote to Sir Gordon Downey on 18 June 1997, and expanded his criticism of Wareing's conduct in another letter on 24 June saying that 'it seems to me that Bob Wareing ... has committed a very serious breach of the rules and resolutions relating to the standards that should apply to a Member of Parliament'. Wareing had controlled a company which had been dealing with firms linked to the Bosnian Serb regime and failed to declare the interest. His conduct was found to be 'wrong' by the Select Committee and in July 1997 he was given a week's suspension and forced to make a personal statement. The Wareing case was the sign of a harsher new regime – the leadership had cracked down on misconduct in its ranks rather than suppressing the facts. However, Wareing was an obscure backbencher, and his association with such a repellent cause as the Bosnian Serbs was relatively easy for the leadership to denounce.

The party leadership were also seriously worried by Scottish sleaze. Two incidents early in the Parliament drew attention to the rancid state of Labour politics in parts of the west of Scotland. Mohammed Sarwar, the newly elected MP for Glasgow Govan, was accused of bribing a potential opponent to stand down as a candidate and fraudulently registering voters in Govan who were not entitled. Sarwar was suspended from the Labour Party and faced criminal charges resulting from the Govan election campaign. Sarwar was acquitted in April 1999 and readmitted to the Parliamentary Labour Party. The Labour MP for Paisley South, Gordon McMaster, committed suicide in summer 1997. He had been depressed and accused a fellow MP, Tommy Graham, of waging a smear campaign against him. McMaster had also clashed with Paisley local politicians, and there were murky allegations about the involvement of organized crime in a council-funded community project. Together with a scandal over councillors' expenses in Glasgow, the Paisley affair added to fears that Scottish Labour politics needed cleaning up. The Scottish Labour Party has been particularly rigorous in vetting prospective Scottish Parliament candidates, but it remains to be seen how effective it has been at suppressing sleaze, rather than left-wingers.

The first allegations of sleaze in the new Parliament that looked like having British, as opposed to Scottish, national political implications concerned Formula One. Labour in Opposition had been critical of the tobacco industry and tended to support measures to restrict cigarette advertising. In government, the party inherited a European-wide policy which was heading towards a complete advertising ban. As well as direct advertising on billboards, indirect advertising through sponsorship of sports events was to be phased out. Motor racing was particularly affected by any changes to indirect advertising because tracks, cars and drivers are heavily sponsored by cigarette firms, so much so that the sport looks to the casual observer as if motorized cigarette boxes are the main feature of a race.

Formula One is a worldwide sport, which unlike many others would be perfectly able to pull out of any country which became an inhospitable business climate. In government, Labour health ministers found themselves arguing through gritted teeth that Formula One should have a temporary exemption from the advertising ban under the EU Directive so that it would have more time to diversify. By October 1997 there was general agreement on the matter in Britain and Germany, which was also affected. Britain applied to the European Commission for an exemption for Formula One on 4 November.

The problem arose because Bernie Ecclestone, the boss of Formula One, had given the Labour Party £1 million in January 1997, and had offered a further donation in summer 1997. The January donation was accepted, but the summer donation was regarded as more complicated because the government was considering the tobacco advertising exemption; on 7 November 1997 Labour wrote to Sir Patrick Neill, who had taken over the Committee on Standards in Public Life from Lord Nolan, to ask his advice.

So far, so good. The problems were caused by the way that information about the Ecclestone donation and its proposed sequel dribbled out publicly over a period of a few days in November rather than being announced publicly. The party gave the impression that it had something to hide, and details such as the huge size of the donation and the possibility of a second emerged only gradually. The result was the worst of all worlds for Labour.

The party's General Secretary Tom Sawyer had told Neill that the donation was 'substantial' but did not give a figure. Neill replied to Sawyer and Blair that:

> *my own opinion is that, while no criticism can fairly be made of the receipt of the first donation, in the light of the way in which government policy has developed, ministers could well conclude that, in the special circumstances of this case, their freedom of action would be, and would be seen to be, enhanced, if the donation were to be returned.*

There was no way that Labour could hold on to the money after this, so it had to be returned to Ecclestone. Then the amount became public, and the question of the second donation arose, as did the interdepartmental dealings involving the Health ministry and Number 10. Tony Blair was given a rough ride in Prime Minister's Question Time on 12 November. Martin Bell, the sleazebuster of Tatton, asked pointedly: 'Have we slain one dragon only to have another take its place with a red rose in its mouth?'

On the same day, Blair extended the remit of the Neill Committee to cover party funding. It reported in October 1998. In retrospect, the Ecclestone affair does indeed seem a storm in a teacup. Nobody seriously suggested that the changing government line on Formula One was really in response to payments from Ecclestone, or that the businessman had given the money in the hope of buying influence. Ecclestone later complained that foreign coverage of the affair was oversimplified and falsely asserted that he had attempted to bribe the British government. The letter in which Sir Patrick Neill advised Labour to return the donation was about appearances, and the necessity of being seen to be above reproach. Ecclestone's motive, he told Neill, had actually been to support Tony Blair's position that Labour should not increase income tax, and to reduce the party's dependence on union funds. He had previously been a donor to the Conservative Party. Ironically, Ecclestone claimed later, he would personally benefit from the phasing out of tobacco sponsorship because it would have to be replaced by higher earnings from TV rights, out of which he personally was paid a proportion.

*

Given the sensitivities aroused by the Hamilton case and the activities of Ian Greer Associates, it was perhaps predictable that there would be an incident involving lobbying. The lobbying and communications industry was as aware as anyone else by 1996 that Labour was likely to win the next election and being too closely identified with the Conservatives would be bad for business. There was a gold rush in the lobbying industry for people who understood how New Labour worked and the sort of language and appeal that would impress a future Labour government. The stampede was at its height just after the 1997 election. 'The phones just rang off the hook. Just about everybody got three or four offers of a job with the private sector', one insider told *The Times*. It was a dizzying time. Bright recent graduates in their twenties were paid around £20,000 a year for their campaign work by Labour, but were offered twice as much or more, sometimes salaries into six figures, by private firms. Part of the reason for the extreme salaries was that there was a relatively small number of people who fitted the bill, because New Labour people were rather a closed circle, almost as hostile to opponents within the Labour Party as to Conservatives. The limited numbers drove up their value; cliquishness and the value of exclusivity were built into 'the Project' at the start.

The inexperience of the young New Labour *apparatchiks* (dubbed 'the Millbank Tendency' in honour of the campaign headquarters) when they turned to lobbying was not helped in most cases by a lack of guidance in the behaviour expected from a reputable lobbyist. For the most part, this took the form of arrogance and exuberance being allowed free rein rather than the sort of institutionalized sleaze that had developed by the late 1980s under the Conservative government. As the more experienced lobbyist Douglas Smith puts it: 'Everybody who knows the system of government knows there's a massive Civil Service behind ministers. To assume that it could suddenly be avoided and that you could do things by moving in, meeting people and making phone calls was presumptuous and idiotic and they were heading for a fall.'

Derek Draper became the emblematic figure of the arrogance of New Labour. He was a smooth young protégé of Peter Mandelson turned senior lobbyist. Unlike some others of the Millbank Tendency, Draper's Labour credentials were of long standing: he had endured over a decade of unglamorous constituency activism and student politics before becoming part of the metropolitan political class. He was also, for all his errors, a cleverer lobbyist than most. He had helped set up a consultancy called Prima Europe when he left Mandelson's service in 1996. Prima was absorbed by another lobbying company, GPC, in February 1998 and merged in turn with another firm, Market Access. The Prima deal brought Draper into the big time as a lobbyist. In June 1998, as reported in *The Observer*, Derek Draper was boasting to an American called Gregory Palast, whom he believed to be an executive of an energy company, about his connections with the New Labour establishment: 'There are seventeen people that count, and to say that I am intimate with all of them is the understatement of the century ... What I really am is a commentator-fixer. Your Mayor Daley [of Chicago] has nothing on me.'

It is dangerous to take Draper's self-estimation (especially as filtered through a journalist's notebook) at face value; but although he is hardly in the Daley class as a party boss, his New Labour connections were second to none. One of Draper's closest contacts was Roger Liddle, who had joined the Downing Street Policy Unit when Labour won the election. Liddle had previously been Managing Director at Prima Europe but, on joining, his 25 per cent stake in Prima Europe had been placed in a blind trust and sold when GPC took over the company. According to Palast, Liddle said, 'There is a circle, and Derek is part of the circle. And anyone who says he isn't is the enemy ... Whenever you are ready, just tell me what you want, who you want to meet, and Derek and I will make the call for you.' The language and the implication that Liddle would perform introductions are vigorously disputed by Liddle and Number 10, and in any case the comments were lubricated by champagne at a GPC reception. Liddle was cleared of misconduct by a Downing Street investigation.

Corinne Souza, author of *How to be a Lobbyist*, puts the Draper affair in perspective:

Cronyism is the modern phrase for the old boy network and for patronage. Ian Greer did not invent this system by having the keys to [Thatcher's] Number 10 any more than Derek Draper invented the system by having the keys to Blair's Number 10 ... Derek Draper was employed by a lobbying company for his address book, whom he knew. You cannot blame him for delivering, it is up to those he knew to live in some form of purdah.

Draper knew the boom could not last: 'I think there will be a scandal here eventually. The curtain is going to come down. I'm sure it will happen.'

He spoke more truly than he realized. Gregory Palast was actually a journalist working for *The Observer*, and Draper's remarks duly appeared on the pages of the newspaper on 5 July 1998. The resulting small scandal was dubbed 'cash for access' which is really a description of the lobbying business from start to finish.

Palast's investigation caused embarrassment to other lobbyists with New Labour connections. Karl Milner of GJW government relations, a former adviser to Chancellor Gordon Brown, told Palast that he had leaked a Select Committee report to a putative client. This sounded bad, but lobby journalists did not take it very seriously. Select Committee reports are, perhaps unfortunately, not very influential, and advance copies are scattered around quite liberally in Westminster.

Another New Labour firm was LLM – Lawson, Lucas, Mendelsohn – set up in 1997 by three former aides to Tony Blair. Ben Lucas was allegedly able to offer the undercover journalist advance access to official announcements, particularly those coming from the Treasury, but for the most part the LLM approach was more considered and intellectual than Draper's. The firm, as is the proper function of a lobbying concern, aimed to give the client a detailed ideological analysis of New Labour and the 'Third Way', and the sort of language that would carry weight with the government. It was rather cynical stuff, according to Palast's recollection of Neal Lawson's pitch: 'on big issues especially, they don't know what they are thinking. Blair himself doesn't always know what he is thinking.' If the government was this uncertain, the role of the lobbyist was extremely important.

The Draper affair was damaging but short-lived as far as the government was concerned. As with Ecclestone, the affair produced no evidence that the government's policies were for sale, and the main revelations boiled down to the unsurprising conclusion that lobbyists boast about how well connected they are and how important their work is. GPC Market Access endured a sticky few months of restructuring, but Derek Draper was not involved. He resigned his position at the firm and was denounced as a rogue elephant in the lobbying industry by an inquiry commissioned by the trade association the Association of Professional Political Consultants. It was rather a harsh verdict, and some of Draper's friends think he walked the plank to spare the government greater embarrassment. He was also fired from a £70,000 a year column for *The Express* – 'Inside the Mind of New Labour' – when it was alleged that it was vetted by Peter Mandelson. One of nature's survivors, Draper has started a media career, although it has been derailed by his exuberant call to his radio station from an Amsterdam brothel.

The Draper disclosures were followed by the imposition of new rules governing relations between civil servants, including politically appointed special advisers, and lobbyists. They were warned that leaking confidential or sensitive material to a lobbyist, or helping a lobbyist by arranging privileged access, would lead to disciplinary proceedings and dismissal. 'Modest hospitality' such as a reception would be allowed. Blair also expressed interest in the suggestions that at long last a register of lobbyists should be established and that a 'quarantine period' should be applied to Opposition advisers going into lobbying.

The problems caused by bringing wealthy businessmen into government were also predictable. Harold Wilson had fallen into this trap in 1974 when he gave his former landlord Lord Brayley a junior ministerial job. The minister resigned within months when his conduct as a company director was made the subject of a DTI inquiry. New Labour, in turn, had attempted to demonstrate its new relationship with business at the highest level, but the culture clash between business and the austere rules demanded of public servants generated bad publicity. Sir David Simon left a job at BP paying £750,000 to become Lord Simon, an unpaid Minister for Trade and Competitiveness attached to the Department of Trade and Industry, and Geoffrey Robinson became Paymaster-General.

Lord Simon's position was the first to come under criticism on two fronts from the Opposition. His financial affairs had taken some time to be unwound, a situation complicated by his ownership of a large tranche of BP shares. During the 1980s and 1990s progressively tighter legal curbs on insider dealing had been enacted, and Simon feared that he might have fallen foul of these rules had he moved immediately to sell off the BP shares. Questions were raised and rapidly dismissed about the propriety of his taking decisions or advising on issues involving the gas industry during this transitional period. In July 1997 *The Sunday Times* reported that Simon had £1 million in offshore funds and William Hague, now Conservative Leader, accused him in the House of Commons of 'tax avoidance'. He declined the opportunity of repeating this allegation outside parliamentary privilege. In August 1997 Simon sold his holding in BP, placing the £2 million capital in a blind trust and donating the profits since the election (roughly £350,000) to charity. The government's handling of Lord Simon's business affairs was anything but sure-footed and, although Simon remained a minister, it gave a bad impression.

Geoffrey Robinson was elected Labour MP for Coventry North West in 1976. Before this he was a business executive with Jaguar. Robinson was one of the rare Labour MPs who continued an active business career while sitting in Parliament. He had rather despaired of the party's chances in the 1980s and stepped down from the front bench in 1986 to take a job as Chairman of an engineering company, Trans-Tec. In 1991 Robinson suddenly stopped being merely comfortable and became really rich. He was the beneficiary of an inheritance valued at over £9 million from a Belgian millionaire, Madame Joska Bourgeois, whom Robinson had known through the motor industry.

Robinson had used his newfound riches since 1991 in a way he thought would be helpful to the Labour Party, particularly after he came back into political favour with the election of Tony Blair as Labour leader in 1994. According to colleagues, he was 'suddenly all over the place' in 1996. He bought the *New Statesman* with the intention of ensuring that the house magazine of the British left stayed in business and took a broadly positive view of Tony Blair and New Labour. Despite its influence the *New Statesman* has, to put it kindly, never been a commercial goldmine and Robinson was not expecting to make money on the deal. He was also generous in providing hospitality in Britain and abroad, particularly at his villa in Tuscany, to his friends among the Labour Party leadership. He was a gracious and prolific host, giving lavish parties and inviting political friends, some of them of recent provenance, to sporting events. He had recently bought Coventry City Football Club. Robinson's friends were never sure about why he was so liberal with his fortune. It would be too easy to say that he was trying to buy his way into a prospective Labour government; when he was appointed he warned Blair that it might prove problematic because the left and journalists did not like what he represented.

Robinson was made Paymaster-General in May 1997, a flexible ministerial post that in his case was a brief to redraw the system of tax-free savings – a task that by all accounts he accomplished successfully. His work as a minister was obscured by the problems that his complex business affairs had caused. Robinson was repeatedly investigated by the Parliamentary Commissioner for Standards – three times in 1998. The first occasion was about the non-declaration of a trust based in Guernsey; the second was about failure to register a company directorship of an engineering firm, Swiss EDM/Agie UK, during the 1983–87 Parliament. On neither occasion did the Select Committee find that he deserved the imposition of a penalty. The third was about a more recent unregistered shareholding in a firm called Stenbell.

The number of minor complaints against Robinson eventually told against him with the Select Committee in November 1998: 'the cumulative effect of the shortcomings identified in two reports is such that we recommend that Mr Robinson should make an apology to the House by means of a personal statement'. Robinson did as he was obliged, but his apology was so graceless and so short – fifty-four seconds – that it won him little sympathy in the House. He was also questioned by the Prime Minister's Chief of Staff over his chairmanship of Hollis Industries, a firm linked with Robert Maxwell which had gone into administration in 1991. Robinson's political support had been worn away by months of adverse publicity and he was left in a severely exposed position when the next blow hit him. It came from an unexpected direction.

Peter Mandelson received a £373,000 loan from Robinson to help him buy a house a few months before the Labour election victory of May 1997. Mandelson was not a consultancy or directorship collector and was reliant on his pay as an MP. During his parliamentary career in 1992–96 he shared a flat with two colleagues and had a house in his Hartlepool constituency, but this style of life hardly reflected Mandelson's impending status as one of the most powerful people in Britain. Mandelson was increasingly moving in high society circles, and his former colleagues in broadcasting like John Birt were earning salaries many times his pay as a backbencher. Unlike Reggie Maudling and the 1980s Tories who had felt similarly inadequate among the rich, Mandelson did not hire himself out for money. He thought he had a cleaner solution. Robinson's money offered a short-cut to the trappings of success he desired and to which he felt entitled. He was able to buy a house in Northumberland Place, a pleasant street in west London, with the loan and a mortgage from the Britannia Building Society for a total cost of £475,000.

The details of the arrangement between Robinson and Mandelson emerged on 22 December 1998, *The Guardian* again in the lead in publishing a story about the financial affairs of politicians. The house was described, rather inaccurately, as being in Notting Hill – it is actually in a neighbouring area called Westbourne Park – but Notting Hill's reputation as London's most expensive and celebrity-ridden district was more attractive to headline writers. Mandelson had feared the disclosure for some time, and knew that his political career depended on the response of his colleagues and the next day's press. His colleagues were less than fulsome in backing him, and the reaction from the other papers to the house loan story was strongly hostile.

Mandelson's resignation on 23 December – followed within hours by Robinson's – came as a surprise. Mandelson's reputation for deviousness equalled that of Talleyrand, who remarked, 'I wonder what he meant by that?' on hearing of the death of a rival diplomat. Many concluded that Mandelson decided that in the long term his career would be better served by resigning rather than hanging on.

Mandelson was perilously dependent on the favour of Tony Blair. He had been a backroom operator in the Labour Party from 1985 to 1990 under Neil Kinnock, and played a considerable part in dragging the party back to electability. His most noted change as Director of Communications was to replace the tattered red flag with a red rose as the party's symbol. He surprised many colleagues when he left the job (although he continued to be an important player behind the scenes) and was selected as Labour candidate for Hartlepool. Elected in 1992, Mandelson had been one of Blair's most important backers in the 1994 leadership election. This fact had to be concealed from the Labour Party internal electorate and Blair played a cryptic tribute to him as 'Bobby' (Kennedy, to Blair's JFK) only after winning. The widespread dislike for Mandelson in the Labour Party was only partly for political reasons. He was widely regarded as a cold, even rude, person; for an expert communicator his personal image was extremely poor. Although those close to him paint a very different picture of his character,

Mandelson did not have deep reserves of loyalty in the Labour Party he could call upon in trouble. Many Labour MPs regarded him with respect rather than affection, and some were positively delighted by his downfall.

The Conservatives were gleeful; in that party he was hated for the triumphs for which Labour did not give him sufficient credit. Ian Greer and Michael Brown were amused and not particularly sympathetic to Mandelson's admission that in hindsight he should have registered the Robinson loan. Greer finds it 'very sickening, because he had been one of many Labour Opposition members who had thoroughly enjoyed the embarrassment of Tory MPs because they had made the same mistake. He had apparently learned nothing.'

Mandelson could probably have survived the story had it been quietly announced in May 1997. What made the difference by December 1998 was the steady stream of adverse publicity that had poured over Geoffrey Robinson and the fact that Mandelson's Department of Trade and Industry was responsible for business regulation. On 23 September 1998 Mandelson had informed his Conservative shadow David Heathcoat-Amory that the question of the inaccurate accounts of Hollis Industries, a Robinson company, 'is being considered' by the DTI. Within the Department, Mandelson had distanced himself from an inquiry into a fellow minister.

The loan became caught up in party infighting. Robinson and Mandelson were not particularly close, personally or politically, despite the loan. The third casualty of the affair, Gordon Brown's press spokesman Charlie Whelan, resigned in January 1999 because it was widely believed that he had 'spun' the story against Mandelson. According to the somewhat tortuous analysis of *The Sunday Times*, the imminent sinking of Robinson would damage Gordon Brown and therefore Mandelson would gain an even stronger position with the Prime Minister. To prevent this change in the balance of power, the Brown camp torpedoed Mandelson by leaking the loan story to his unauthorized biographer Paul Routledge (now occasionally writing for Robinson's *New Statesman*). How it ended up in *The Guardian* is still a matter of dispute.

Mandelson returned quickly to an influential position; as early as 8 January 1999 he acted as Tony Blair's personal envoy in talks with the German government. He had been boosted by an announcement by the Britannia Building Society that it had not upheld the most serious allegations against him. It had been claimed that his application for his mortgage had been false because he did not declare the Robinson loan, but the Britannia stated that 'the information given to us at the time of the mortgage application was accurate'. The new Parliamentary Commissioner for Standards, Elizabeth Filkin, disagreed and thought Mandelson had 'breached the code of conduct for MPs'. Mandelson protested strongly that the ruling was 'illogical' and in July 1999 the Select Committee agreed that he had not breached the code, saying that he had acted without dishonest intent. In future, however, loans between MPs must be registered. Mandelson sold the house for £725,000 in June, having made £200,000 after paying his debt. Local estate agents were divided on whether the notoriety of the house added to its value or not: 'Notting Hill is so full of movie stars that Peter Mandelson is not that extra-ordinary', one told the *Financial Times*. Blair set the seal on Mandelson's return to favour by appointing him Northern Ireland Secretary in October 1999.

The resignations of Mandelson and Robinson were expected to end the Labour government's long electoral honeymoon. Labour had been consistently ahead in the opinion polls since September 1992. It is unprecedented for a party to sustain a six-year ascendancy, and for nearly two years of government to have gone by without the electorate's voting intentions to shift against the ruling party. Surprisingly, when the first polls of 1999 were taken, the Conservatives had suffered more than Labour from the re-emergence of sleaze as a political issue.

The reason for this surprising state of affairs is that memories are still fresh from the Tory sleaze of the previous government. Sleaze, particularly cash for questions, seems to be linked to the Tories in the same sort of way that strikes, especially the 1979 winter of discontent, was linked with Labour in the early 1980s. However much doubt is cast on the standards of the Labour government, very few voters seem willing to believe that the situation would improve if the Conservatives were brought back to power. The Conservative tactic of hyping any minor transgression into a public issue, copied from Labour's assault on the Major government, looks like the pot calling the kettle black. The Tories had presided over a deep recession in 1990–92 which had led to job losses, high mortgage rates and poverty, and the idea that Tory MPs were living the high life was offensive to many voters. In addition, the public are not looking for reasons to dislike what is still a new government. In 1994 the Conservatives were a tired crew who had been in power for fifteen years; the previous occasion when sleaze had been an important issue for voters was in 1963, after a similar long spell in government.

In recent British history, scandal has only weakened governments which were already undermined by the staleness of a long period in power and which had lost control of the political agenda. Fresh governments with a strong sense of direction, like the Attlee Labour government in 1948 (Sidney Stanley) or the Thatcher Conservative government in 1986 (the Westland affair) can ride out even scandals which briefly capture the popular imagination. The Blair government seems strong enough to do the same.

Conclusion

THE FUTURE OF SLEAZE 2000-

I t is always dangerous to predict the future: history is littered with confident predictions that rapidly bit the dust. But I think the following sketch is a reasonable enough vision of likely developments.

Sexual behaviour will cease to be an important factor in political careers, once a politician has become established at Westminster. Labour regards homosexual relationships as more or less equivalent to heterosexual relationships. Privacy is more and more difficult to maintain, so a gap will open up between what counts as a good tabloid story and what counts as politically damaging. Footballers and popular musicians have long survived tabloid revelations about their sex lives with the most minor career problems, and the same will eventually become true of politicians. The failure of the bizarre attempt to impeach President Clinton over his relationship with Monica Lewinsky dealt a blow to moralizers across the Western world.

Similarly, some forms of sexual behaviour now regarded as borderline resignation cases, principally cruising for sex in public places and paying to indulge kinks, will be treated by Westminster society and the public in a similar way to drunk driving and drunk and disorderly offences which cause momentary embarrassment but are quickly forgotten. The Conservative Party remains ambivalent about these social trends and, particularly at the grass roots, will continue to be so.

The remaining sexual taboos for politicians will then approach the criminal law more closely. Rape and paedophilia will of course be unacceptable conduct. The only likely growth area in accusations of sexual misconduct would be workplace sexual harassment cases. There are no precedents for how the political class would handle such a matter.

Recreational drug use among politicians is likely to be a growth area for future scandals. There is a ready public interest angle given that politicians insist on maintaining the illegal status of cannabis and other drugs and preaching about the evils of drugs to the electorate. Calls for reform of the law in this area are met with polite and reasoned resistance from Jack Straw at the Home Office and hysterical mockery from some Conservatives. The shift over the years in the composition of the political élite has brought to power the first generation who went to university at a time when cannabis use was common, and the trend will only continue. It is probable that a certain proportion of MPs still enjoy the occasional joint. In January 1999 the

Conservative MEP Tom Spencer admitted that he occasionally used drugs while in Amsterdam. His absent-minded failure to throw the drugs away before returning to Britain was detected by customs officers and led to a withdrawal of support from his Conservative colleagues. There will be more of the same.

Financial corruption will be even more infrequent than it has been in the past, although it will not seem that way. The most serious problems will involve local government. The compulsory competitive tendering for a range of council services which was introduced in the 1980s increased the number of commercial decisions taken by amateur local councillors. In the 1960s the construction industry was the biggest such interface, and it involved systematic corruption centred on John Poulson and other building firms such as Crudens and Bryants. During the 1980s contract cleaning, information technology and waste disposal were boom areas. It would be extremely surprising if there were, if not another Poulson, one or two significant cases of corrupt influence on contract decisions. Whether the evidence will surface is another matter. It depends mainly on the efforts of local and business journalists, and future cases are unlikely to involve the equivalent of the thorough archive Poulson bequeathed to the bankruptcy court.

The strict regime imposed on Parliament in 1995–98 has changed the institution more than is generally realized. Monitoring of ethics and conduct has passed outside the control of Parliament to the Parliamentary Commissioner for Standards and the continuing Neill Committee on standards in public life. Both institutions now have a life of their own. The publication of the Commissioner's findings stops any temptation on the part of the Commons Select Committee on Standards and Privileges to return to the cosy arrangements that discredited the system over Poulson and during the 1980s. The political class has drawn the message from the 1997 election that public tolerance of financial irregularity is very low, and it will not forget quickly. New areas such as indebtedness and transactions between members are being brought into the system as quickly as they seem to arise. Allegations that were trivial, even vexatious, were investigated during the 1997–98 session.

A balance has yet to be struck between the need for scrutiny and transparency and the need for the results of openness to be handled responsibly by the Opposition and the media. But the great imponderable remains how much we will ever know. The full truth about the activities of extremely prominent figures in the 1960s such as Bob Boothby, Jeremy Thorpe, Reginald Maudling and Tom Driberg was only revealed many years later, in the case of Boothby and Thorpe only in the 1990s. Each of the dominant political movements since 1945 has now had some of its dark side exposed. The 1945–51 Labour government combined high rectitude with an undercurrent of spivs and hospitality. The 1951–64 Conservative government posed as moral leaders and guardians of British interests in the Cold War, but some of its members lived in a louche climate of sexual licence and lax security. Harold Wilson had the corrupt figures of Lord Kagan and Eric Miller at his side; Edward Heath allowed City spivs to run riot and had Maudling as his deputy. Under Thatcher, a climate of freeloading and dubious get-rich-quick enterprises flourished among Conservative MPs, and Major's government became synonymous with sleaze. New Labour stands accused of being built on a network of cronies.

One wonders how much more, and how much worse, in recent political history is still hidden. Britain's reputation as one of the cleanest political systems in the world has been sustained by strict libel laws and official secrecy. As society and government become more open, this reputation faces even more testing times in the years ahead.

Select Bibliography

Several compendiums of scandal have been published in the last few years, of which the best is Matthew Parris' *Great Parliamentary Scandals* (Robson, 1995). I have found this book a constant reference point for its accuracy and sympathy. Alan Doig's *Westminster Babylon* (Allison & Busby, 1990) is also a painstaking – as well as hilarious – book by one of the few political scientists to take an interest in the dark side of British political life.

Chapter 1
The age of austerity 1945–62
The Board of Trade 'corruption' affair is described in Stanley Wade Baron's *The Contact Man* (Secker & Warburg, 1966) and in the memoirs of Hartley Shawcross, *Life Sentence* (Constable, 1995). Harold Wilson's *Memoirs 1916–64* (Weidenfeld & Nicolson, 1986) adds some detail on postwar controls and austerity. Robert Rhodes James' *Bob Boothby* (Hodder & Stoughton, 1991) is a sympathetic account of its subject. Peter Hennessy's *Whitehall* (Secker & Warburg, 1989) is the definitive work on prevailing ministerial standards, including Crichel Down and *QPM*. Paul Ferris' *The City* (Gollancz, 1960) describes Bank Rate.

Chapter 2
'Honourable Members' 1945–74
Mark Hollingsworth's *MPs for Hire* (Bloomsbury, 1991) and Alan Doig's *Corruption and Misconduct* (Penguin, 1984) were very useful for this chapter. Samuel Finer's *Anonymous Empire* (Pall Mall, 1965) is a contemporary account which missed most of the underside of the industry that existed even then. On specific politicians in this time I have consulted Philip Ziegler's *Harold Wilson* (Weidenfeld & Nicolson, 1993), Kenneth Morgan's *Callaghan: A Life* (Oxford University Press, 1997), Peter Walker's *Staying Power* (Bloomsbury, 1993) and Charles Raw's *Slater Walker* (André Deutsch, 1977). The King payments to George Brown are in Christopher Mayhew's *Time to Explain* (Hutchinson, 1987), Peter Paterson's *Tired and Emotional: The Life of Lord George Brown* (Chatto & Windus, 1993) and Cecil King's *Strictly Personal* (Weidenfeld & Nicolson, 1969). Lewis Minkin's *The Contentious Alliance* (Edinburgh University Press, 1991) is a full account of Labour's relations with the unions. Michael Gillard and Martin Tomkinson's *Nothing to Declare* (John Calder, 1980)

and Eddie Milne's *No Shining Armour* (John Calder, 1976) deal mainly with the Poulson affair – Chapter 6 – but also cover the areas of dubious PR and consultancy contracts, as does Richard Crossman's *Diaries of A Cabinet Minister, Vol. 3* (Hamish Hamilton and Jonathan Cape, 1977). Gordon Winter's *Inside BOSS* (Penguin, 1981) and *The Naked Spy* by Yevgeny Ivanov with Gennady Sokolov (Blake, 1992) are memoirs by spies.

Chapter 3
Private lives 1945–62
Cate Haste's *Rules of Desire* (Pimlico, 1994) is a general history of sex in Britain in the twentieth century, and both Matthew Parris' book and H. Montgomery Hyde's *A Tangled Web* (Futura, 1986) were particularly informative. Political divorces are described in Robert Rhodes James' *Anthony Eden* (Weidenfeld & Nicolson, 1986), the same author's *Bob Boothby*, and Somerset de Chair's *Buried Pleasure* (Merlin, 1985). For Gaitskell and Fleming, see Brian Brivati's *Hugh Gaitskell* (Richard Cohen Books, 1996) and Andrew Lycett's *Ian Fleming* (Weidenfeld & Nicolson, 1995). Edward Short's *Whip to Wilson* (Macdonald, 1989) revealed the existence of the dirt book. Anne Chisholm and Michael Davie's *Beaverbrook: A Life* (Hutchinson, 1992) is a revealing account of that bizarre figure; and on press morals see also Colin Seymour-Ure's *The British Press and Broadcasting Since 1945* (Blackwell, 1995) and Patrick Marnham's *The Private Eye Story* (André Deutsch, 1982). Brian Brivati's *Goodman: A Life* (Richard Cohen Books, 1999) deals with the Venetian Blind and its sequels; see also Richard Crossman's *The Backbench Diaries of Richard Crossman* (Jonathan Cape, 1981) and Anthony Howard's *Crossman: The Pursuit of Power* (Jonathan Cape, 1990) on this episode and Crossman's sexual history. Homosexuality is the theme of Ian Harvey's *To Fall Like Lucifer* (Sidgwick & Jackson, 1971) and Tom Driberg's suitably outrageous *Ruling Passions* (Jonathan Cape, 1977). Francis Wheen's *Tom Driberg: His Life and Indiscretions* (Chatto & Windus, 1990) is a spectacularly good biography: who could resist a book with a chapter called 'Distant Trousers'?

Chapter 4
The climate of scandal 1962–63
While John Vassall's *Vassall: The Autobiography of a Spy* (Sidgwick & Jackson, 1975) is practically alone, the Profumo affair has spawned a multitude of books. Of the principals, Christine Keeler's *Scandal* (Xanadu, 1989) was joined by Yevgeny Ivanov's book in 1992 (see Chapter 2). Anthony Summers and Stephen Dorril's *Honeytrap* (Weidenfeld & Nicolson, 1987) and Philip Knightley and Caroline Kennedy's *An Affair of State* (Jonathan Cape, 1987) are investigative works about the affair; Wayland Young's *The Profumo Affair: Aspects of Conservatism* (Penguin,

1963) is an excellent piece of instant history. Richard Lamb's *The Macmillan Years: The Emerging Truth* (John Murray, 1995) had the benefit of papers from Lord Denning and the Public Record Office. Bill Deedes' *Dear Bill* (Macmillan, 1997) describes the panicked government response. *George Wigg* by himself (Michael Joseph, 1972), Crossman's *Backbench Diaries* (see Chapter 3) and David Thurlow's *Profumo: The Hate Factor* (Robert Hale, 1992) about John Lewis concern the Labour figures who exposed the affair; for Henry Kerby, see Joe Haines' *The Politics of Power* (Jonathan Cape, 1977) and Chapman Pincher's *Inside Story* (Sidgwick & Jackson, 1978); for the press, see John Pilger's *Hidden Agendas* (Vintage, 1998) on King, and Charles Wintour's *The Rise and Fall of Fleet Street* (Hutchinson, 1989) on Murdoch. In the course of research for *Rinkagate* (see Chapter 7) Simon Freeman and Barrie Penrose tied up a loose end from the Denning Report.

Chapter 5
The Wilson circle 1963–76

John Pearson's *The Profession of Violence* (HarperCollins, 1995 – 1st edn 1972) describes the criminal career of the Krays, as do several books written by gang members. Only in the later versions is there an accurate story of the Boothby affair and Boothby's official biography by Robert Rhodes James, published in 1991, dismissed the story. The memoirs of Bill Deedes add to Pearson's account. Brian Brivati's *Goodman* (see also Chapter 3) describes the lawyer's place in the Wilson circle. Simon Freeman and Barrie Penrose's *Rinkagate* (see Chapter 7) contains the definitive quote from Lady Falkender. Leo Abse's *The Man Behind the Smile* (Robson, 1996) is mainly an attack on Tony Blair but takes a sideswipe against Wilson. Susan Crosland's *Tony Crosland* (Jonathan Cape, 1982) is a brave and profound account of her husband; other stories in this section come from Paterson's biography of George Brown and a series of articles in *The Spectator* in autumn 1998 on Wigg.

The Wilson plot is dealt with in Stephen Dorril and Robin Ramsay's *Smear! Wilson and the Secret State* (Fourth Estate, 1991) – a book replete with stories from the underside of British politics in 1945–76; David Leigh's *The Wilson Plot* (Heinemann, 1988); and Paul Foot's *Who Framed Colin Wallace?* (Pan, 1990), from which comes the smear chart on leading politicians of the time. Joe Haines' *The Politics of Power* (Jonathan Cape, 1977) recalls the 'slag heaps' outcry and *Westminster Babylon* covers the 'lavender list' and the downfall of Kagan. The 'big fat spider' talk is in Barrie Penrose and Roger Courtiour's *The Pencourt File* (Secker & Warburg, 1978).

Chapter 6
Poulson: corruption by design 1957–77

Ray Fitzwalter and David Taylor's *Web of Corruption* (Granada, 1981) and Michael Gillard and Martin Tomkinson's *Nothing to Declare* (John Calder, 1980) were constant reference points in writing about the complex Poulson affair. John Poulson's *The Price* (Michael Joseph, 1981) conveys the character of its author if nothing else. Reginald Maudling's *Memoirs* (Sidgwick & Jackson, 1978) is predictably defensive on this matter, but an appealing read on other things. Eddie Milne's *No Shining Armour* (see Chapter 2) deals with some of the ramifications of the scandal. Susan Crosland's book describes the effect of the inquiry's error on Tony Crosland (see Chapter 5), and Dorril and Ramsay deal with some of the murkier aspects of the case. Michael Gillard's *A Little Pot of Money* (Private Eye Productions, 1974) is the farcical story of REFA.

Chapter 7
Sleaze in the 1970s

Slater Walker is the subject of a book of that name by Charles Raw (André Deutsch, 1977) and is mentioned in Peter Walker's *Staying Power* (Bloomsbury, 1993). Other City operations are covered in Edward du Cann's *Two Lives* (Images Publishing, 1995) and the Lonrho scandal is in Tom Bower's *Tiny Rowland: The Rebel Tycoon* (Heinemann, 1993). Tom Bower's *Maxwell: The Outsider* (Heinemann, 1991) is also relevant. John Stonehouse wrote his own strange story in *Death of an Idealist* (W. H. Allen, 1975). One of the most remarkable and little-known stories of 1970s financial sharp practice, the Rossminster affair, is covered in Michael Gillard's *In the Name of Charity* (Chatto & Windus, 1987). Tony Benn on speed is taken from his own remarkably open diaries *Years of Hope 1940–62* (Hutchinson, 1994).

Several books were written about Jeremy Thorpe in the late 1970s, starting with the confusing *The Pencourt File* (see Chapter 5) and continuing after the trial with *Jeremy Thorpe: A Secret Life* by Lewis Chester, Magnus Linklater and David May (Fontana, 1979). Peter Bessell's *Cover Up* (Simons Books, 1980) is a rare, fascinating and scurrilous book. Simon Freeman and Barrie Penrose's *Rinkagate* (Bloomsbury, 1996) fills in a lot of the gaps left by legal worries twenty years ago. Peter Chippindale and David Leigh's 'Thorpe: the politician as tycoon' in *New Statesman* (6 July 1979) is probably still definitive on his financial affairs. Jeremy Thorpe's own memoirs *In My Own Time* have recently been published (Politico's Publishing, 1999).

Chapter 8
The enterprise culture 1979-92

Peter Riddell's *Honest Opportunism* (Hamish Hamilton, 1993) describes the rise of the career politician, and Anthony Sampson's various *Anatomies of Britain* (1962–92) examine the changing Establishment. Cecil King's *The Cecil King Diary 1970–74* (Jonathan Cape, 1975) contains Stonehouse's hypocritical comment on modern Tory MPs. Paul Foot's *Words as Weapons* (Verso, 1990) contains articles written at the time raising concerns about outside interests. Mark Hollingsworth's *MPs for Hire* (Bloomsbury, 1991) is a useful account of the lobbying industry in the 1980s and the Browne case in particular. The Downey Report and the reports of the House of Commons Select Committee on Standards and Privileges are the main sources for much of what follows, in this chapter and in Chapter 10, on greedy MPs and cash for questions. Ian Greer's *One Man's Word* (André Deutsch, 1997) adds some colour.

Chapter 9
'Family values' 1979–97

Specific episodes are often well described in Parris and Doig. Martin Durham's *Sex and Politics: The family and morality in the Thatcher years* (Macmillan, 1991) is an overview of the political effect of moral campaigners. Woodrow Wyatt's *Confessions of an Optimist* (Collins, 1985) talks about MPs and secretaries; Sara Keays wrote her side of the Parkinson affair in *A Question of Judgement* (Quintessential Press, 1985), and Margaret Thatcher's *The Downing Street Years* (HarperCollins, 1993) also comments. Stephen Jeffery-Poulter's *Peers, Queers and Commons* (Routledge, 1991) is the story of gay law reform since the 1950s and is eye-opening about 1980s homophobia. Norman Fowler's *Ministers Decide* (Chapmans, 1991) discusses AIDS. Michael Gove's *Michael Portillo* (Fourth Estate, 1995) is intriguing about the gay scene at the Conservative Research Department. On the press see Colin Seymour-Ure's book (see Chapter 3), Gerry Brown's *Exposed!* (Virgin Books, 1995) and the incomparable Peter Chippindale and Chris Horrie *Stick It up Your Punter!* (Mandarin, 1992). On Back to Basics see *Major: A Political Life* by Anthony Seldon with Lewis Baston (Weidenfeld & Nicolson, 1997) and Steven Norris' *Changing Trains* (Hutchinson, 1996).

Chapter 10
Cash for questions 1987–97

The case against Hamilton is put by David Leigh and Ed Vulliamy's *Sleaze* (Fourth Estate, 1997). The book was recognized as an important source during the Downey investigation. Hamilton put his own case before Downey, but has also been supported by Jonathan Boyd Hunt's *Trial By Conspiracy*

(GreeNZone, 1998). Hunt's book posits a bizarre plot involving the fabrication of evidence by *The Guardian* journalists to frame Hamilton. Tom Bower's *Fayed* (Macmillan, 1998) does not seem to come to a conclusion on the matter. I have for the most part relied upon the Downey Report and the Commons Select Committee reports, and the first Nolan Report. Analysis of the impact of sleaze on politics in the 1990s is in *New Labour Triumphs: Britain at the Polls 1997* by Anthony King, *et al.* (Chatham House, 1998), and *Sleaze: Politicians, private interests and public reaction* by F. F. Ridley and Alan Doig (Oxford University Press, 1995). The dramatic Tatton election campaign is recounted in John Sweeney's *Purple Homicide* (Bloomsbury, 1997) and Brian Cathcart's *Were You Still up for Portillo?* (Penguin, 1997).

Chapter 11
The culture of sleaze 1992–97
On Scott see Brian Thompson and F. F. Ridley's *Under the Scott-light* (Oxford University Press, 1997) and Richard Norton-Taylor's *Truth is a Difficult Concept* (Fourth Estate, 1995). Jonathan Aitken is the subject of *The Liar* by Luke Harding, David Leigh and David Pallister (Penguin, 1997 and 1999), and Saïd Aburish's *The House of Saud* (Bloomsbury, 1995) is a vivid description of Saudi business culture. Party finance is covered in the Neill Report (Fifth Report of the Committee on Standards in Public Life, *The funding of political parties in the United Kingdom* Vol. I Cm 4057-I October 1998), Colin Challen's *The Price of Power* (Vision, 1998), Alistair McAlpine's *Once a Jolly Bagman* (Weidenfeld & Nicolson, 1997) and A. J. Davies' *We, the Nation* (Little, Brown, 1995). On Serbia see *The Sunday Times* 19 May 1996 and the Leigh and Vulliamy sleaze book. Michael Crick's *Jeffrey Archer: Stranger than Fiction* (Hamish Hamilton, 1995) more than lives up to its subtitle, and Judith Cook's *The Sleaze File* (Bloomsbury, 1995) has interesting accounts of misconduct in quangos.

Chapter 12
New Labour, new sleaze? 1997–
On New Labour generally, see Paul Anderson and Nyta Mann's *Safety First* (Granta, 1997) and on Mandelson see Don Macintyre's *Mandelson: The Biography* (HarperCollins, 1999) and Paul Routledge's *Mandy* (Simon & Schuster, 1999). To the despair of politicians in the 1990s the press has become expert at detecting sleaze and anyone writing about recent events has to acknowledge a debt to *The Guardian* and *The Observer* in particular. Of the rest of the press *The Sunday Times*, the *Electronic Telegraph* and the *Financial Times* on the Internet, and *Private Eye* have been particularly useful.

Index